KNOW YOUR CUSTOMER:
New Approaches to Understanding Customer Value and Satisfaction

Robert B. Woodruff
Sarah Fisher Gardial

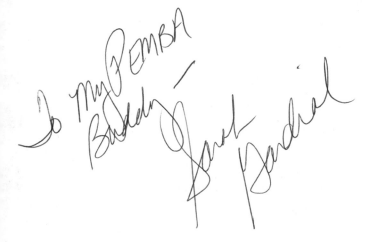

D1516523

BLACKWELL
Business

First published 1996

Reprinted 1996

Blackwell Publishers Inc.
238 Main Street
Cambridge, Massachusetts 02142, USA

Blackwell Publishers Ltd
108 Cowley Road
Oxford OX4 1JF, UK

Library of Congress Cataloging in Publication Data
Woodruff, Robert B.
Know your customer : new approaches to customer value and
satisfaction / Bob Woodruff, Sarah Gardial.
p.   cm.
Includes bibliographical references and index.
ISBN 1–55786–553–1 (Pbk)
1. Consumers' preferences. 2. Consumer satisfaction. 3. Quality of products.
4. Marketing—Management. I. Gardial, Sarah, 1957– . II. Title.
HF5415.32.W66   1996   95–45437
658.8'12—dc20   CIP

British Library Cataloguing in Publication Data
A CIP catalogue record for this book is available from the British Library

Typeset by Cornerstone Composition Services.

Printed in the United States of America on acid-free paper.

TQM SERIES FOREWORD

In August of 1991, six US corporations with substantial global operations, American Express, Ford, IBM, Motorola, Procter & Gamble, and Xerox, sponsored The Total Quality Forum. The Forum was an annual gathering of academic leaders and corporate executives. Its purpose was to discuss the role of Total Quality Management in the United States and its role on US campuses, especially in business and engineering schools.

The chief executive officers of the six sponsoring companies summarized the importance of the topic in the November-December 1991 issue of the *Harvard Business Review*, "An Open Letter: TQM on Campus."

"We believe business and academia have a shared responsibility to learn, to teach, and to practice Total Quality Management. If the United States expects to improve its global competitive performance, business and academic leaders must close ranks behind an agenda that stresses the importance and value of TQM. Working together, companies and institutions of higher education *must* accelerate the application of Total Quality Management on our campuses if our education system and economy are to maintain and enhance their global positions." (94–95)

In 1989: 14 leading European corporations founded the European Foundation for Quality Management. By 1993 the membership had grown to nearly 300 European organizations (corporations and universities). The September 1993 Membership Information brochure included the following objective and vision.

"The European Foundation for Quality Management (EFQM) believes that, through Total Quality Management, Western Europe will become a leading force in the world market. Our objective is to create conditions to enhance the position of European industry by strengthening the role of management in quality strategies. EFQM's vision is to become the leading organization for promoting and facilitating Total Quality Management in Western Europe. This vision will be achieved when TQM has become an integrated value of the European society, and European management has achieved a global competitive advantage."

The commitment of the Japanese to quality management is legendary. Herein lies the theme of this series of books on TQM. As a system of management, whether in the Americas, the Pacific Rim, or Europe, TQM has become important for global competitive positions. Therefore, learning about TQM models and practices is relevant in universities, in corporate training centers, and in individual development.

Michael Stahl
Series Editor

CONTENTS

Contents

Section II: Learning About Customer Value and Satisfaction

3 A New Perspective on Customer Value 51

4 Linking Customer Value to Customer Satisfaction 84

Contents

Section III: Customer Value Determination Techniques

7   Measuring Customer Value   157

8   Analyzing Customer Value Data   191

9 Measuring Customer Satisfaction 220

10 Analyzing Customer Satisfaction Data 251

Contents

Appendix III: Customer Value Change
Forecasting Techniques

325

Index

333

PREFACE

For quite a few years now, we have been conducting research on customer value and satisfaction. At first, we just wanted to learn how customers understand value and satisfaction and how these concepts linked together in their minds. Our research has helped us do just that. Over time we became more and more concerned with how organizations learn about their customers. Most of our research has been done in partnership with companies that have graciously allowed us to test our ideas using their managers and customers. We have interacted with many organizations on consultation projects and in executive education. We also have attended a number of practitioner conferences where companies and research firms talk to each other about how to do customer research. All these experiences have been instrumental in helping us develop invaluable insights into how organizations try to know their customers.

We have been asked for our ideas on customer value, satisfaction, and techniques for learning about customers quite often – in business briefings, MBA classes, executive education programs, and by our corporate research partners. While we have published numerous articles in journals and proceedings that discuss our work, such publications are not the best means to reach students or practitioners in a timely way. So we felt the need to put our thoughts into this book, which hopefully will better communicate with our intended audience – students in advanced undergraduate and master's business courses and practitioners in organizations. We know that it is difficult to write a book for both students and practitioners, but we decided to try because both are so concerned with the same issue: how to improve the value that an organization delivers to its customers.

One of the most important things that we learned early on is how organizations understand the concepts of customer value and customer satisfaction. We never asked managers what these concepts meant directly; instead, we looked at the research that their organizations do. We found two things. Surprisingly, many organizations use rather similar techniques to know their customers, reflecting a great degree of commonalty in how value and satisfaction are conceptualized in industry. Consider the impact on competitive advantage. If every organization uses similar ways to know their customers, all competitors learn about the same things. Their research may not gain any edge in customer knowledge over competitors.

Secondly, many companies are not entirely happy with their current processes for learning about customer value and satisfaction. In the book, we discuss important reasons for this dissatisfaction. Fortunately, on both accounts our research suggests that there are opportunities to improve current practice. This book is intended to provide guidelines for those organizations that want to pursue these opportunities.

The book offers several ideas that we think will lead to improvements. We discuss a new way of thinking about customer value, one that delves into the customer's world. We show how customer value is linked to customer satisfaction. In fact, both value and satisfaction provide the conceptual foundation for an expanded process for learning about customers. In addition, this book presents new techniques for getting customer value information from customers and demonstrates how this information can be incorporated into satisfaction surveys. We also discuss the difficult challenge of predicting how customer value is likely to change in the future, among other ideas. Hopefully, every reader will come away from reading the book armed with new information.

Like any effort of this kind, this book could not have been completed without help from others. First, we thank our families, who provided the support and understanding that we needed to spend all the hours that we have on this project. In addition, we are grateful to be part of a very productive Customer Value Research Team at the University of Tennessee. We especially appreciate the contributions of David Schumann, who, along with the authors, codirects this team. David's ideas, leadership, and constant encouragement are a source of inspiration for us. We have benefited in many ways from other members of this team who have been our collaborators on research projects. Many thanks to Joseph Rentz, Pratibha Dahbolkar, James Foggin, Richard Reizenstein, Mary Jane Burns, Scott Clemons, Linda Wright, Bob Graves, Amy Cathey, Dan Flint, and Mike Garver.

We also want to thank Ernest Cadotte, David Cravens, and Al Shocker for their suggestions on the manuscript and to Pat Pecorella, Bill Barnes, Tina Davis, Bill Adams, Al Carey, John Mariotti, Al Cole, and Michael Stahl for their support for our research. In addition, Blackwell Publishers has been a joy to work with, particularly in giving us the freedom to write what we felt was important. We especially appreciate the help that we have received from Rolf Janke and Mary Riso in developing the manuscript. Finally, we would like to thank the Center for the Advancement of Organizational Effectiveness of the College of Business Administration at the University of Tennessee for providing initial funding for our early research. Thanks also go to Charles Cwiek and Rick Beckley for their expert help on the figures.

Our research on customer value and satisfaction is in progress, and we know more learning is yet to come. For that reason, we do not view this book as complete. It addresses only those customer value issues on which we have focused for the past several years. There are others, and hopefully in our future research we will begin to tackle them.

Section I

BUILD A COMPETITIVE ADVANTAGE BY KNOWING YOUR CUSTOMER

CHAPTER 1

ACHIEVING A COMPETITIVE ADVANTAGE THROUGH CUSTOMER VALUE DELIVERY STRATEGIES

Baxter Healthcare Corporation, a subsidiary of Baxter International, is a major player in the medical products industry. Baxter's managers continuously search for ways to increase *customer satisfaction*[1] through superior value delivery. In one case, management wanted to improve on-time delivery service to a key hospital customer. Baxter had been focusing inward by measuring the quality of its delivery service in terms of the percentage of product delivered after two and three shipments. Based on these data, its on-time delivery service met or exceeded internally derived standards. Yet management was puzzled because it knew that this customer was not entirely satisfied.

Baxter decided to talk directly with the customer. Its management learned that the hospital measured on-time delivery differently. The hospital recorded the percentage of a total product order that was delivered on the *first* shipment, explaining why Baxter's service did not live up to the customer's standard. With an eye toward better responsiveness, Baxter sat down with the hospital's managers to discuss ways to resolve the difference between their respective measures of on-time delivery service. The key issue was how much of a product order had to be included in the first shipment. Eventually, the two companies agreed on the same measure. Baxter changed its delivery service process accordingly. Now the hospital is much more satisfied with Baxter's service. Incidents like this one have encouraged Baxter to allocate more than twenty people to working on ways to improve customer service.

If a company understands value from its customers' perspective, ways usually are found to deliver that value to their satisfaction. Often, the more difficult task is to find out exactly what it takes to satisfy customers. As Baxter learned, a *competitive advantage* through superior value delivery starts with information from customers.[1]

Introduction

Most observers agree that competition in industry after industry is becoming increasingly intense. More and more companies worldwide are searching for ways to build sustainable advantage to counter this threat. In the 1980s, many firms turned to quality improvements in products and internal processes in order to achieve competitive advantage.[2] The impact of such quality initiatives on competitiveness has been impressive. However, some believe that the point has been reached where organizations will have to deliver quality just to stay even with competitors.[2] New sources of competitive advantage are needed, and we believe that these will come from creating, communicating, and delivering superior value to carefully targeted customers.[3]

Value delivery strategies concentrate on ways to help customers meet their needs. A supplier's challenge is to enhance value from the customer's perspective – by learning, for instance, how the customer defines on-time delivery – or to help customers solve product use problems.

Importantly, emphasizing customer value does not mean giving up on quality initiatives. Rather, customer value complements the quality imperative to continuously improve products and internal processes. An understanding of how customers define value becomes the guiding force for determining *what to improve*. Consider the Baxter case described previously. It would have done little good to improve the quality of on-time service after the second or third shipment – that was not what the hospital customer wanted. Only after receiving input from the customer did management know what to improve.

Conceptually, customer value has been linked to company performance for a long time. In the 1950s, for instance, Peter Drucker argued that the customer's perception of value plays a decisive role in business performance.[3] However, only recently have many organizations become serious about making superior quality and value the driving force in formulating strategies and implementing processes. Anecdotal evidence of this change comes from advertising, a kind of "window" into a company's strategic thinking, where quality and value are the core ideas in many slogans and themes:

> "Metlife Healthcare Means Quality." (Metropolitan Life Insurance Company)

> "Escort has always been able to separate itself from the pack by establishing a strong tradition of value." (Ford Motor Company)

> "Quality means the world to us." (Motorola, Inc.)

> "What makes it a *business decision* is value." (Toshiba)

> "Performance, compatibility, and room for the future – three reasons the i486 DX2 processor is today's best value." (Intel)

Many managers believe that quality and customer value initiatives are critical to achieving improved performance.[4,5] Recent research is proving them right.[6,7] We can see the rationale for this relationship in the customer satisfaction and performance cycle shown in Figure 1.1. By being responsive to customers' needs, customer value delivery strategies are instrumental in building strong customer satisfaction. This satisfaction, in turn, can have a double-barreled impact on "bottom line" performances. First, satisfied customers are more likely to want to maintain a long-term relationship with a supplier. As many organizations are finding out, the economic worth of a customer over a long period of time is substantial. In addition, it is becoming widely accepted that retaining customers is much less expensive than replacing them.[8,9] There also is a side benefit to keeping customers satisfied. They are more likely to speak favorably about your organization to other potential customers. This positive word of mouth can make the job of acquiring new customers much easier.

Another reason for the success of customer value delivery strategies comes from the realities of today's market. Customers are more demanding than ever before.[10] They want to deal with a company that is responsive to all their needs and that takes

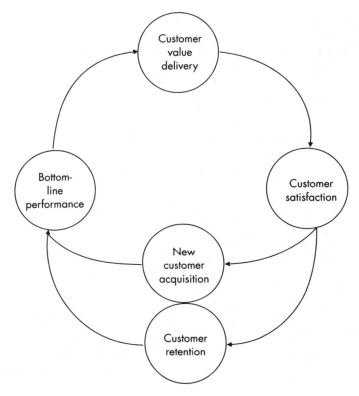

Figure 1.1. The customer responsiveness cycle.

a personal interest in their well-being. For instance, business travelers rate a feeling that an airline cares about them as being just as important as baggage delivery and check-in services, and fast-food customers place courtesy ahead of speed of service as the most sought-after restaurant service.[11] The implication is inescapable: organizations must find new ways to deliver superior value by satisfying their customers' needs.

This book details how organizations should approach learning about their customers. In this chapter, we lay the groundwork for thinking about this learning process as a critical input into customer value delivery strategies. We argue that an important source of competitive advantage lies in how well managers use customer information to develop and implement effective value delivery strategies. We then introduce a process for obtaining and analyzing information to help managers learn what customers value and how that value translates into customer satisfaction. This process, which we call customer value determination, provides the framework for the rest of the book.

Customer Value Delivery Strategies

A Value Delivery Strategy Process

Every customer value delivery strategy is the outgrowth of a series of key decisions. Figure 1.2 identifies these decisions and shows how they are linked together. We find this process useful as a way of thinking about how to attain competitive advantage in markets.[12,13] Let's look at what is involved in each activity in the process.

Delivering value requires a clear understanding of exactly what kind of value is desired by customers. Importantly, customer value is not inherent in products or services themselves; rather it is experienced by customers as a consequence of using the supplier's products and services for their own purposes. For example, the driver of a car may want to feel in control in bad weather situations. Or an aluminum company's auto manufacturer customer may want to increase promised gas mileage by designing a lighter car.

Value is as your customers perceive it, and so every organization must find ways to draw out from customers how they see value – now and in the future. For this reason, "identify the value" is where planning a customer value delivery strategy must begin (see Figure 1.2). For instance, a beverage business unit of a large food company conducted research with consumers to learn about what occurred as they participated in sports and exercise activities; how various kinds of drinks were purchased, stored, and used; and why drinks were being used in these situations. From this research, the company's management learned about a whole range of different kinds of value desired from various segments of its customer base.

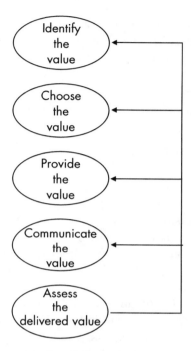

Figure 1.2. A process for planning a customer value delivery strategy.

Source: Adapted from Mary Jane Burns and Robert B. Woodruff, "Delivering Value to Consumers: Implications for Strategy Development and Implementation," in Chris T. Allen et al, eds., *Marketing Theory and Applications*, Chicago: American Marketing Association, 1992, 209–216.

The next activity shown in Figure 1.2, "choose the value," begins translating this customer learning into a value delivery strategy. Out of all the various customer segments and the many kinds of value desired, on which ones are you going to focus? This decision is complicated. Your organization's capabilities must be considered in relation to the value sought by different markets or segments and the strengths and weaknesses of important competition. The challenge is to match what your organization does (or potentially can do) best – its core competencies – with the value sought by customers in each different market segment. For instance, the previously mentioned beverage business unit wanted to know from where its competitive advantage would most likely come. It examined the many kinds of value being sought from different segments and compared its competencies with other similar brands as well as other types of drinks (e.g., water) used in athletic situations. Out of this analysis came decisions about the consumer segments and kinds of value on which the business unit should focus.

The next activity shown in Figure 1.2, "provide the value," requires translating a value delivery strategy into action. Every aspect of an organization's offering is considered, including (1) products or services designed to meets customers' needs, (2) support services (e.g., repair, use suggestions, warranties, customer "hot lines," and the like) that enhance customer satisfaction with the product, (3) distribution services to help customers acquire and receive the product conveniently, and (4) pricing to enhance value. Each of these value delivery offerings should be linked to internal processes through which a supplier provides the chosen kinds of value. To illustrate, the beverage business unit is now in this phase of the process. It is examining each aspect of its business to determine how the key kinds of value will be delivered to selected consumer segments.

It usually is a mistake to assume that customers will immediately and fully understand the value that your company offers. You have to "communicate the value" that customers will experience from your organization's offering.[14] An integrated communications campaign combines several promotion activities in a concerted effort to help customers learn about this value. For instance, the management of the beverage business unit is considering how advertising might incorporate vignettes taken from personal interviews with consumers to demonstrate how the drink enhances their athletic performance and how displays in distribution outlets could be used to reinforce the same messages.

The last step shown in Figure 1.2, "assess the value," monitors how well the planned value delivery is being implemented. Are customers satisfied with the value that they are getting? Is that value perceived as being superior to that delivered by competitors? "Bottom line" measures of value delivery performance, such as sales, market share, and profitability, may provide some answers to these questions. However, satisfaction surveys, customers' complaints, and follow-up interviews with selected customers about problems that they encountered provide more useful insight into what is going on. These data uncover specific value delivery performance strengths and problem areas, as well as the reasons for them. For instance, the beverage business unit regularly tracks consumer satisfaction with strategically important kinds of value that were selected in the prior "choose the value" activity.

Gaining Advantage with Value Delivery

It is all too easy to think that a competitive advantage lies only in what you uniquely offer to customers. It is true that you want customers to think that you offer something that your competitors do not. This view is limited, however, because there is an additional, complementary way to seek an advantage. An organization may develop a superior ability to design and implement key internal processes that are clearly linked to customer value.

Look back at Figure 1.2 for a moment. You can strive for superiority throughout the entire process of planning and implementing value delivery strategies. Each activity offers potential for building an advantage.

Consider the first step, "identify the value." Superior information capability results when managers learn about customer value more deeply and/or more quickly than their competitors. For example, how did Japanese automobile manufacturers make such impressive inroads into the luxury car market in the United States with the Acura, Lexus, and Infinity lines? Why did Cadillac, Lincoln, Mercedes, and BMW lose ground? One can argue that the Japanese companies learned about the kind of value desired by luxury car buyers in the United States more deeply than did either American or European automobile manufacturers. Acura, followed by Lexus and Infinity, offered cars with comparable quality and performance at lower prices that were sold by dealerships that delivered superior service. This value delivery strategy apparently offered just what many American consumers wanted.

A competitive advantage may come from sound "choose the value" decisions as well. Perhaps this fact explains why many companies are returning to their core competencies in order to compete more effectively. It takes concerted attention to detail to provide superior value delivery. For instance, Promus Corporation spun off most of its casino business in order to better focus management attention on its profitable overnight and extended stay accommodation businesses.

Providing and communicating value are activities with which organizations typically do look for a competitive advantage. These activities depend on the organization's ability to implement strategy in selected markets; such implementation can be a major difference among competitors. For instance, it is one thing for an auto manufacturer to say that it wants to be known for highly service-oriented, personally attentive dealerships (a value delivery strategy), but it is quite another thing to implement processes in those dealerships that ensure consistently high responsiveness to individual consumers' requests.

Finally, "assessing the value" creates opportunity for advantage by enabling superior responsiveness to customers' problems. Of course, you must know where problems are cropping up before you can resolve them, and it is here that timely and accurate information from customers is critical. The benefits of being responsive are well known. For one thing, it creates a positive feeling among your customers. Part of this feeling comes from solving the immediate problem, but it also comes from customers believing that the supplier can be counted on in the future.

Assessing value also helps you better understand the strengths of your company's offering. Customers need to be reminded of these strengths, and so this information is a source of ideas for integrated communications. We know of a survey conducted by a luxury pleasure boat company that revealed that customers loved the beauty of its sport cruisers. In this case, "value" lies in the enjoyment that boat owners get from experiencing that beauty and from the compliments received from

11

others. This information provided the rationale for the company to continually reinforce – through advertising, brochures, and dealer displays – these feelings primarily by highlighting the cruiser's design profile.

Competitive Advantage through Customer Value Information

We believe that organizations too often overlook the opportunity to gain a competitive advantage by *developing superior processes for understanding their customers.* Competing on customer value delivery is a highly information-driven way to manage, and all those involved must be adept at learning about their customers. While every organization has some process in place for this purpose, we believe that they can be improved substantially. Most managers with whom we have talked agree. The question is *how* to improve these processes.

Typically, it is not enough to change a research technique here and there. Long-term improvement in an organization's customer value learning process requires re-examining the entire process from one end to the other. However, you must have some idea of what the process *should be like* before you can spot strengths and weaknesses in what is currently being done. In the next section, we overview a process for learning about customer value that we recommend for this purpose. By discussing the activities in this process in subsequent chapters of the book, we intend to raise a number of issues that must be addressed in order to improve the processes by which an organization gets to know its customers.

The Customer Value Determination Process

We start this section with a caveat: by the time you begin a customer value determination process, you must already know which current or potential customers are strategically important to your organization. Identifying these customers is one activity in a *market opportunity analysis* (MOA) and customer value determination should be considered part of the larger MOA as well. We come back to this point in Chapter 2, where we talk about how to integrate customer value determination into an

MOA process. For now, think about a particular market or segment of customers that is important to you. How should you go about learning about these customers?

Customer Value Determination

Knowing your customers takes time, effort, and persistence. No one source of information will suffice. The best companies bring together several sources, such as experience derived from customer contacts and data from various kinds of research, into an integrated process for learning about customers. Figure 1.3 diagrams such a process that we call *customer value determination* (CVD).

Identify Customer Value Dimensions. CVD begins by identifying what your customers want or value. You can be assured that customers want more than a few things out of a relationship with a supplier. These "things" are called *customer value dimensions*, and it is absolutely essential that you understand what they are. A customer value dimension may be some component or feature of your product (e.g., quality, durability) or services (e.g., on-time delivery, completeness of an order). But they are also likely to be more intangible experiences, such as a customer's feeling of trust in the supplier or a belief that the supplier can be counted on in times of difficulty. In general, how you conceive of customer value is crucial to the entire CVD process because it drives everything that is done. For this reason, we devote all of Chapter 3 in this book to developing a framework for thinking about customer value.

Identifying customer value dimensions requires interacting with customers. You can learn about these dimensions from contact with customers during the regular course of business, but this by itself may not be enough. Research is usually needed to explore more fully customers' perceptions of value. We believe that qualitative measurement techniques, such as indepth personal interviews, focus groups, and observation, are absolutely essential for this activity. Chapters 7 and 8 and Appendix I discuss these important techniques.

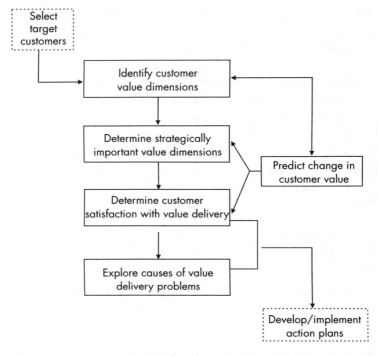

Figure 1.3. The customer value determination (CVD) process.

Determine Strategically Critical Value Dimensions. Quite likely, a large number of value dimensions will emerge from the previous activity in the CVD process. Though customers are demanding, not all dimensions have the same impact on their decisions to buy from one supplier over another or on their satisfaction. The second CVD activity searches through these dimensions to discover the most important of these. This search depends heavily on what "importance" means and how you decide to measure it. We come back to these issues in sections of Chapters 7 and 10 and in Appendix III.

Predict Change in Customer Value. The prior two activities are good for discovering a customer's *current* perceptions of value desired. We know that these perceptions change, but rarely do organizations try to predict that change ahead of time. Yet, if we know in advance what changes in value are likely, we can then respond with corresponding improvements in customer value delivery strategies. CVD allocates effort to customer value prediction in order to develop this lead time for improvement decisions. Like any forecasting task, the challenge is to bring several sources of data to bear on making the most accurate predictions possible. Chapter 9 and Appendix II discuss ways of making these predictions.

Determine Customer Satisfaction with Value Delivery. The previous three activities focus on understanding what customers value, but that is only part of the story. We need to know what customers think of our value delivery as well. The next activity, customer satisfaction measurement (CSM), accomplishes this purpose. We cannot assume that customers within a target segment will have similar evaluations of what we do. CSM queries relatively large, representative samples of customers to learn the range of satisfaction feelings across the segment. CSM also can be used to validate the value dimensions uncovered in prior customer value identification research. We discuss issues and techniques for satisfaction research in Chapters 4, 10, and 11.

Explore Causes of Value Delivery Problems. The results of satisfaction studies are good at uncovering the degree of satisfaction that customers perceive with specific aspects of your value delivery. High satisfaction scores indicate strengths, while low satisfaction or dissatisfaction scores signal performance problems, either with your value delivery or the communication of value. Even the best of these studies, however, do not give much insight into *why these problems exist*. A follow-up CVD activity uses small scale, qualitative studies to probe the reasons for these problems (see Chapters 10 and 11). These results are essential for deciding how best to improve in the eyes of customers.

Key Features of the CVD Process
The CVD process is an on-going, never-ending process that must

be managed over time. It has several important features that we stress throughout this book. These include:

- The integration of measurements of customer value and customer satisfaction.
- The measurement of current customer value and the prediction of future customer value.
- The gathering of information on the motivations and rationales for customers' perceptions of value and satisfaction.

First, the CVD process combines analyses of what customers want (customer value measurement) with analyses of how well they think you are delivering value to them (customer satisfaction measurement). Too often, organizations conduct customer value research and satisfaction research separately (or conduct only one, typically satisfaction) and overlook the opportunity to combine these efforts. In fact, value data are incomplete without satisfaction data, and the reverse is true as well.

Second, while most of the CVD process is concerned with customers' current perceptions of value, one activity focuses entirely on predicting the changes in these perceptions that are likely to occur in the future. At the outset, we believe that you have to improve your organization's process for understanding current value and satisfaction. However, once that part of CVD is in place, you must then look for ways to anticipate the future. Again, lengthening lead time for changing customer value delivery can be a significant source of competitive advantage.

Third, CVD goes well beyond measuring customers' value and satisfaction perceptions. It also delves into *why* customers think and feel the way they do. What are customers' underlying motivations and rationales? In what situation or context do customers use your products and services? We believe that understanding these motivations, rationales, and situational contexts increases the value of CVD data. They help a supplier think more creatively about how to increase the value delivered to customers. For instance, a luxury boat manufacturer learned that sport cruiser owners frequently forgot their training on how to do routine on-board maintenance, repair, and operation activities. Managers brainstormed about how they could help owners remember to perform these activities. One idea was to develop videotapes of the procedures for each activity. Since all sport cruisers are equipped with a VCR, these tapes could easily and quickly be used on board the boat.

Finally, CVD should be an ongoing process. Again, customers change. What you learn about customer value and satisfaction today may not carry over to next quarter, much less next year. The best of companies learn this lesson. For example, in the mid-1980s all indications were that the Granite Rock Company was performing well. Its management believed that its customers' perceptions were in line with the company's offerings. In spite of this seemingly rosy picture, Granite Rock initiated research to learn more about its customers. One result was reassuring – customers liked the company's product quality. But in a surprise finding, it was discovered that customers perceived Granite Rock as being inflexible when it came to meeting special needs. Management made pervasive changes in the way it dealt with customers and became much more responsive to all their needs. As an outgrowth of these changes, the company applied for and won the 1992 Malcolm Baldrige National Quality Award. No matter how good you think you are doing, you cannot rest on your laurels. You have to keep up with what customers want and ensure that they perceive you to be responsive to their needs.[15]

Summary

In this chapter, we argued that organizations face increasingly intense competition and much more demanding customers than ever before. Successful suppliers in this environment will continuously search for new ways to achieve a competitive advantage. Focusing on customer value delivery strategies encourages managers to think outward toward external customers and about ways to achieve greater responsiveness to their needs. We think that, ultimately, a competitive advantage comes to those who develop superior strategies that deliver the kinds of value that customers want. Organizations must focus on those internal processes that are instrumental in implementing these strategies.

A competitive advantage based on customer value depends heavily on learning about external customers and what they perceive value to be. While most organizations have in place some process for knowing their customers, indications are that there is widespread dissatisfaction with them. This fact strongly suggests that one important source for gaining a competitive advantage can come from implementing a process for knowing your customers more deeply than do your competitors. However, this advantage will come only to those organizations that periodically evaluate and improve their process for learning about customers. This book is devoted to helping organizations accomplish this evaluation and improvement.

In this opening chapter, we introduced a process for learning about your customers that we call *customer value determination*. This process offers a standard or benchmark for evaluating the customer learning process that your organization has in place. We discuss each part of this process in the following sections of the book. Section II provides the conceptual logic for the CVD process. In it we lay out a way of thinking about (1) how the customer perceives value, (2) how customer value is linked to customer satisfaction, (3) how a CVD process is managed over time, and (4) how knowing your customer can translate into business decisions. In Section III we discuss techniques for measuring customer value, predicting customer value change, and measuring customer satisfaction. Before getting to these sections, we think it is important to place CVD in perspective within a larger market opportunity analysis process. Chapter 2 discusses this perspective.

References

[1] Bennett, Amanda, "Making the Grade with the Customer," *Wall Street Journal*, November 12, 1990, B1.
[2] Petersen, Donald E., "Beyond Satisfaction," in *Creating Customer Satisfaction*. New York: The Conference Board, Research Report No. 944, 1990, pp. 33–34.

[3] Drucker, Peter F., *The Practice of Management*. New York: Harper & Brothers Publishers, 1954.

[4] Anderson, Eugene W. and Mary W. Sullivan, "The Antecedents and Consequences of Consumer Satisfaction for Firms," *Marketing Science*, 12 (Spring 1993), pp. 125–143.

[5] Jacob, Rahul, "TQM – More Than A Dying Fad?" *Fortune*, October 18, 1993, pp. 66–72.

[6] Narver, John C. and Stanley F. Slater, "The Effect of Market Orientation on Business Profitability," *Journal of Marketing*, 54 (October 1990), pp. 20–35.

[7] Webster, Frederick E., "The Rediscovery of the Marketing Concept," *Business Horizons*, May–June 1988, pp. 29–39.

[8] Birch, Eric N., "Focus on Value," in *Creating Customer Satisfaction*. New York: The Conference Board, Research Report No. 944, 1990, pp. 3–4.

[9] Sellers, Patricia, "Getting Customers to Love You," *Fortune*, March 13, 1989, pp. 38–49.

[10] "Meet the New Consumer," *Fortune*, Autumn/Winter 1993, pp. 6–7.

[11] Sellers, Patricia, "What Customers Really Want," *Fortune*, June 4, 1990, pp. 58–68.

[12] Bower, Marvin and Robert A. Garda, "The Role of Marketing in Management," in *Handbook of Modern Marketing*, Victor P. Buell, ed. New York: McGraw-Hill, Inc., 1986, Chapter 1, pp. 3–13.

[13] Burns, Mary Jane and Robert B. Woodruff, "Delivering Value to Consumers: Implications for Strategy Development and Implementation," in *Marketing Theory and Applications*, Chris T. Allen et al, eds. Chicago: American Marketing Association, 1992, pp. 209–216.

[14] Waldrop, Judith, "Educating the Customer," *American Demographics*, September 1991, pp. 44–47.

[15] Triplett, Tim, "Satisfaction is Nothing They Take for Granite," *Marketing News*, May 9, 1994, p. 6.

Notes

1. In this chapter, we use several terms that are more fully explained in subsequent chapters. For those readers who want to see how we define these terms, we provide a glossary of terms at the end of the chapter.

2. Throughout the book, we use the term "product" very broadly to mean both tangible products and more intangible services. We believe that everything the book has to offer about customer value determination applies equally well to suppliers of products and of services. In

each case, management's focus must be on being responsive to its customers' perceptions of value.

3. In practice, managers use a variety of terms to refer to those who buy from a supplier. In business-to-business industries, the term "customer" means an end-use business that buys from a supplier. But in industries selling to individuals or households, the end-use buyer is a "consumer." Sometimes the same term can mean different things to managers in different industries. For instance, in consumer products industries, a "customer" means a trade buyer such as a distributor or a retailer. We believe that our approach to customer value determination applies equally well to all industries, and so we looked for a single term that could be used to refer to all of these different kinds of buyers. For convenience, we chose the term "customer."

Glossary of Key Terms

Customer value delivery strategies are the decisions that an organization makes about the kinds of value that their targeted customers should receive.

Customer value is the customers' perception of what they want to have happen in a specific use situation, with the help of a product and service offering, in order to accomplish a desired purpose or goal.

Customer satisfaction is a customer's positive or negative feeling about the value that was received as a result of using a particular organization's offering in specific use situations. This feeling can be a reaction to an immediate use situation or an "overall" reaction to a series of use situation experiences.

Competitive advantage is the value delivered by an organization that customers' perceive as superior to corresponding value delivered by competitors.

Responsiveness is the organization's action taken to satisfy specific requests made by customers.

Customer value learning process is all information gathering, analysis, and interpretation activities that an organization uses to learn about the value desired by its customers

Customer value determination process is a particular customer value learning process that combines measurement of current customer value, customer satisfaction, and prediction of future customer value into a systematic set of information activities.

Market opportunity analysis is a systematic process for learning about potential target markets and those forces that are acting on or in those markets to impact the organization's performance in them.

Customer value dimensions are the particular aspects of a product and service offering and/or the consequences of its use which are desired by customers in specific situations.

CHAPTER 2

CUSTOMER VALUE IN MARKET OPPORTUNITY ANALYSIS PROCESSES

Banks in the United States historically have profited from full-service financial strategies, but now they are under fire. The first signs of a real threat came from innovative services introduced by nontraditional competition. Mutual funds sell higher yield and equally liquid money market products that compete with the savings accounts offered by banks. Giant companies like General Motors and General Electric offer popular commercial loan services, and brokerage firms provide financial planning services. Both federal and state governments have encouraged this new competition through deregulation. To make matters worse, many customers are getting more comfortable with shopping for individual financial services from different suppliers. Banks can no longer expect that their full-service strategies will remain as attractive to these more knowledgeable customers as they once were.

Just how serious is the threat from these changing market conditions? One bank learned a valuable lesson from putting its top managers through a competitive exercise in which they were asked to play the role of different competitors and to design strategies to take away market share from their own bank. The shocking conclusion was that the bank's current approach could not succeed against these new strategies.

Many banks are looking for ways to regain an advantage in markets. Some are trying to become more responsive to customers. This approach, however, will require improving the information processes by which managers learn about customers, markets, and market opportunity. At a minimum, a bank must understand what customers value and how to create, communicate, and deliver that value to them. But there is more to it than that. Customers are influenced by many market forces, and banks must understand all of them. Only then can superior value delivery strategies be tailored to meet customer needs in the face of highly dynamic market conditions.[1,2]

Introduction

The markets in which organizations compete for customers have changed dramatically in the past decade. As we noted in Chapter 1, competition is becoming increasingly global and intense, which has expanded the choices available to customers. Customers, in turn, are becoming more sophisticated in choosing among a larger variety of offerings. Both competitors and customers are having to cope with slower growth economies. In many areas of the world, these forces combine to make customers ever more demanding as they seek higher value in satisfying their needs. Organizations that do not change to meet these dynamic market conditions will struggle at best. Even such world-class firms as General Motors, IBM, and Sears are finding that the old ways of operating are not working, and they are having difficulty achieving the levels of performance that formerly made them great.[3]

How should organizations go about dealing with today's dynamic markets? As more and more organizations refocus on their core competencies, success will be defined by the quality of such decisions as which customers should be targeted, how these customers should be served, and what is superior performance relative to competitors. How will these decisions be made? There is no simple answer to this question, but one thing is clear. Market strategy and tactics decisions are inevitably based on what managers "know" about customers, markets, and opportunity. "Knowing" is an information activity, and so information drives decisions.

At the risk of oversimplification, let's consider the two basic types of data available to most managers. *Internal data* measure aspects of operations inside the organization, such as production, new product development, logistics, sales, support services, and advertising. Data on costs, process effectiveness, sales, asset utilization, and the like make up a database intended to help you learn about how your organization works. In contrast, data from market research and market intelligence activities provide another, very different database for decisions. These *external data* allow you to look outward to learn about customers, markets, and the forces affecting them.

Managers differ in their preferences for internal versus external information.[1] These preferences create orientations and affect how decisions are made in departments, business units, and entire organizations. Take a minute to look at Figure 2.1. Four different management orientations are possible, depending on whether high versus low emphasis is placed on each type of data. Remember, the difference among the categories is not dependent on what data are *available*; rather, managers differ on which type of data *drives* their decision making.

Let's start with the upper-left cell of the classification shown in Figure 2.1, *intuitive-oriented managers*. These managers place a low emphasis on both internal and external data. Consequently, they tend to base decisions on personal intuition and experience. For instance, an entrepreneur in a newly formed business may be driven by a personal conviction about how best to operate. A new or small business may have very weak internal and external data processes in place, and so management has little choice except to adopt this orientation. But, even in larger, more established organizations, we have seen managers who seem to take pride in their intuitive abilities and tend to rely largely on personal judgment.

In contrast, *internally oriented managers* (shown in the lower-left cell in Figure 2.1) rely heavily on internal data but pay much less attention to information about markets. Consequently, they know a lot about what goes on inside their organization but less about external market dynamics. Even managers who have adopted total quality initiatives may fall into this category, particularly if they concentrate on process improvement without a strong understanding of what customers value or of how internal processes are linked to delivering that value. For in-

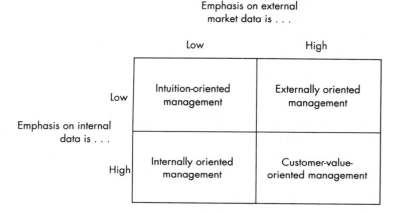

Figure 2.1. Managerial orientations.

stance, we know of one company in which product design engineers spent considerable time and resources improving the performance of a product only to learn later that customers could not see the difference between the performance of the old and new products. Even though the engineers thought the improvement was important, it did not deliver noticeable value to customers.

Externally oriented managers (shown in the upper-right cell in Figure 2.1) rely most on what they learn about markets. This category is complicated because the following three variations are possible:

- *Competitor-oriented managers* place the greatest weight on external data about competitors. They often look for a competitor's weakness that they can exploit. They may try to control competitors or follow their lead by reacting to their moves. Competitor benchmarking of internal products, services, and processes becomes a favorite information tool of such managers.
- *Customer-oriented managers* base their decisions on what they have learned about customers through measurements such as satisfaction research. These managers

tend to do what the customer wants because "the customer is always right." They give only cursory attention to competitors. They seem to believe that "if we satisfy our customers, we won't have to worry about what competitors do."

- *Market-oriented managers* place more balanced emphasis on what they know about both customers and competitors. They want to satisfy customers but also keep track of what competitors are doing to influence customer buying. The performance of competitors is studied in relation to customer needs to determine what is superior value.

In all these variations on externally oriented management, internal data plays a less important role in decisions. At worst, this may result in a limited understanding of how internal processes are linked to specific value that customers seek. A division sales manager, for instance, once touted what he thought was a data process core competency. His division had accumulated considerable data on the characteristics of geographical areas in which the company did business, and he was willing to make that data available to customers. When asked what value the data would have for customers, however, the manager was hard pressed to come up with an answer. He did not fully understand how the data might be used by customers to improve *their* business performance.

Finally, we are beginning to see *customer-value-oriented managers* emerge (shown in the lower right cell in Figure 2.1) who require both internal process data and external market data describing both customers and competitors. Their way of achieving a competitive advantage is to constantly seek ways to improve those processes that are critical to delivering value to selected customers. Nonvalue processes are limited or curtailed. For instance, a large industrial company is developing an information system that will link internal process data with external customer value and satisfaction data to help business unit managers focus on those processes that create value and encourage customer loyalty. Information system managers are helping to foster a much stronger customer-value orientation among business unit teams.

Out of all the possibilities shown in Figure 2.1, which management orientation do you use? Are you where you want to be? How do you transition to a different orientation? What role should information activities and processes play in that transition? Every organization should grapple with these questions. Because management orientation affects performance in markets, it is important to decide which one is best for you and your organization. If you are like a lot of managers in today's organizations, you can benefit most by improving processes for learning about external customers, markets, and opportunity. Overhauling the customer value determination (CVD) process on which you will depend is a start, but there is more to it than that.

The plan for this chapter is to show how customer value determination (or CVD), the major topic for this book, fits into a larger market opportunity analysis (MOA), an integrated external information process aimed at helping managers learn about opportunity in markets. In the next section, we argue that management orientation affects how MOAs are done in organizations. We compare two different approaches and then briefly discuss the MOA activities that are needed in the CVD process. Finally, we end the chapter by discussing how to manage MOA processes.

Approaches to Market Opportunity Analysis

All managers with market-related decision responsibility have "mental models" of their markets.[4] Essentially, a mental model is a set of beliefs about how various forces in markets operate to create opportunity. These models are absolutely crucial in decision making because they affect how managers interpret what they see going on in markets. Years ago at General Motors, for instance, managers apparently believed that Americans would not buy smaller cars and that Japanese automobile manufacturers could not make cars that would seriously threaten GM's market position. These beliefs influenced key decisions for a long time and were instrumental in allowing Japanese brands to make significant inroads into the U.S. automobile market. GM is only now beginning to recover from the resulting loss in market share and reputation.[3]

Too often, the mental models of individual managers can have a disastrous impact on strategy. Here is what Peter Drucker has to say on this point:

> A serious cause of business failure is the common assumption that conditions – taxes, social legislation, market preferences, distribution channels, intellectual property rights, and many others – *must* be what we think they are or at least what we think they *should* be. An adequate information system has to include information that makes executives question that assumption.[5]

Formal Models of Market Opportunity

Some organizations are turning to information tools to try to overcome their managers' over-reliance on their own mental models. One such tool is a formal, conceptual model of market opportunity. There are several such models available, and they can be very effective in guiding the development of information processes used to gather and organize data on external market opportunity.[2] Michael Porter's five forces model is a popular alternative.[3]

In his influential work on competitive advantage, Porter laid conceptual groundwork for understanding what forces operate in markets. He argued that industries should be the core unit of analysis. Based on his studies, Porter identified five major forces that determine opportunity in an industry: (1) bargaining power of customers, (2) bargaining power of suppliers, (3) threat of new entrants, (4) threat of substitute products and services, and (5) rivalry among firms in the industry. He recommended that managers learn how these forces work to create opportunity – or a lack of it – before deciding whether to compete in an industry or how to best achieve a competitive advantage.

We believe that Porter's model is an important contribution. Within an organization, it can replace the managers' more personal and diverse mental models of market opportunity with a shared framework. Adopting such a framework (1) encourages consistency across the organization in the way market analyses are performed and reported, (2) provides a checklist of data needed to analyze opportunity, and (3) ensures that important factors are not overlooked. We know of quite a few organizations that have redesigned their MOA processes to incorporate data about these five forces.

Every mental model is based on underlying assumptions, and Porter's model is no exception. For instance, this model assumes that players in an industry (i.e., buyers, suppliers, competitors, new entrants, and substitutes) do not have common goals or interests but instead are concerned with preserving and enhancing their own interests. They rely on "relative power," the ability of each party to affect how well the other can achieve its goals, during transaction bargaining. Assumptions like these color the way one looks at opportunity. If you accept that power drives opportunity, for example, you will tend to be wary of other players, whether they be competitors or customers, and to associate with those over which you can exercise the most power.

It is not hard to look at business practice and conclude that power is a major force in markets. Bargaining is common, and power may help one side involved in a transaction to extract concessions from the other. Large U.S. consumer products manufacturers, for instance, historically took advantage of their size and clout in dealing with organizations in distribution channels. The more recent successes of large-scale, low-price-for-value retailers such as Kmart, Target, and Wal-Mart has shifted the balance of power in most of these channels. Because of this change, even large manufacturers like Frito-Lay and Magnavox have had to redesign their ways of dealing with the trade. Increased use of selling teams, sharing of product flow information, concessions on price, and relationship building are just some of the ways in which sellers are responding to powerful trade customers.

A mental model's assumptions also influence external information processes. Certain data are given the highest priority. For instance, if you believe that power drives opportunity, you are likely to pay attention to data describing weaknesses in suppliers, competitors, and customers. You look for a power imbalance that works in your favor and then exploit it to enhance your organization's power. A manufacturer driven by power may temporarily sell at artificially low prices in order to weaken another competitor or sabotage a competitor's test market for a new product in order to distort what the competitor learns about market opportunity. A large retailer may threaten to stop buying from a smaller manufacturer in order to gain a price concession.

There are different formal models of market opportunity available, and each tends to be more consistent with some management orientations than others. Think a minute about which of the decision-making orientations in Figure 2.1 is most consistent with Porter's model. If you are a competitor-oriented manager, you probably will feel comfortable with this model. Suppose, however, that you want to make a transition toward a customer orientation or a customer-value orientation. In this case, you may want to consider alternative models.

Value-Exchange-System Model of Market Opportunity

Clues that another, very different mechanism than power operates in markets come from the growing number of organizations that are forging long-term relationships with other players. Think about what the following organizations want to accomplish:

- Procter & Gamble and Wal-Mart have established an ongoing supply relationship, merging parts of their organizations for greater total performance.
- General Electric has established over 100 collaborative relationships with other firms.
- Whirlpool created a large 1-800 customer service operation to make it easy for consumers to communicate requests and complaints and get fast response.
- A consortium of European firms formed Airbus Industries to compete in the global aerospace market.

In each of these instances, competitors, suppliers, and customers strive for long-term relationships where mutual benefit comes through cooperation. Relationships require thinking beyond an individual transaction. Organizations must develop a common sense of commitment and loyalty to each other over many interactions. In today's markets, we believe that cooperation is becoming a critical force that influences the nature of opportunity. What would a model of market opportunity look like if it was based on cooperation? The value-exchange systems model, shown in Figure 2.2, suggests an answer.

This model assumes that market opportunity originates with end users because it is their needs that create demand. These customers are linked to sellers through channels that extend back to trade customers (e.g., retailers, distributors, wholesalers, and so forth), producers, and eventually to their suppliers. For example, consider the running shoes market. Competitors such as Adidas, Nike, New Balance, and Reebok offer shoes and support services targeted for both consumer and organizational (e.g., university sports programs) end users. These firms sell directly to organizational customers and distribute their products through retailers, such as specialty sports stores and large discounters. Running shoe manufacturers work with many suppliers to obtain a variety of components, materials, and service.

Though independent organizations, participants in distribution channels must work together to deliver value to end users. In turn, end users deliver value back to the entire channel through their behavior, such as purchases, loyalty, commitment, positive word of mouth, and the like. Cooperation influences these interactions. As channel participants think more about mutual benefits, they explore such relationship practices as electronic data interchange, just-in-time delivery, and mutually agreed upon quality standards.

There are some very good reasons why cooperation is gaining favor in business practice. For one thing, there is a cost advantage to building long-term relationships. From a supplier's perspective, it has been estimated that it costs about one-fifth as much to retain an existing customer than it does to acquire a new one.[6] In addition, cooperating organizations can combine core competencies to jointly reduce the risk inherent in today's dynamic markets.[4] The important point is that all participants in

31

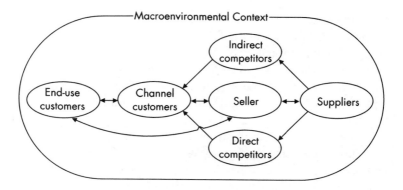

Figure 2.2. The value-exchange-system model of market opportunity.

the system must pay attention to relationship building through value exchange if the system as a whole is to work effectively. A model of market opportunity founded on cooperation will facilitate that effort.

An MOA Framework for Customer-Value-Oriented Organizations

The value-exchange-system model suggests an alternative MOA process to Porter's five forces analysis. The former model advocates a rather different combination and sequencing of information activities (see Figure 2.3).[7] Starting at the top of Figure 2.3 and working down, you will see that the MOA process links together four major phases. Phase I analyzes the macroenvironment in which a market's value-exchange channel system operates. The purpose of Phase I is to help managers learn about how market opportunity is being shaped by economic, cultural, social, technological, governmental, and natural forces. Consider the recession of the early 1990s. Many predict that this downturn will prove to have made a lasting impact on buying habits in the United States and elsewhere around the world. Consumers are expected to spend less, seek more benefits, have less desire for material goods, and show more concern for future

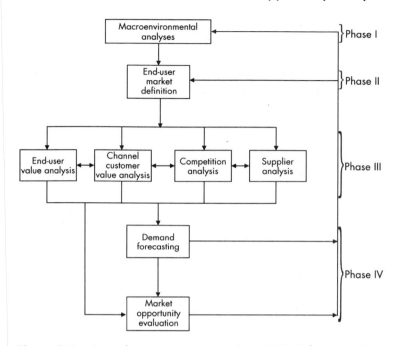

Figure 2.3. A market opportunity analysis (MOA) framework.

financial security.[8] Creative strategies will be needed to take advantage of these new realities.

Phase II of the MOA identifies markets and customers with specific opportunities. This activity lays out the alternative markets within which opportunity lies. Arguably, it is the most critical phase. For one thing, the results greatly affect an organization's strategic decisions on target markets. For another, all other MOA phases follow from it. For instance, which competitors become the focus for analysis depends on which markets and customers are of most interest to managers. Suppose an important segment of potential buyers of luxury boats also consider buying houseboats. If you are in the luxury pleasure boat business, you will have to understand the relative value delivered by houseboat competitors as part of your strategic thinking.

Phase III helps managers understand the nature and dynamics of the interactions between key participants in markets.

Market Opportunity Analysis

Information activities focus on understanding the exchange of value between suppliers, competitors, trade customers, and end users. CVD is a key process in this phase for both end users and channel customers. What value do customers seek, how satisfied are they with value delivered by sellers, and how is that satisfaction related to desired customer behaviors such as repurchase, positive word of mouth, sales, and loyalty? Value delivery by competitors also must be analyzed to identify their strengths and weaknesses.

Finally, Phase IV of the MOA concentrates on evaluating opportunities in identified markets. In part, evaluation requires forecasting the future demand from these markets. Revenue potential is an important criterion for assessing opportunity. Other criteria for evaluation are also needed to ensure that all aspects of opportunity are explored. These include:

- Financial criteria
    - Sales growth
    - Market share growth
    - Profit potential
    - Return on investment
    - Cash flow
- Sustained advantage criteria
    - Industry entry barriers keep out competition
    - Untapped segments available
    - Evidence of relative strengths
    - Protection from weakness
- Synergistic criteria
    - Enhance opportunities for complementary products
    - Keep customers with shifting preferences in the firm's sales
    - Fill niches to discourage competitors
- Company and brand image criteria
    - Consistent with corporate image
    - Enhance corporate image
    - Enhance product line image

For instance, opportunity may come from the synergy between products in a product line or the product mix. Honda recognized the importance of this kind of opportunity when it introduced a new entry into the U.S. luxury car market. The company capitalized on the goodwill built up among its Accord customers by offering the Acura line for those who wanted to trade up to a luxury car.

The value-exchange-based MOA model provides a framework for designing and implementing an external information process. Its most critical feature is the interrelationship between the various phases and activities of an MOA. For instance, CVD both depends on and contributes to other MOA activities. In the next section, we explore some of these interrelationships.

Positioning Customer Value Determination in an MOA

We position CVD as the core process in the "end user value analysis" and "channel customer value analysis" components of the MOA shown in Figure 2.3. The rest of this book expands on CVD activities. At this point, however, it is important to understand that each MOA component must fit together with the others into a larger picture of market opportunity, and CVD is no exception. Let's see how CVD interrelates with some of the other MOA components. (Before reading further, you may want to review the CVD process shown in Figure 1.3.)

Customer Value Determination and Macroenvironmental Analysis

Because the types of value desired by customers will change, a hallmark of customer-value-oriented management is its focus on the future. You must devote part of your time to anticipating likely change scenarios.[9] CVD contributes to this information need by predicting customer value changes. Macroenvironmental analysis is a key information source for this activity.

As we discuss in Chapter 9, one major impetus for customer value change comes from shifts in the macroenvironment. Consider the revolution in information technology. Computer, telephone, and cable TV technologies are merging to create new and different opportunities for suppliers to build relationships with their customers. For instance, telephone companies offer voice mail services, which have become serious competitors to the answering machine. These services, which demonstrate the benefits of using the telephone as a multipurpose tool, cause customers to change their perception of value and open the door for telephone companies to offer a variety of other services.[5] Technology is but one of many such macroenvironmental forces that must be considered in predicting changes in how customers perceive value.

Customer Value Determination and End-User Market Definition

Not all customers value the same things. For instance, customers who use their pleasure boats to entertain business associates have different sets of values than those who use their boats for family outings. Such differences require that you decide which customers are important prior to launching a CVD process. The MOA process takes this relationship into consideration by sequencing end-user market definition to precede the start of the CVD process.

It is beyond the scope of this book to discuss the market definition process. However, there are some observations that we can offer. We find that the diagram in Figure 2.4 is helpful to think about what you need to know from the market definition phase.

Selecting Markets. CVD can be applied to learn about customers in both existing markets and new markets. Every organization should determine what resources should be spent on studying customers in each type of market. Hopefully, the markets already served by an organization will be well-defined. Identifying new markets is more difficult. There are several directions in which a company can look for these new opportunities. One is toward the markets served by a company's competitors. For instance, Japanese automobile manufacturers are trying to break into markets in Western Europe, which are now dominated by their American, British, and Western European competitors. Similarly, Mariott devoted six months to studying

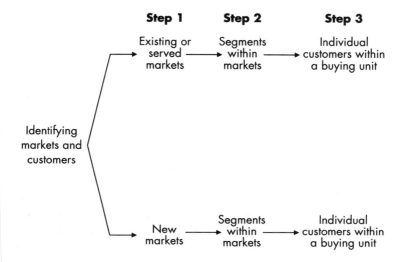

Figure 2.4. Identifying markets and customers.

markets currently served by economy hotels in the United States and Europe before deciding to enter them.[10]

Another type of new market is that being served by different types of products. By definition, product types serve similar needs, and each one's market potentially can be entered by the others. Perrier, in a very successful market entry, demonstrated that image-based bottled-water products could make significant inroads into markets targeted by soft drink companies. More recently, Coke, with its "Coke in the Morning" promotional campaign, captured sales that would have otherwise gone to coffee companies.

Finally, new markets may emerge when customers place priority on a new need. Your organization may have core competencies well-suited to delivering value to these emerging markets. Consider the impact on bicycle demand when U.S. consumers began placing increasing importance on personal health and fitness. Bicycle manufacturers, who were accustomed to serving children's markets, saw new markets emerge as adults discovered that bicycle riding is a great way to improve their strength and aerobic fitness.

Selecting Segments. Markets, whether existing or new, are often comprised of segments. If so, customer value will differ across these segments. For instance, business travelers have different needs for accommodations than do family vacation travelers. To learn about these differences, CVD must be applied to each priority segment separately. Fortunately, techniques for segmenting markets are well known and widely used.[6] Most market research firms can help you design research programs to uncover actionable segments.

Sometimes, CVD data cause a reevaluation of prior segmentation. We have seen several cases where the value sought by customers in existing or served segments is so similar as to bring into question just how actionable these segments are. If customers in two segments want the same things, it does not make sense to have different value delivery strategies for each of them. In this case, you should recycle from CVD back to the market definition phase of the MOA. CVD data may help in suggesting a different, more actionable segmentation.

Selecting Respondents. Finally, CVD requires that you identify the people in a customer unit (e.g., a household, an organization) who need to be researched. If the segment is comprised of consumers, who in each designated household should be interviewed? For example, the head of service operations for an automobile dealer noticed that the number of women who were coming to the service center was increasing. Consequently, market research was conducted to learn more about the value that women seek from dealer service centers.

The same issue comes up for industrial customer segments. Who in customer organizations should be studied? Because these customers typically are larger than households, there may be more people involved in the study. A few may have formal purchase decision responsibility, but others may influence the decisions of which suppliers to use. All of these people form the "buying center" in a customer organization. It is not unusual to have to contact four, five, or more respondents from a single organization in order to fully understand the value sought by buying centers.

In general, you are going to get more insightful information from CVD processes if you, in advance, carefully select who to study. It is the value desired by high priority customers that should weigh most heavily in strategy and tactical decisions.

Customer Value Determination and Competitor Analyses

In Chapter 1, we mentioned the fact that customer value research often reveals a large number of value dimensions. It is quite likely that you will not be able to work on all of them at once. The CVD process recognizes this reality by helping you select and concentrate on the strategically most important customer value dimensions (see Figure 1.3). One criterion for determining strategic importance is whether you can achieve a competitive advantage through the delivery of a particular value dimension. Implementing this criterion requires knowing how well competitors are delivering that value dimension, and it is at this point that competitor analyses contribute to CVD.

We are most interested in uncovering how customers view our competitors' strengths and weaknesses. Competitor analyses provide this insight by assessing how well specific value dimensions are being delivered within an industry and by key competitors. You can go directly to customers for this information. Ask them to rate one or more key competitors as to how well they perform on various value dimensions. Then compare these ratings with corresponding ratings of your organization's value delivery.[5] For instance, a county hospital conducted a study to learn about a key competitor's strengths and weaknesses. Management found that this competitor was not rated highly by patients on the value dimension, " helps me feel that I am a valued person." Apparently, that hospital created a very impersonal atmosphere for patients, and they did not like it. The sponsoring hospital saw an opportunity to build advantage by delivering to patients a feeling that the hospital's staff cared about them as individuals.

In general, organizations that are most skilled at MOAs recognize that all of its components must be integrated into a comprehensive evaluation of opportunity. Information from one component often makes a contribution to the analyses in another component, and this is especially true for CVD. You will get the most benefit from CVD if you manage the entire MOA process well.

Managing MOAs in Organizations

MOAs, including customer value determination, must be actionable. Unless this external data influences strategy and implementation decisions, resources are being wasted. This point is obvious, but we continually hear managers complain that too many resources are spent on market research data that are not influential in key decisions. This complaint is real, and there are many reasons for it. However, most of these reasons reflect problems with the management of MOA processes, and they are correctable. Like any other internal process, an MOA needs continuous improvement.

A Gaps Model of MOA Processes

When working properly, an MOA should kick in when managers request data to help with an important decision. (See the left column in Figure 2.5.) This request comes in the form of questions about market opportunity. How well a question is answered depends on the quality of the MOA concepts, tools, and techniques brought to bear on it. Data are generated, analyzed for information content, and translated into a decision. The outcome, in terms of performance, depends on both the soundness of the decision relative to market opportunity and the effectiveness of the decision's implementation.

We think that managing an MOA boils down to making this information-based decision process work smoothly. You have to anticipate where there may be problems so that you can prevent them. The right column in Figure 2.5 identifies where these problems may occur. We call them "gaps" because they are most likely to occur during the transition from one step to the next.

MOA Information Gap. The first gap arises when managers are unsure of the questions that should be asked. MOAs cannot help

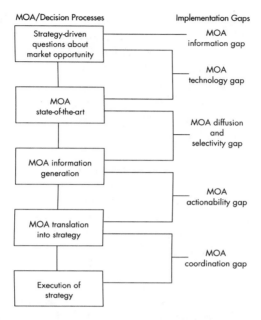

MOA/Decision Processes | Implementation Gaps

Strategy-driven questions about market opportunity

MOA information gap

MOA technology gap

MOA state-of-the-art

MOA diffusion and selectivity gap

MOA information generation

MOA actionability gap

MOA translation into strategy

MOA coordination gap

Execution of strategy

Figure 2.5. Managing MOA processes in an organization.

if you do not ask the right questions. Suppose you are accountable for creating and delivering superior value to targeted customers. You ask, however, about which of a competitor's internal operating weaknesses makes it the most susceptible to tactics to drive it out of a market. A competitor analysis may uncover such weaknesses, if they exist, but is that data really answering the right question? Probably not. Decisions driven by this data may not have much to do with delivering value to customers. In fact, the data may actually distract you from your primary responsibility or even lead to charges of unfair competitive practices.

MOA Technology Gap.   Even if the right questions are asked, someone must select the right information to provide answers. Of course, you have to consider whether it is possible to answer a critical question given the current MOA state of the art. Most of the time it is, but there are exceptions. Suppose, for example, that a new product design team wants to know what value customers will desire ten years from now, but the technology for forecasting value for these customers ten years into the future does not exist. You face a technology gap, and in the short run, it may not be correctable. While tremendous progress has been made over the past several decades in advancing MOA technology, there are some questions that cannot be answered. You will have to ask different questions.

MOA Diffusion Gap.   The technology may exist for answering a question about market opportunity, but does someone in your organization know about that technology? If you do not know about a technology, it will not get used. For example, conjoint analysis techniques, which are very useful for determining which of several product or service attributes or benefits are most important to customers (see Appendix III), have been available for well over a decade. However, only recently have applications of this technique become widespread. Unfortunately, it may take a decade or more for MOA techniques to diffuse into widespread business practices.

MOA Selectivity Gap.   Collecting and analyzing MOA data only creates a potential for actionability – managers may elect not to rely on the information generated. There are several reasons why this happens. For instance, a particular technique may be undervalued. We argue in Chapter 7, for example, that some questions about customer value are best answered by qualitative research techniques such as in-depth personal interviews, focus groups, and direct observation. However, we know of cases where managers feel that data collected by these techniques are not valid and thus have consistently ignored reports of results from qualitative research.

Sometimes, this selectivity problem can have deeper roots. Intuition-oriented and internally oriented managers do not place a high priority on most external data. They tend to select it out when making decisions. In addition, we know that some managers feel threatened by certain kinds of MOA information and thus avoid using it. Satisfaction research is an example. A manager simply may not want to know whether customers are dissatisfied with services for which he or she is responsible. In general, it does not matter what the reason is. If you choose to ignore data, it cannot influence decisions.

MOA Actionability Gap.   Let's say you get MOA data and take the time to study what it means. There is still the challenge of translating that data into strategic or tactical actions, and problems can come up at this point. Perhaps the data are incomplete. For instance, branch managers at one bank were expected to improve performance on those value dimensions receiving low customer satisfaction scores. Too often, however, managers did not know exactly how to make such improvements because no follow-up research had been done to explain why customers were not satisfied. So the managers had to guess at what actions to take. This trial-and-error approach was frustrating.

Sometimes, data gathered by one department for its own purposes are examined by managers from another department. Actionability is hindered when the data are not well suited for the latter's purpose. For instance, suppose an auto manufacturer's advertising department learns that consumers desire a "feeling of security while driving in bad weather." That information may be highly actionable for creating an advertising message. But product design engineers may look at that same finding and feel that it is too vague or general to help with product improvement decisions. Actionability lies in the eyes of the user.

MOA Coordination Gap.   Finally, suppose strategy decisions made by one management team are implemented by others within an organization. Those managers who implement strategy may look at customers, markets, and opportunity differently. For instance, in the publishing industry it is common practice for a textbook to be designed by an editorial team. When a text is ready for introduction, a member of this team presents it to the sales organization at an annual sales meeting. At this point, responsibility for the textbook shifts from the editorial team to the sales force. We know of one new product introduction where MOA data were not fully shared between the design team and sales. Unfortunately, sales managers decided to target customers who were different from the ones for whom the textbook was designed. The result was confusion in the marketplace.

The potential threat from the six gaps just discussed is real, but it can be managed. Each gap represents an opportunity to improve the MOA process by finding ways to narrow or close it. In the next section, we suggest some of these ways.

Managing Ongoing MOA Processes

Each gap responds to different improvement activities. The following is a list of some options that can be implemented.

- Develop organizational ways to speed up diffusion of MOA knowledge.
- Implement organizationwide training based on a common MOA process model template.
- Change the corporate culture and reward systems to encourage managerial participation in and use of MOAs.
- Assign clear ownership responsibility for MOA processes.
- Ensure that the MOA processes are ongoing.
- Periodically review and evaluate the MOA system for completeness, sharing of data, managerial ownership and involvement, the use of state-of-the-art tools and techniques, managerial relevance, cost versus benefit balance, data timeliness and accuracy, and so forth.

We believe that organizations should develop ways to speed up the diffusion of MOA technology. There are many ways to accomplish this objective. For example, one advertising agency employs a technical expert to read specialty literature in marketing and consumer behavior in order to cull out applicable concepts, theories, tools, and research results and then present them to management. There are other ways to affect diffusion as well. You might consider (1) routing MOA technique articles around to potential users, (2) attending executive education programs, (3) participating in practitioner conferences such as the American Marketing Association's annual conference on customer satisfaction measurement, and (4) picking the brains of new hires and consultants.

Notice that some improvement activities help to reduce more than one gap. For instance, MOA training should be offered for all potential users in an organization. Everyone should start with the same perspective on how to do MOAs and why they are actionable. Further, every organization must have a culture and a reward system in place that encourages mangers to treat MOAs as a critical information source for decisions. Remember, customer-value-oriented managers are data driven.

Perhaps the most important suggestion in the list given earlier concerns the ownership of the design, execution, and application of the MOA process. Too often this ownership is not clearly assigned. Instead, we find that individual departments or functions in an organization develop their own approach to MOAs and that there is very little consistency across the organization. Or the market research function assumes de facto ownership even though this function does not have strategic decision-making accountability. We believe that the lack of organizationwide ownership unfortunately tends to widen the various MOA gaps. For instance, you can count on having serious coordination gap problems when different departments have their own MOA processes.

There has been virtually no attention given to finding answers for the ownership issue. Different opinions abound. One view is to assign ownership for MOAs high up in the organization. After all, top management should be accountable for the design and implementation of all internal systems and processes. Further, top management is in the best position to ensure that MOA processes are effectively used for decision applications across functions. An alternative view is to assign MOA ownership to cross-functional teams who have decision-making accountability for customer-value-based strategies. This approach ensures that all managers involved in developing and executing strategy for the same customer segments have a common process for learning about market opportunity. Whichever view is chosen, the important thing is to clearly assign ownership so that the MOA process will be improved.

Summary

The purpose of this chapter is to present a larger informational framework within which to position customer value determination. We started by arguing that how well CVD is used depends on the orientation of management. Although there are several different orientations possible, we showed that external market data are critical for managers who plan and execute value delivery strategies. An MOA process is the means by which managers learn about customers, markets, and opportunity.

Next, we discussed two quite different models used to conceptualize what drives opportunity in markets – Michael Porter's five forces industry model and our value-exchange-system model. Because each model translates into somewhat different MOA processes, it is important to chose the appropriate one. We favor the value-exchange-system model for those organizations that want to build long-term relationships with customers. Based on this model we introduced an MOA process framework that lays out the sequence and types of information subprocesses needed to evaluate opportunity in end-use markets.

The most important feature of this MOA is the interdependence of the various MOA information subprocesses. We illustrated this point by discussing how customer value determination is dependent on (1) macroenvironmental analyses, (2) market definition, and (3) competitor analyses.

Finally, the chapter raised an important issue concerning the management of MOA processes. Just collecting and analyzing external data is not enough. We argued that MOA processes must be managed to maximize their contribution to management's decisions. Most importantly, we argued that ownership for MOAs be explicitly assigned to ensure that continuous improvements are made in this critical information process.

In the next section of the book, we narrow our focus to the customer value determination process component of an MOA. In Chapters 3 and 4, we discuss an important perspective on the nature of customer value and how it relates to customer satisfaction. This relationship was instrumental in designing the customer value determination process introduced in Chapter 1 and developed more fully in Chapter 5. In Chapter 6, we suggest a number of ways in which CVD information can be applied in organizations.

References

[1]   Bacon, Kenneth H., "Banks' Declining Role in Economy Worries Fed, May Hurt Firms," *Wall Street Journal*, July 9, 1993, A1, A5.

[2]   Brannigan, Martha, "Two Big Rival Banks in Southeast Take on New-Age Competitors," *Wall Street Journal*, July 8, 1993, A1, A4.

[3]   Loomis, Carol J., "Dinosaurs?," *Fortune*, May 3, 1993, pp. 36–42.

[4]   Senge, Peter M., "The Leader's New Work: Building Learning Organizations," *Sloan Management Review,* 12 (Fall 1990), pp. 7–24.

[5]   Drucker, Peter F., "The Information Executives Truly Need," *Harvard Business Review*, 73 (January-February 1995), p. 61.

[6]   Sellers, Patricia, "Getting Customers to Love You," *Fortune*, March 13, 1989, pp. 38–49.

[7]   Cravens, David W., Shannon H. Shipp, and Karen S. Cravens, "Analysis of Cooperative Interorganizational Relationships, Strategic Alliance Formation, and Strategic Alliance Effectiveness," *Journal of Strategic Marketing*, 1 (March 1993), pp. 55–70.

[8]   Sellers, Patricia, "Winning over the New Consumer," *Fortune*, July 29, 1991, pp. 113–126.

[9]   Hamel, Gary and C. K. Prahalad, "Competing for the Future," *Harvard Business Review*, 72 (July/August 1994), pp. 122–130.

[10] Dumaine, Brian, "Corporate Spies Snoop to Conquer," *Fortune*, November 7, 1988, pp. 68–76.

Notes

1. For more discussion of this point, see Day, George, *Market Driven Strategy*. New York: The Free Press, 1990, Chapter 6.

2. It is beyond the scope of this chapter to review all formal models of market opportunity. For other discussions of market analysis models, see Day, George S., *Analysis for*

Strategic Market Decisions. St. Paul, MN: West Publishing Company, 1986; and Donald R. Lehmann and Russell S. Winer, *Analysis for Marketing Planning.* Burr Ridge, IL: Richard D. Irwin, Inc. 1994.

3. Comments in this section on Porter's model are based on material in two books: Porter, Michael E., *Competitive Advantage: Creating and Sustaining Superior Performance.* New York: The Free Press, 1985; and Michael E. Porter, *Competitive Strategy: Techniques for Analyzing Industries and Competitors.* New York: The Free Press, 1980.

4. For a similar framework, see Woodruff, Robert B. and Ernest R. Cadotte, "Market Opportunity Analyses for New Ventures," *Survey of Business,* 12 (August 1990), pp. 1–12.

5. For more on this topic, see Rayport, J.F. and J.J. Sviokla, "Managing in the Marketspace," *Harvard Business Review*, 72 (November/December 1994), pp. 141–153.

6. For more on segmentation, see Cravens, David W., *Strategic Marketing.* Burr Ridge, IL: Richard D. Irwin, Inc., 1994, Chapters 5 and 6; and Wind, Yoram, "Issues and Advances in Segmentation Research," *Journal of Marketing Research*, 15 (August 1978), pp. 317–337.

7. We discuss this kind of analysis more fully in Chapter 11.

Section II

LEARNING ABOUT
CUSTOMER VALUE
AND SATISFACTION

CHAPTER 3

A NEW PERSPECTIVE ON CUSTOMER VALUE

One of the chief determinants of satisfaction for customers of service organizations is length of waiting time. This is true for a number of businesses, whether it be a grocery's check-out line, a doctor's waiting room, or the service call on a broken copier. How service suppliers respond to this problem, however, depends very much on how they define it. For example, a hotel might define the problem as "the lines are too long at our registration desk." As such, its management would likely consider solutions that focused on the registration desk and procedures and that might include everything from adding personnel to adopting high-technology solutions.

What if the problem was defined differently? For instance, a hotel could see a broader goal: to reduce (or even eliminate) the time between the guests' arrival and when they get to their rooms. Given this problem definition, which focuses more on the consequences to the customer and less on one particular aspect of the business operation, management might think more creatively about ways to create customer value. One hotel recently did this when they began to register customers in the hotel courtesy van on the drive from the airport. By the time its customers arrive at the hotel, they have been checked in and provided a room key, allowing them to bypass the front desk altogether and go straight to their room.[1] This is an example of what can happen when a business stops organizing its efforts around improving attributes or features of its existing offering and instead defines its mission as determining and delivering customer value.

Introduction

"What is customer value?" "What is it that *our particular customers* value?" "How do I know if we are delivering value to our customers?" In whatever form they are asked, these questions are fundamental to any business organization, whether it sells a product or a service, whether it is a profit or nonprofit organization, whether it is a relatively young organization or one that has been in business for years. These are questions that must be asked and asked continually, for the answers are complex and dynamic. More importantly, these are questions that, when answered correctly and insightfully, can ensure the long-range survival of an organization. Likewise, organizations that answer these questions incorrectly – or, worse yet, fail to ask them at all – are probably doomed to failure in the long run, if not sooner.

As fundamental and basic as these questions are, too many organizations cannot answer them as well as they should. Organizations that don't understand what their customers value typically suffer from one of two problems: (1) failing to ask customers the right questions and/or (2) failing to disseminate and use customer information effectively across the organization.

First, it has been our experience that many managers never ask the right questions to begin with. This manifests itself in many different ways within organizations.

- Some managers aren't asking customers any questions at all. The most obvious cases (although they are becoming more rare) are those where organizations do not have any processes in place for systematically gathering customer feedback.
- More typical are cases where managers have tried existing customer information processes only to give up on them. This may occur because the existing process fails to provide actionable data or because the managers feel that it is impossible to keep up with rapid marketplace change, including mercurial customer attitudes. More arrogant managers are those who feel that they know the answers *better* than their customers, who can be "coached" into the correct mindset. (The experiences of the American automobile manufacturers in the 1970s and '80s are classic examples of this attitude.)

- Finally, an increasing number of organizations are trying to answer these questions via customer satisfaction measurement (CSM). CSM has multiplied at an astounding rate over the last decade. While we will argue in Chapter 4 that customer satisfaction is important and worthy of attention, we will also contend that traditional customer satisfaction measures, by themselves, are incapable of fully addressing customer value issues. In short, they are typically more concerned with evaluating product features than with understanding the customer's perception of value.

Second, many organizations do not have information systems and processes in place which are capable of effectively promoting the dissemination and use of customer data. These systems and processes may not exist at all. Or existing systems may be deficient for several reasons, including: (1) the data may not be updated often enough, leading to information that is outdated and static, (2) information systems may not effectively integrate customer information from different organizational sources (e.g., customer satisfaction surveys, salesperson call reports, complaint data, and so forth), leaving it to be analyzed in a piecemeal fashion, (3) the information may not get into the hands of the managers who need it to make strategic decisions, (4) if the information gets into the right hands, the users may not know what to do with it, or (5) organizations may not encourage appropriate managerial use of customer information because they fail to tie responsibilities, performance evaluation, and rewards to it. Unfortunately, managers are often lulled into thinking that existing information systems are working effectively when in fact they may not be.

In this chapter, we address the first problem cited previously: the failure of many organizations to ask the right questions at the outset. If this problem isn't resolved, it does no good to pursue subsequent problems related to information dissemination and use. To do this, we must begin by helping the reader understand what customer value is.

First, we define value through the eyes of the customer and

in terms of the interaction that occurs between the product and the customer in a use situation. Next, a value hierarchy is proposed that provides a way for managers to organize their thinking about customer value. This hierarchy encourages a broader perspective on value that goes beyond a narrow focus on product attributes or features and instead considers higher order outcomes that the customer experiences. Finally, to explore the advantages and managerial implications of a customer value perspective, a comparison is made between a customer value perspective and more traditional ways of thinking about the customer.

Defining Customer Value

What is customer value? The question is deceptively simple. Although we all believe we know what "value" means, in fact there are a multitude of different definitions and perspectives.[1,2] The concept of value is one that has its roots in many disciplines, including psychology, social psychology, economics, marketing, and management. Even when we narrow our interest more specifically to consider the "customer value" of a particular product or service, there are multiple meanings. For instance, for many organizations customer value means "value-added," which is the economic cost (price) necessary to build certain attributes and features into a product or service for customers. While economic value is certainly part of the puzzle, it is necessary to define value more broadly in order to understand its richness from the customer perspective.[3]

The following definition of value has been adopted for our purposes: *Customer value is the customers' perception of what they want to have happen (i.e., the consequences) in a specific use situation, with the help of a product or service offering, in order to accomplish a desired purpose or goal.* There are three important elements of this definition.

- Products are means of accomplishing the customers' purposes. The purposes of product use can be broadly classified as *value-in-use* or *possession value*.

- Products create value through the delivery of consequences (the outcomes that are experienced by the customer), rather than through their inherent characteristics.
- Customers' value judgments are highly influenced by and best determined within the constraints of a particular use situation. These judgments are subject to change across use situations, over time, and due to specific "trigger" situations.

These three elements will be explored in more detail below.

Consumption Goals: Value in Use and Possession Value

One of the most important aspects of the value definition just given is its suggestion that, for customers, products are merely means to an end. In fact, what managers need to understand first and foremost is not the product per se, but what the customer wants to accomplish – the ultimate purpose or goal that is being served. The specific purposes and/or goals that customers are attempting to achieve are as many and varied as the products and consumption experiences themselves, but they can be more generally understood in two broad classifications: *value in use* and *possession value*.[1,4]

"Value in use," as the name suggests, is a functional outcome, purpose, or objective that is served directly through product consumption.[5] For example, drinking a cup of coffee helps the customer to wake up in the morning, using a word processor increases a user's productivity, and using a particular supplier's materials in a manufacturing process can increase product reliability. Other examples of value in use might include time efficiency, thirst quenching, dependable transportation, entertainment, easy clean-up, and so forth. The specific type of value in use that the customer requires will obviously vary considerably by type of product or service. However, even for a specific product or service there may be a number of value-in-use objectives which the product must meet. For example, consumers of the same microwave dinner may have different and often competing purposes in mind – including, nutrition, low cost, good taste, quick preparation, and so forth.

Customers can also derive value simply from possessing a product. This notion of possession value acknowledges that products can contain important symbolic, self-expressive, and aesthetic qualities that accrue to the customer through proximity and association.[6,7] This type of value is often associated with products that have a very high "pride of ownership" component, such as family heirlooms or a firm's expensive office furnishings. In addition to the obvious luxury items, consumers may have pride of ownership attached to relatively inexpensive items (e.g., a bargain from a garage sale, a clothing fashion item, or any product with which the consumer has a high involvement because of his or her specific interests). Services have a parallel "pride of usership" component. Consider the status and prestige that can accrue to the individual who dines at a fine restaurant or the business organization that retains a prestigious legal counsel.

Of course, these two goals are not mutually exclusive. Many products deliver both value in use and possession value. Consider the owner of a Mercedes-Benz or a corporate jet, or a fashion innovator's purchase of a new suit, or a firm's new office building. These classifications are not meant to imply an either/or mentality, but to alert you to the multiple purposes that may be associated with the use of your products.

The Consequences of Product Use

The ability of customers to attain their desired purposes or goals is determined by the *consequences* of product use. As opposed to characteristics of the product itself, consequences are *outcomes that are experienced by the customer as a result of product use.* Customers will seek consequences that are linked to a desired purpose or goal and avoid those that are not.

Some consequences of product consumption are positive. These are the desired outcomes, or benefits, that the customer enjoys as a result of product/service possession and consumption, and they can be far-reaching in scope. Some positive consequences may be relatively objective in nature – for example, infrequent trips to the service department, minimal time and effort involved in assembly, a lower inventory, and the like. In contrast, many positive consequences are quite subjective in nature, including stress relief, self-confidence, efficiency, productivity, and so forth. Positive consequences may result from the presence of a single product or service attribute (e.g., front-wheel drive to provide better handling on snow). They may also accrue across a number of product attributes and features. For example, many features of a car might combine to determine the consumer's perception of "a comfortable ride," including its suspension, size, upholstery, climate control, and so forth.

Like positive consequences, negative consequences can be both objective (e.g., price, time) and subjective (e.g., "difficult to use"). The most frequently considered negative consequence of product consumption is the price. However, negative consequences go well beyond monetary considerations. Thinking more broadly, for every positive consequence associated with the use of a product, there is a corresponding negative consequence that the customer must bear if that benefit is not received. For instance, when ease of use is not perceived, the negative consequence of using the product might well be the conclusion that it is "difficult to operate" or that it "takes too much of my time (or effort)." Negative consequences may include psychological costs (e.g., stress or loss of prestige), the time and effort spent in purchasing and consuming the product, loss of the opportunity (e.g., lost productivity or sales due to choosing an unreliable supplier), and various other sacrifices that might be associated with the product or service.

We consider value to be the result of the trade-off between the positive and negative consequences of product use as perceived by the customer (see Figure 3.1).[8] Product and service providers must keep in mind that customers will receive multiple consequences as a result of using a product and that it would be highly unusual for these consequences to be all positive or all negative. For example, a consumer's new car may provide comfort, a feeling of security and luxury, and better handling. However, these positive consequences may be offset by having to cope with frequent repairs, deal with insensitive service providers at the dealership, or experience psychological stress because of the price. Managers must therefore attempt to under-

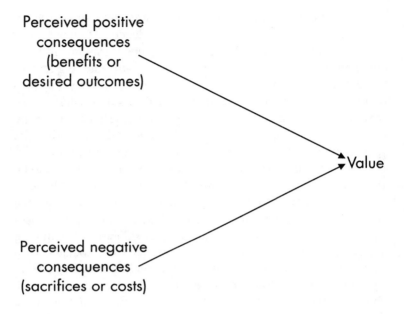

Perceived positive
consequences
(benefits or
desired outcomes)

Value

Perceived negative
consequences
(sacrifices or costs)

Figure 3.1. Value as a trade-off in consequences.

stand the consequence trade-offs that their customers will experience and, thus, the value that is associated with their product. These trade-offs are critical because they determine the extent to which the consumer's ultimate goals and purposes are achieved.

Understanding the value trade-offs customers are willing to make can, in fact, provide strategic opportunities for businesses. For example, in buying home furnishings, consumers have traditionally been willing to pay a premium price so that the seller will, in turn, provide offsetting benefits such as assembly, delivery, and displaying the furniture in elaborate showrooms staffed by helpful salespeople and interior design consultants.

One furniture manufacturer created a strategic opportunity by reconsidering the cost-benefit trade-off for its customers.[9] IKEA has become the world's largest retailer of home furnishings, with a global network of over 100 stores worldwide and

1992 revenues of $4.3 billion. While maintaining certain stand-ards of quality in their furniture, IKEA has encouraged its consumers to make product selections with minimal assistance, to assemble furniture themselves, and to transport it to their homes in exchange for a lower priced product. To be sure, IKEA assists their consumers by providing catalogues, pens, paper, and tape measures, by furnishing carts to transport the ready to assemble furniture to the consumer's car, and by loaning or selling automobile roof racks to get the furniture to the con-sumer's homes. Clearly, the success of IKEA is a result of its understanding the trade-offs its consumers are willing to make as well as its willingness to redefine the value equation differ-ently from traditional industry practice.

The Importance of Use Situation

Value is created when a product and a user come together within a particular use situation (see Figure 3.2).[10,11] This perspec-tive is important because customers' judgments about product value are based upon the requirements of their use situations. In fact, it is difficult to determine whether a product "generally" provides value for an individual or organization without under-standing the many different ways which the product will be used. For example, a consumer may consider purchasing a bottle of wine for one of many use situations: a dinner at home with the family, a picnic, a means to entertain important guests, as a gift for a friend, and so forth. The value that a particular bottle of wine has for the consumer may vary considerably depending upon the demands of these different use situations.

A good example of using this triangulated perspective to create customer value comes from Nissan's development of the Maxima.[12] Positioned as a sedan for families (users), Nissan began to consider the various ways in which their product would be used (situations). One specific situation that was considered was "women loading groceries," which put additional emphasis on the need for a trunk that would be easy to open and close. Therefore, Nissan designed the trunk (product) with a counter-balanced lid so that it would create more value for the user in this situation.

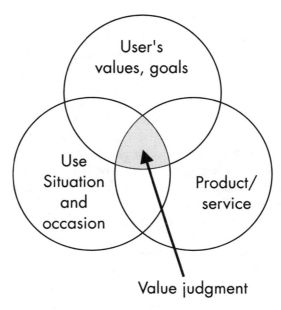

Value judgment

Figure 3.2. Value judgments concern relationships between the product, the situation, and the user.

In another example, NEC asked field researchers to study the situations in which persons use laptop personal computers. Among other things, they found that an individual using a portable computer while on the telephone may need to open the machine with one hand instead of two. Or, that during a conference meeting, that same user might need to show the computer screen to others in the room, and might like the option of a detachable display screen that could be turned to face others. NEC took its sensitivity for the consumers' various use situation requirements seriously in producing its Versa notebook computer, every major component (e.g., display screen, disk drives, power supply, and memory) of which snaps in and out. This design allows the user to reconfigure the machine for different use situations such as home, office, or travel. In fact, NEC built a machine that will adapt to (and create value in) the specific use situations in which the user finds him- or herself.[13]

The influence of use situation on value judgments has important implications. First, it implies that the perceived "value" of a product may, in fact, change over time and across use situations.[14] For instance, while a compact sedan may be entirely adequate (and thus create value) for an individual who is commuting to and from work, its value may diminish when judged within the context of an extended family vacation.

In another example of how perceived value can change over time, we recently interviewed Department of Transportation employees to understand how they judged the value received from suppliers with whom they contract to complete projects, such as building bridges or interstate exchanges. We found that "value" could only be defined by specifying the events occurring during the project. During the often complex, preproject bidding process, the employees judged the value provided by suppliers on the basis of dimensions such as "frankness and honesty during negotiations," "minimal documentation errors," "doesn't try a cookie cutter approach to our unique problems," and "ability to understand our needs." In contrast, after a supplier had won the bidding process and was engaged in actually managing the contract and project, other value dimensions emerged, such as "reduces our lead times," "becomes an extension of our staff," "minimal changeover in personnel," and "communicates well." Product or service providers must realize that value is often less a "snapshot" than it is a moving picture. Figure 3.3 shows how a customer's value perception (represented on the vertical axis) can change over time and use occasions (shown on the horizontal axis).

Second, we believe that some especially important use occasions can be identified that trigger changes in product requirements and corresponding changes value judgments. Notice in Figure 3.3 how value judgments drop significantly at occasion trigger OT_2 and rise dramatically at occasion trigger OT_7. While there are sometimes differences in product performance (such as product failure) that result in changing value judgments, these judgments may also vary due to occasion triggers which signal changes in the customer use situation requirements – even where objective product performance remains stable.

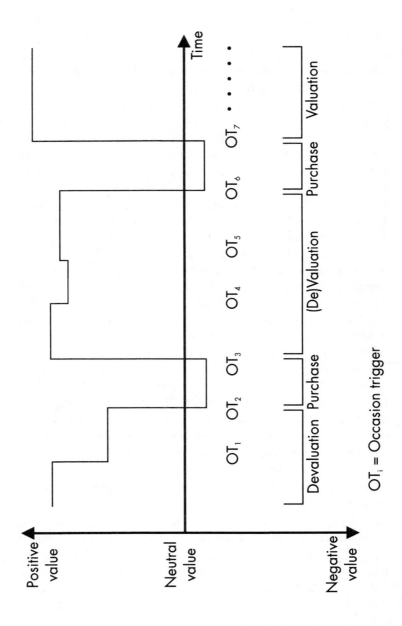

Figure 3.3. Value perception changes over time.

For example, most car dealers understand that a critical occasion trigger is the new car buyer's first visit to the service department after purchase. At this time, it is likely that a completely different set of value dimensions will be used to judge the responsiveness of the dealership than were used during the product purchase. What are those dimensions? How can the dealer track its customers in order to identify exactly when this occasion trigger is reached? What might be done by the service department to respond to these occasion trigger requirements? It is clearly important for managers to know if and when these critical occasion triggers exist for their customers and to know what specific requirements will be used to judge their products in those situations.

Finally, our research has uncovered another interesting phenomenon related to Figure 3.3. We have found that, just as products often have a "honeymoon" period after purchase where they are highly valued by customers. However, use over time and over various situations can sometimes result in a "devaluation" process, where the customer forms increasingly negative value judgments of a product that can escalate into brand or supplier switching.[15] Again, this devaluing may result from product failure. However, it can also result from changing use situation requirements that might not even have existed when the product was first purchased. We believe that once the devaluation mindset has engaged, a downward spiral or a self-fulfilling prophecy exists. The customer may actively construct a case for switching products or service suppliers. In addition to noting this tendency with customers we have interviewed, we have encountered managers who are intuitively and painfully aware of how devaluation has occurred in their customer base.

Summary

Clearly, product value is a complex concept. Because we have now defined value as multidimensional (in that it includes both upon consumption and possession goals), as a trade-off (in terms of a variety of positive and negative consequences), and as dynamic (the judgment can vary across different product usage situations), it is clear that attempting to understand and measure value will be a challenge. To this end, it would be helpful to have an organized and systematic way to think about and determine customer value. Such a framework is provided by the customer value hierarchy.

The Customer Value Hierarchy

A Hierarchical View of Value

The means/end theory suggests a hierarchical representation of how customers view products.[16–19] It says that products, and more specifically, *how products relate to customers*, can be represented by three levels: attributes, consequences, and desired end-states (Figure 3.4). As we will see, these levels become increasingly abstract with movement from the lower to higher levels, as well as becoming increasingly relevant to the customer.

Attributes. At the most concrete level, the customer defines the product in terms of its attributes: what the product/service is, its features, and its component parts or activities. Attributes are typically what would be mentioned if a customer was asked to describe a product ("it is a four door utility vehicle with four-wheel drive, leather interior, and antilock brakes") or a service ("we talk to the receptionist, she dispatches a repair person, he fixes the copier, and we get billed"). One might also consider these as the "options" that are offered by a particular product/ service. Attributes tend to be defined objectively, and there may be multiple attributes and bundlings of attributes that make up a particular product or service.

Figure 3.5 depicts a value hierarchy constructed from an in-depth interview we conducted with a car owner. This hierarchy includes several attributes that the consumer noted in discussing her car. These were associated with both tangible elements of the car itself (location of switches, layout of instruments, size, plushness of the interior, and fuel efficiency) and intangible characteristics of the service surrounding the sale and maintenance of her car (the use of pressure tactics by sales-

Desired End-States

Describes the goals of the person or organization

↑

Consequences

Describes the user/product interaction

↑

Attributes

Describes the product/service

Figure 3.4. A value hierarchy.

people, the competence of the mechanics, the responsiveness of the service department, and so forth).

It should be noted that companies traditionally have defined what they do by focusing on attributes. Customer satisfaction surveys provide compelling evidence of this, as they almost invariably measure satisfaction with product attributes or features. (More will be said about this in Chapter 4.) Make no mistake, understanding and improving product attributes is important, and we will argue later that it is a critical undertaking for organizations. However, as will become evident, when an organization's focus *stops* at an attribute perspective and fails to consider the upper levels of the value hierarchy, that is where difficulties (and failures) lie.

Consequences. At the middle level of the hierarchy are the customers' more subjective considerations of the consequences (both positive and negative) that result from product use: what the product does for the user, the outcomes (desired and undesired).

In interviewing users of a variety of products, we have noted that they frequently speak in terms of consequences when describing their product experiences. For instance, one consumer discussed the effects of inflexible leather soles on a pair of sandals in the following way: "They were kind of stiff. They had the kind of flat-footed effect of a flop, flop, flop because they

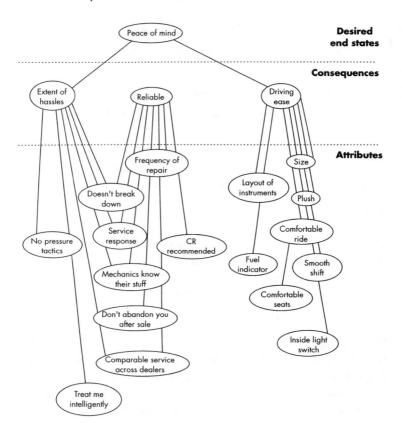

Figure 3.5. Our customer's value hierarchy.

wouldn't bend." Likewise, a boat owner discussed the location of the boat's instrumentation: "You have to be a contortionist to read your autometer. It is usually mounted between the two hatches in the bilge, and you can't get your body in there." These examples highlight the change in perspective from the attribute level. While attributes describe the *product*, consequences are the results and experience that accrue to the *customer* as a result of product consumption and possession.

A good example of a consequence orientation is found in Oldsmobile's description of their product design process for the

Aurora, their 1994 entry into the luxury car market.[20] As early as 1988, Oldsmobile engineers interviewed owners of European luxury cars such as Mercedes-Benz and BMW. To be sure, these owners mentioned attributes such as leather seats and wood trim, multivalve engines, and four-wheel disk brakes. However, the consequences that Oldsmobile designers determined were most critical in defining the "European luxury car experience" were that these cars "inspired confidence and security, gave the vehicles an opulent hush, and isolated drivers from bumps and jolts." It was left to the Oldsmobile engineers to determine which combination of attributes could produce those desired consequences. They eventually decided that the key was a "rock-solid body structure" and began to define the combination of materials, design, and assembly (attributes) that would produce the desired consequences.

Figure 3.6 depicts a different kind of value hierarchy. It is a representation of how a business might perceive the value delivered by one of its suppliers. Again, the distinction between the attribute and consequence levels is highlighted. Under this scenario, the attributes provided by the supplier might include the helpfulness of the staff, on-time delivery, accurate order filling, EDI services, and the like. However, the consequences to the buying organization might be the extent to which the supplier helps the customer deliver value to their downstream customers, inventory reduction, eliminating down-time, and so forth. Figure 3.6 illustrates how the concepts of a value hier- archy can be adapted not only to service providers but to business- to-business and manufacturer-to-customer relationships.

Another way to think about the difference between attributes and consequences is to consider what types of questions one would have to ask in order to understand each one. At the attribute level, one could simply ask the customer to describe the product or service. At the consequence level, however, one would ask questions that focus on the customer, such as "How do you use this product?," "What happens when you use this product?," or "What does this product do for you?"

As stated earlier, the consequences of product use can be both positive (benefits, desired outcomes, or realizations) and

A New Perspective on Customer Value

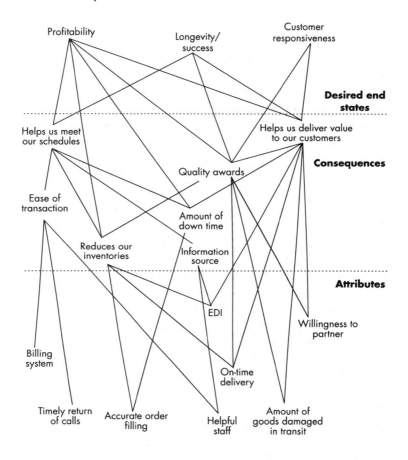

Figure 3.6. A business-to-business value hierarchy.

negative (sacrifices, costs, and undesirable outcomes). They tend to be more abstract in nature than attributes and are more subjectively defined by the product user. Where customers might easily agree on a description of a product's attributes, they may have considerable disagreement over its consequences. For instance, two consumers might objectively describe and agree upon the keyboard design of a particular laptop computer (attribute). However, they may disagree completely on whether the design is user friendly (consequence).

Another characteristic of consequences that must be kept in mind is that, although there may be a one-to-one correspondence between some attributes and some consequences, it is also true that a consequence may be the result of a combination of many attributes. For example, Ford found that many of its consumers complained of scuffed shoes when riding in the back seats of their cars. In responding to this negative consequence, several adjustments were made, including sloping the underside of the seats, widening the space between the seat adjustment tracks, and making the tracks out of smooth plastic rather than metal.[21] One way to think about consequences is that they are the key to understanding why customers prefer certain attributes or attribute combinations over others. Attributes are preferred because of their ability to deliver desired consequences or to avoid undesirable ones.

Desired End States.   At the top of the hierarchy are desired end states: the user's core values, purposes, and goals. These are the most basic and fundamental motivators for the individual, family or buying unit, or organization. They are the ultimate ends that are served by the product or service means. The means/end theory defines this most abstract level as including values that are deeply held, such as security, familial love, and achievement. These values may be directly related to product consumption, e.g., a low fat entree leads to good health. In addition, product consumption may be indirectly instrumental in other aspects of the individual's life, e.g., "a sports drink allows me to compete in league basketball which helps me support my community." While our definition of desired end states would clearly include such core values, we have broadened the definition for our purposes. First, we also include consumption goals or purposes (e.g., variety, productivity, good taste) that motivate the customer. Relative to core values, the latter represent a lower-order, consumption-specific set of concerns that are related specifically to the individual's (or organization's) role as a customer. In addition, we explicitly consider organizational customers as well as individuals. The desired end states of buying organizations might include longevity, a sense of unity or community, customer responsiveness, quality, or shareholder wealth.

Again, examples from our interviews illustrate the conscious way in which customers' desired end states shape their decisions to buy and use products. One boat owner discussed his purchase as a way of achieving family unity: "We got our boat to hopefully keep our teenagers interested in being with us for a few years longer. It keeps us all together." Likewise, a user of a health and fitness center commented, "I feel better about everything, I guess, and my outlook on life is better." Our consumer in Figure 3.5 valued peace of mind very highly both in her life in general and, more specifically in her relationship to her automobile. (It should probably be noted that her history was characterized by a string of undependable and repair-ridden "lemons.") By selecting a car that contained a specific configuration of attributes (of both product and service) and that provided her with three key consequences (the absence of hassles, security, and effortless driving), she was attempting to improve her overall peace of mind.

The Important Characteristics of the Hierarchy

There are several characteristics of the hierarchy that stand out when thinking about applying this concept in practice.

First, as implied earlier, the three levels of the value hierarchy – attributes, consequences, and desired end states – are interconnected in the sense that the lower levels are the means by which the higher level ends are achieved. Product attributes are the "means" by which consequences are delivered to the customer. As shown in Figure 3.5, for instance, instrument layout, size, and seat comfort are three attributes that the consumer felt contributed to driving ease. Another example of the attribute/consequence relationship can be found in the experiences of the Power Tool Division of Stryker.[22] When Stryker employees went into customers' factories to see where and how their tools were being used, they came across a surprising fact: one half of their product users were women. They noticed that one consequence of their product design was that these customers had difficulty gripping their tools. As a response to this negative consequence or "sacrifice," they had to reconsider the related attributes (design and construction) of their products. Stryker subsequently redesigned their tools with variable-size grips made of rubberized plastic that made them easier to grasp. As an unexpected result, they also found that these products sold well among Japanese users, who tend to have smaller hands.

Likewise, each customer forms a perception of the extent to which the consequences derived from product use will help him or her obtain desired end states. For example, cars that provide security and effortless driving help create peace of mind (see Figure 3.5).

Second, as mentioned earlier, the level of abstraction increases at higher levels in the hierarchy. While attributes tend to be the most objectively and concretely defined, consequences (the benefits and sacrifices of use) tend to be more abstract in nature, and desired end states are the most abstract of all. One result of this is that it becomes much more challenging to measure and understand the higher levels of a customer's value hierarchy. Consumers and organizations may not readily articulate their product desires at the higher levels of the hierarchy, and those attempting to understand and measure the customer perspective will have to dig more deeply to get at the consequences and desired end states. (This issue will be addressed more specifically in Chapter 7.)

Another characteristic of the hierarchy has to do with stability over time. There is a tendency for stability to increase at higher levels of the hierarchy. According to psychologists, values are some of the most enduring and stable traits possessed by individuals. While they might change and evolve over time, generally this process is a very gradual one. The same can be said for organizations. At the middle level, the consequences that are desired by customers are probably less stable than valued end states, especially given their tendency to change across situations. Nonetheless, they are much more stable and much less apt to change than product attributes. At the lowest level the actual attributes or bundles of attributes that are available to the customer in the marketplace are continually changing over time;

product life cycles are decreasing, technological change is occurring at an astounding rate, and there is a multiplicity of offerings in any given product category. For example, in 1992 alone some 15,000 new food, health, beauty, and pet products were introduced in supermarkets in the United States. In addition nearly 70 percent of these products were "different varieties, formulations, sizes, or packages of existing brands."[23] Therefore, an attribute level perspective results in a quickly changing target for managers. Consequences and desired end state provide a relatively more stable strategic focus.

Finally, touching back on our previous discussion, we must remember that there is no such thing as "the" value hierarchy for a product or service. Our research shows that use situation will be a critical determinant of value and, therefore, the components of the value hierarchy may change significantly as use situation is altered. For example, Smith and Wesson has competed in the traditionally male-oriented weapons market for years. However, they recently found that as their female customer base has expanded they have had to reconsider how to deliver value in different use situations. For example, women are more likely to carry a weapon in a purse instead of in a holster or inside their clothing. One result of this change in use was that the sharp edges of the guns often ripped the fabric lining of customer purses (a negative consequence), resulting in complaints to the company. Incidents such as this have caused Smith and Wesson to reconsider how to provide value in an expanding variety of use situations.[24]

In an earlier example, we discussed how Department of Transportation employees considered different value dimensions when dealing with their suppliers during different project events, such as the preselection stages (qualifying and bidding) and contract management stage (project implementation). Figures 3.7 and 3.8 show how value hierarchies might differ for these two situations.

Applying Customer Value Hierarchies in Practice

A legitimate question to ask is why managers should go to the trouble to understand and measure the entire value hierarchy.

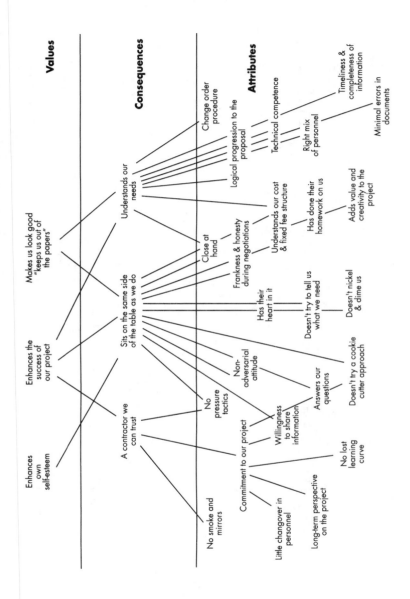

Figure 3.7. Value chain for preselection stage transportation customers.

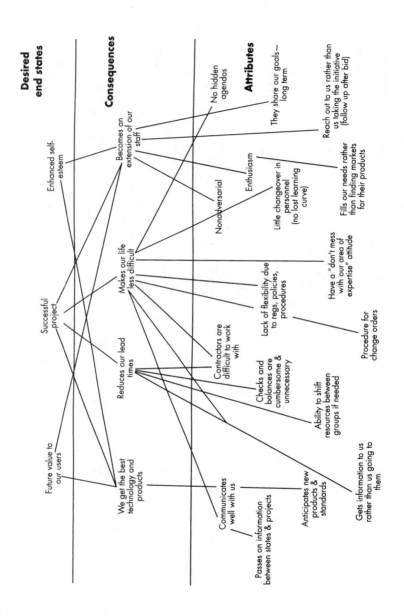

Figure 3.8. Value hierarchy for contract management.

We feel that there are several compelling reasons, including the following.

- Managers should not define their product or service offerings strictly in terms of attributes.
  - Managers must understand that value is judged by customers at the upper levels of the hierarchy, specifically in terms of consequence trade-offs.
  - Managers who have a clear understanding of the entire value hierarchy will have better criteria for comparing the merits of alternative product and service offerings.
  - Understanding the linkages between attributes and consequences can help managers to identify "high-impact" attributes that provide multiple benefits for the customer.
- Rather than a bottom-up approach to decision making, the hierarchy suggests a top-down approach. Managers should first understand the higher hierarchy levels before translating this knowledge into a specific configuration of attributes or features.
- Managers who concentrate their attention on changing, unstable attributes will find themselves chasing a moving target, whereas consequences and desired end states provide a more stable basis for decision making.
- The upper levels of the hierarchy are inherently oriented toward some future state, while the attribute levels focus on historical or current offerings.
- The upper levels of the hierarchy provide more opportunity for significant and creative changes in the product or service, while an attribute focus tends to result in smaller, more incremental change.

The Advantages of a Consequence-Level Perspective. Many product or service providers view their output as a bundle of attributes or features.[25] They produce their product or service by a process that combines component parts, features, or processes, and their research and development efforts are frequently aimed at improving their offering by adding, refining, or deleting attributes. They very often differentiate their products from those of competitors by comparing the attribute options that they offer versus those offered by competitors.

By contrast, the customer value hierarchy clearly shows that in order to understand value one must understand which particular set of consequences are – or are not – desired by product users, as well as what end states are deemed desirable. Unless these upper levels of the hierarchy are understood, there is no "north star" to guide managers in the selection and choice of which attributes should be incorporated into the product or service; nor is there any way to judge the relative attractiveness or importance of alternative offerings. One research study concluded that the most important product characteristics that are related to choice are those at the higher consequence level.[26] It is clear that many business practitioners are increasingly viewing the creation of "value" as a competitive advantage, and, more specifically, are feeling that providing sustainable superior value has a direct impact on profitability.[27]

Understanding value hierarchies will also remind the product or service provider that no two customer's – or segment's – value hierarchies will be exactly alike and that these differences provide both challenges and opportunities. For example, Safety Kleen, a commercial waste disposal business, found that their sma..er customers required a great deal of face-to-face service tailored to their needs. This was largely a result of their lack of understanding of regulatory requirements associated with commercial waste. In contrast, these needs were not in the value hierarchies of larger businesses, which tend to have staffs more astute to these issues. Consequently, Safety Kleen was able to offer their larger customers a "stripped-down" service that met their unique needs.[28]

In addition, if a manufacturer truly understands the customers' value hierarchy, they might be able to identify "high-impact" attributes or features that serve multiple consequences for the customer, thus enhancing value. For example, LCD readouts may provide several benefits for an automobile driver, including the fact that they are easier to read, that they provide pride in owning the most recent technology, and so forth. Manufacturers may consequently find that they are undervaluing (and, in some instances, underpricing) some of their product or service features by failing to recognize all the benefits that they offer to the customer.

"Top-Down" Product Design. Second, the customer value hierarchy suggests a "directional" approach to product or service design. Many organizations that are product-driven start at the bottom of the hierarchy, bundling attributes and setting design engineers to work to "build better mouse traps." Later, the organizations go in search of customers or markets that might desire their offerings. The hierarchy suggests, instead, a "top-down" approach where the organization begins with an in-depth understanding of the consequences and end states that are important to the customer and then works backward to try to design a bundle of goods or services to deliver those consequences (as in the example of the Oldsmobile Aurora mentioned previously).

Stability at the Higher Levels of the Hierarchy. Third, it was mentioned earlier that the hierarchy represents increasing stability at higher levels. One obvious implication of this characteristic is that managers who are focused at the attribute level will always be chasing a target that is moving and changing very quickly. An attribute focus can introduce a frantic sense of keeping up or staying ahead of the competition, often without producing strategic advantage for the product or service provider.

One example of this is the technological one-upmanship that has been practiced in the consumer electronics industry. Manufacturers are finding that their "innovations" provide only a short-term advantage, as they can often be quickly imitated by competitors. On the other hand, by concentrating on the higher levels of the hierarchy, the strategic goals are more stable and are less apt to change. While management will still have various opportunities to pursue how they can deliver desired consequences to customers, the objectives can remain more focused for longer periods of time. Again, consider the Oldsmobile Aurora. If engineers are focused on creating a sensation of "cocooning" the driver from the road, there may be a multitude of ways to deliver this perception. Rather than a one-shot design change, the quest for this consequence could be an evolutionary, continuous improvement process that includes making changes in several product dimensions over time.

"Future" Perspective. While customers are pretty good at responding to a particular product design or idea that is put in front of them, they are not very good at answering in the abstract, "What should a product (service) look like in five years?" Ask any manager who has tried. Customers are not well equipped to project, create, and imagine offerings that they have not experienced.[29,30] There are probably several reasons for this, but two are most obvious.

First, customers are very oriented toward "what is." They tend to think in terms of what they already know or have experienced, and this often limits their ability to see beyond the obvious. (Similar effects have been noted in memory research studies in the field of psychology, which have shown a person's ability to generate responses to a question can be limited by first suggesting what some of the responses might be.) This tendency to ground responses in "what is" obviously has the limitation of leading to incremental or marginal improvements in existing offerings. However, in many cases product and service providers are looking for more dramatic breakthroughs that literally redefine the product or service. It is such breakthroughs that lead to significant improvements in customer value as well as a competitive advantage. Consumers are simply not very good at visualizing such breakthroughs.

The other reason why consumers are not particularly good prognosticators is the fact that they have limited knowledge. In many cases they lack the technical, mechanical, chemical, process, systems, or resource know-how to understand or even imagine what the possibilities of a product are. In fact, in most instances it is the product or service provider who is much more knowledgeable about its potential.

A fourth benefit of pursuing the higher levels of the hierarchy is that it is inherently more concerned with the future. An attribute focus has a greater tendency to focus on "what is." For example, a consumer would probably design a future computer by improving existing features, such as size, keyboard, and memory. As stated earlier, incremental changes to attributes are not an uncommon route for new product development. However, consumers can more accurately predict what their needs will be at the consequence level (e.g., the ability to network computer users at various locations, the need to integrate databases represented by a variety of different formats, accessibility, portability, and so forth). Once a manager has a keener understanding of these future consequences, he or she can turn an eye toward delivering the endless possibilities and alternatives at the attribute level.

Opportunities for Significant, Creative Product Improvements. Finally, it is increasingly evident that the objective of delivering consequences creates more opportunity for creativity and for significant or dramatic change than a concentration on improving attributes. It is at this higher level that managers can free up their organization to consider many – and sometimes very different – options for the customer. It allows them to think beyond their current attribute offerings and systems capabilities, as illustrated by our hotel example at the beginning of this chapter. Instead, it challenges them to think much more broadly in terms of future directions and opportunities for serving the customer.

One example of this notion is found in the fast-growing child care industry.[31] Historically, these centers have defined themselves as "baby-sitters," an attribute-level description of what they do ("We are caretakers for children."). However, some child care centers have begun to define their role more broadly in terms of the consequences to the parents – as "surrogate extensions of the family." This latter definition provides many opportunities to add and expand services that might meet the needs of their customers. For instance, some child care facilities have begun providing gym and swimming classes, health care and child-rearing information for parents, transportation to ball games or to and from schools, prepared meals that parents can take home and reheat, and even regular visits by a doctor who can provide immunizations to children.

Another example of this may be found in Apple's development of a laptop computer.[23] Their initial efforts (which ultimately failed) concentrated solely on making a smaller and lighter version of their existing desktop machines (an attribute focus). Once the market rejected these, Apple turned to consumers for redirection. By observing consumers using laptops in a variety of situations – on airlines, in cars, and even in bed – they were able to come away with a clearer understanding of the consequences of certain product designs. For instance, a mouse is of little use when the user is working on a small airplane tray table or in his or her lap. From this observation, the inclusion of a built-in tracking ball was born, a design feature that is now being copied by Apple's competition. A successful redesign of Apple's laptops would probably have been less likely had the company gone out and directly asked consumers what kind of attributes they wanted on their laptop or, worse yet, simply sent their design engineers back to the drawing board to try something different.

In short, we feel that a substantive, radical, and strategically sustainable advantage is more likely to result when organizations step back from a narrow focus on attribute improvement and consider the broader issues of consequence and value delivery. In turn, this type of radical product improvement is likely to provide a more strategically sustainable competitive advantage than would result from simply improving attributes on the margins.

Summary

We began this chapter by discussing the need for a customer value orientation to guide business strategy. It is our contention that most companies have difficulty understanding what their customers value. We then defined customer value as (1) the result of value in use and/or possession value goals, (2) a function of the requirements of a particular use situation, and (3) a trade-off between the positive and negative consequences that result from product use. This chapter showed how determining customer value, specifically through a value hierarchy perspective, can provide a rich and meaningful way to understand the needs and desires of customers. We feel that if companies are to address value issues more effectively they will have to reorient their thinking (from a product/attribute to a customer/consequence perspective) and reexamine and possibly revise their current market information gathering systems. Finally, we highlighted some of the managerial benefits that we think are inherent in the adoption of a value hierarchy perspective.

At several points in the chapter, we touched on the difficulty of measuring customer value. Higher levels of the hierarchy are not as straightforward to measure as are attribute-level attitudes. Likewise, existing customer feedback systems do not always set out to measure these dimensions; often they are inadequate for such measurements. In Chapter 7 we explore some of the specific techniques that are best used to capture your customer's value dimensions.

References

[1] Burns, Mary Jane and Robert B. Woodruff, "Value: An Integrative Perspective," Curtis P. Haugtvedt and Deborah E. Rosen, eds., *Proceedings of the Society for Consumer Psychology*. Washington: American Psychological Association, 1991, pp. 59–64.

[2] Sheth, Jagdish N., Bruce I. Newman, and Barbara L. Gross, *Consumption Values and Market Choices – Theory and Applications,* Cincinnati, OH: South-Western Publishing Co., 1991.

[3] Woodruff, Robert B., David W. Schumann, and Sarah Fisher Gardial, "Understanding Value and Satisfaction from the Customer's Point of View," *Survey of Business*, 28 (Summer/Fall 1993), pp. 33–40.

[4] Burns, Mary Jane and Robert B. Woodruff, "Delivering Value to Consumers: Implications for Strategy Development and Implementation," *1992 American Marketing Association Winter Educator's Conference Proceedings*, Chicago, IL: American Marketing Association, 1992, pp. 209–216.

[5] Holbrook, Morris B. and Kim P. Corfman, "Quality and Value in the Consumption Experience: Phaedrus Rides Again" in *Perceived Quality: How Consumers View Stores and Merchandise,* Jacob Jacoby and Jerry

C. Olson, eds., Lexington, MA: D.C. Heath and Company, 1985, pp. 31–57.

[6]   Holbrook, Morris B., "Aims, Concepts, and Methods for the Representation of Individual Differences in Esthetic Responses to Design Features," *Journal of Consumer Research*, 13 (December 1986), pp. 337–347.

[7]   Prentice, Deborah A. (1987), "Psychological Correspondence of Possessions, Attitudes and Values," *Journal of Personality and Social Psychology*, 53 (6, 1986), pp. 993–1003.

[8]   Jacobson, Robert and David A. Aaker, "The Strategic Role of Product Quality," *Journal of Marketing*, 51 (October 1987), pp. 31–44.

[9]   Normann, Richard and Rafael Ramirez (1993), "From Value Chain to Value Constellation: Designing Interactive Strategy," *Fortune*, July-August, pp. 65–77.

[10] Woodruff, Robert B., David W. Schumann, D. Scott Clemons, Mary Jane Burns, and Sarah F. Gardial, "The Meaning of Consumer Satisfaction and Dissatisfaction: A Themes Analysis from the Consumer's Perspective," Working Paper Series, Customer Value and Satisfaction Research Program, University of Tennessee, Knoxville, TN 1990.

[11] Zeithaml, Valerie A., "Consumer Perceptions of Price, Quality and Value: A Means-End Model and Synthesis of Evidence," *Journal of Marketing*, 52 (April 1988), pp. 35–48.

[12] Melcher, Richard, "A New Era For Auto Quality," *Business Week*, October 22, 1990, pp. 88–95.

[13] McWilliams, Gary, "A Notebook That Puts Users Ahead of Gimmicks," *Business Week*, Sept. 27, 1993, pp. 92–96.

[14] Sinden, J. A. and A. C. Worrell, *Unpriced Values: Decisions Without Market Prices*, New York, NY: John Wiley and Sons, 1979.

[15] Woodruff, Schumann, Clemons, Burns and Gardial Working Paper, op. cit.

[16] Gutman, Jonathan, "A Means-End Chain Model Based on Consumer Categorization Processes," *Journal of Marketing*, 46 (Spring 1982), pp. 60–72.

[17] Gutman, Jonathan and Scott D. Alden, "Adolescents' Cognitive Structures of Retail Stores and Fashion Consumption: A Means-End Chain Analysis of Quality," in *Perceived Quality: How Consumers View Stores and Merchandise*, Jacob Jacoby and Jerry C. Olson, eds., Lexington, MA: D.C. Heath and Company, 1985, pp. 99–114.

[18] Perkins, W. Steven and Thomas J. Reynolds, "The Explanatory Power of Values in Preference Judgments: Validation of the Means-End Perspective," *Advances in Consumer Research*, Vol. 15, Michael J. Houston, ed., Provo, UT: Association for Consumer Research, 1988, pp. 122–126.

[19] Vinson, Donald E., Jerome E. Scott, and Lawrence M. Lamont, "The Role of Personal Values in Marketing and Consumer Behavior," *Journal of Marketing*, 41 (April 1977) pp. 44–50.

[20] Kerwin, Kathleen, "GM's Aurora: Much Is Riding On The Luxury Sedan – And Not Just For Olds," *Business Week,* March 21, 1994, pp. 88–95.

[21] Phillips, Stephen, Amy Dunkin, James B. Treece and Keith Hammonds, "King Customer," *Business Week*, March 12, 1990, pp. 88–94.

[22] Nussbaum, Bruce, "Hot Products: Smart Design in the Common Thread," *Business Week*, June 7, 1993, pp. 54–57.

[23] Miller, Cindee, "Little Relief Seen for New Product Failure Rate," *Marketing News,* 27 (June 21, 1993), p. 1.

[24] Zinn, Laura, "This Bud's For You. No, Not You – Her," *Business Week*, November 4, 1991, pp. 86–90.

[25] Sullivan, L. P., "Quality Function Deployment," *Quality Progress*, June 1986, pp. 38–50.

[26] Geistfeld, Dennis H., G. B. Sproles, and S. B. Badenhop, "The Concept and Measurement of a Hierarchy of Product Characteristics," in *Advances in Consumer Research*, Vol. IV, W. D. Perreault, Jr., ed., Provo, UT: Association for Consumer Research, 1977, pp. 302–307.

[27] Narver, John C. and Stanley F. Slater, "The Effect of Market Orientation on Business Profitability," *Journal of Marketing*, 54 (October 1990), pp. 20–35.

[28] Higgins, Kevin T., "Business Marketers Make Customer Service Job For All," *Marketing News,* 23, (January 30, 1989), pp. 1–2.

[29] Bennett, Amanda, "Making the Grade With the Customer: Firms Struggle to Gauge How Best to Serve," *Wall Street Journal*, November 12, 1990, B1, B3.

[30] McGee, Lynn W. and Rosann L. Spiro, "The Marketing Concept in Perspective," *Business Horizons*, 31, (May-June 1988), pp. 40–45.

[31] Trost, Cathy, "Marketing-Minded Child Care Centers Become More Than 9–5 Baby Sitters," *Wall Street Journal*, June 18, 1990, pg. 1, Section B.

Note

1. Parr, William, presentation delivered at the Management Development Center, University of Tennessee, Knoxville, TN.

CHAPTER 4

LINKING CUSTOMER VALUE TO CUSTOMER SATISFACTION

Hyundai, the automobile manufacturer, has spent a great deal of time pursuing customer satisfaction and its measurement. Beginning with the premise that satisfied customers lead both to referrals and repeat sales, this company actually had its "advanced customer communication program" in place before it sold its first car in the United States. This program included an early warning system that used extensive telephone interviews with charter customers and even required service technicians to check features that were *not* complained about during routine maintenance checks. Their customer satisfaction measurement program includes surveys at six weeks, 12 months, and 24 months after purchase. These questionnaires are returned to dealerships on a weekly basis, a customer satisfaction index is provided for sales and service performance, customer satisfaction ratings are tracked over time, and dealers are provided with survey summary reports. Dealers are also required to respond to each customer's survey, both for positive and negative evaluations. Hyundai's commitment to customer satisfaction measurement can be summarized by Hyundai Motor America's manager of market planning and research: "We strive to go beyond the prerequisite of measuring customer satisfaction by providing additional avenues of communication with our customers and future prospects."[1]

Introduction

The question we most often get after describing our framework for understanding customer value is "What is the difference between customer value and customer satisfaction?" It is a natural question for two reasons: (1) the current popularity of, and manager familiarity with, customer satisfaction measures and (2) the fact that both value and satisfaction measure aspects – albeit different ones – of the customer's interaction with products and services.

First, clearly distinguishing customer value from customer satisfaction is important because individuals and businesses are far more familiar with the latter and may mistakenly confuse the two. Customer satisfaction measurement programs have become enormously popular in the last decade. Efforts to track spending on these programs indicated a 28% increase from 1991 to 1992, and that was on top of an increase of 28% between 1990 and 1991. Revenues in fourteen large U.S. market research firms alone were $132.8 million in 1992.[2] Other evidence of the popularity of these programs is the frequent mention of customer satisfaction in the management literature (both popular and academic) by the likes of Tom Peters, Michael Porter, W. Edwards Deming, and others.

Perhaps as a result of this attention, in the 1980s the American Marketing Association and the American Society for Quality Control began to jointly conduct an annual conference on customer satisfaction and its measurement. This conference has been attended by hundreds of mostly business practitioners who are seeking information on techniques for more accurately gauging customer satisfaction as well as success stories from organizations that have instituted a strong customer satisfaction orientation. Attendance for the 1993 conference was 833, significantly up over the 1992 conference attendance.[2]

For most customers, the most obvious evidence of the popularity of customer satisfaction measurement has been experiential. In recent years household and industrial buyers have been asked to respond to an increasing number of customer satisfaction surveys, either in the mail, over the telephone, or face to face. Some consumers who have recently purchased automobiles report being almost overwhelmed by the number of customer satisfaction measures they have been asked to complete within the first few months of ownership; measuring satisfaction with the car, the buying process, the dealership, the salesperson, the service after the sale, and so forth. Many consumers no longer even notice the short customer satisfaction surveys that appear regularly on tables at restaurants, in hotel rooms, or inside the packaging of products. And the occurrence of these surveys is no less frequent for the business buyer. For example, Procter & Gamble routinely measures satisfaction levels of retailers and other partners within their distribution channels, and Eastman Chemical Company continuously tracks the satisfaction of their industrial customers.

Defining the distinction (and linkage) between customer value and customer satisfaction is also critical because of the natural affinity of the two concepts. As we will explain in more detail below, these concepts are related but different. We believe that customer value describes the nature of the relationship between user and product, while customer satisfaction is a representation of the customer's *reaction to* the value received from a particular product offering. While this distinction may seem subtle or a matter of semantics, we will show that it is an important one, and that value and satisfaction orientations yield very different kinds of information with different uses for managers.

This chapter will clarify the distinction and linkage between customer value and customer satisfaction. First we will define customer satisfaction and discuss some of the more important issues related to its theory and measurement. Next, the linkage between customer satisfaction and customer value is explicitly explored and the limitations of measuring customer satisfaction alone are discussed. Finally, the case is made that value and satisfaction are complementary types of information that benefit from being integrated into a larger customer value determination process. (This relationship is explored further in Chapter 5.)

Customer Satisfaction Defined

In contrast to customer value, a great deal of research, both academic and practitioner based, has been done in the area of customer satisfaction and its measurement. The following discussion summarizes the traditional thinking on customer satisfaction theory. It addresses the way customer satisfaction and its measurement are currently viewed and practiced by business organizations, and it raises some important issues for managerial consideration. This traditional approach to customer satisfaction will be contrasted in Chapters 5 and 9 with a new orientation that we advocate.

The Expectancy-Disconfirmation Model

The expectancy-disconfirmation model is the most dominant theory of customer satisfaction.[3–6] Figure 4.1 graphically represents this theory.

Determining whether a product is satisfying or dissatisfying is essentially an evaluation process. The customer is required to make a performance judgment. Note that it doesn't matter how the product actually performed, or even less so how the product provider believed the product performed. Satisfaction is strictly tied to the customer's *perception* of product performance. For instance, how many visits to the service department are "acceptable" before the car becomes a lemon in the consumer's eyes? Five? Three? One? Only the customer can – and will – make that judgment. As many have said, customers' perceptions are their reality. This fact is often difficult for management to accept, because it means that their own perceptions of satisfactory performance are largely irrelevant to consumers' satisfaction judgments.

Next, perceived product performance is compared with a standard representing the product performance that the customer expected. For instance, a woman in one of our studies formulated an expected repair frequency for a car she was purchasing based largely upon her reading of *Consumer Reports*. As we will discuss in more detail below, comparison standards can vary across as well as within customers, and they may come from a variety of sources.

The comparison of perceived performance with the comparison standard results in disconfirmation, or the difference between what was expected and what was received. This comparison process is graphically represented in Figure 4.2.

First, note that an area immediately surrounding the comparison standard is labeled the "zone of indifference." This zone indicates that, from the customer's perspective, there may be some latitude within which product performance may vary but

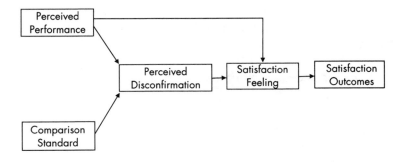

Figure 4.1. The customer satisfaction theory.

will still be evaluated as "meeting expectations." For example, a consumer visiting a fast-food outlet typically has an idea of how quickly the food will be delivered, perhaps "around five minutes" (his or her comparison standard). However, the food might arrive within three minutes or even up to eight minutes and still "meet" the consumer's expectation. The magnitude of the zone of indifference will obviously vary by the type of product, by the specific product dimension being judged, by the individual, and even by use and consumption situation.

Of great importance is what happens when the performance of the product or service deviates significantly from the standard of comparison and falls outside the zone of indifference. If the performance falls well short of expectations (depicted as movement to the left in Figure 4.2), the consumer will experience what is known as "negative disconfirmation" – the expected product performance is disconfirmed (the product did not meet the comparison standard goal), and the direction of the disconfirmation is negative (i.e., is significantly *less* than what was expected). Negative disconfirmation is critical for managers to recognize, as it represents the largest threat to customer loyalty, word-of-mouth recommendations, repeat purchases, and other desirable customer responses.

In the other direction to the right of the zone of indifference is product performance that increasingly exceeds the compari-

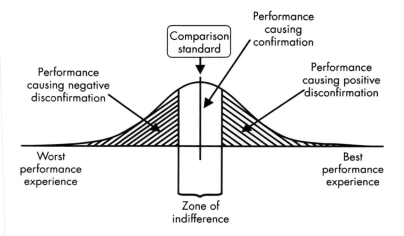

Figure 4.2. The disconfirmation process. (Adapted from [7].)

son standard and thus represents superior or unexpectedly good product or service performance. This is known as "positive disconfirmation" – while expected performance is not confirmed, the direction of the disconfirmation is positive, or better than what the consumer expected. Increasingly, management is encouraged to take the performance of their product or service offerings *beyond* what is expected and move the consumer into the area under the right side of the curve.[8,9]

Satisfaction, then, is the evaluation or feeling that results from the disconfirmation process. It is not the comparison itself (i.e., the disconfirmation process), but it is the customer's *response* to the comparison. As will be discussed later, satisfaction has an emotional component. This implies that larger gaps between perceived performance and the comparison standard might evoke stronger emotion and therefore stronger satisfaction and dissatisfaction responses. Looking at the far-right side of Figure 4.2, we might expect satisfaction judgments to result in customer "delight," while results shown at the extreme left could lead to consumer dissatisfaction in the form of anger, frustration, or disappointment. More importantly, various attitude and behavioral outcomes can be associated with the feeling of satisfaction that is evoked in the customer, including repeat purchase intentions, word of mouth, brand loyalty, and the like.

The Importance of Comparison Standards

One issue that is receiving increasing attention concerns the nature of comparison standards. Exactly what types of standards do customers use to judge product satisfaction? Where do these standards come from? Are different standards used for different product dimensions or at different times? These are important questions, because clearly the customer's feeling of satisfaction is dependent upon which comparison standard he or she uses to judge the product. Different comparison standards can and often do lead to very different satisfaction judgments.

Initially, customer satisfaction theory conceptualized comparison standards simply as "expectations," or beliefs about how the product will perform.[10] However, our research has shown that the comparison standards which customers use may be more diverse[7] and may even vary across stages in a consumption process (from prepurchase to purchase to use to disposal).[11]

An example may help to highlight differences in these standards. Consider a car owner. One important dimension in her value hierarchy might be fuel economy. Thus, postpurchase satisfaction with her car will be significantly influenced by the number of miles per gallon that the car achieves. How might different comparison standards influence her satisfaction judgment?

The following sections detail the different types of comparison standards that may be adopted by the car owner. In addition to expectations, these may include ideals, other competitors, marketing promises, other product categories, and industry norms.

Expectations. *Expectations represent how the customer believes the product will perform.* Our customer may believe that her car will get 30 miles per gallon on the road. This expectation may have originated from several sources, including her own experience, word of mouth from other owners, *Consumer Re-*

ports, and so forth. Regardless of the source of this standard, if the owner's car actually gets 30 miles to the gallon (or something close to that in the zone of indifference), then she will be satisfied with its performance.

Ideals. *Ideals represent how the customer wishes the product would perform.* Our consumer's ideal might be 40 to 50 miles per gallon, significantly higher than her expectation. If her ideal is used as the comparison standard, then she will be dissatisfied with a car that gets 30 miles per gallon, although this level of performance would have been perceived as satisfactory had her expectation been used as the standard.

Competitors. *Consumers may adopt the performance of competitors in the same product category as a standard of comparison.* For example, our consumer might compare the performance of her car with the performance she would have gotten from a competitor that advertised 35 miles per gallon. In this case, she might be dissatisfied with 30 miles per gallon, depending upon her zone of indifference. In some instances, a customer's comparison standard might be based upon the highest performance level of the available competitors. Under this circumstance, it behooves the product provider to deliver performance that is at least as good as, if not better than, other competitors in the field. Again, competitors as comparison standards may yield standards that are different from either expectations or ideals.

Other Product Categories. *Interestingly, customers may look to products in completely different product categories to provide standards of comparison.* For instance, our consumer might compare the performance of her car with the gas mileage she gets from her family's pickup truck, which gets only 15 miles per gallon. In this case, our consumer may be delighted to get 30 miles per gallon. In one instance in our own research, we encountered owners of luxury cruisers who compared the reliability of their boats with the performance of their luxury automobiles (much to the chagrin of the boat manufacturer). Likewise, Chrysler discovered that the Jeep Cherokee's most common garage mate was a Mercedes Benz, prompting comparison through proximity (comparing a sport utility vehicle designed for off-road performance with a luxury car). "No one realized when Cherokee was born that it would be compared to a Mercedes."[12]

Marketer Promises. The comparison standard that the customer adopts may also be based on promises that were made by the salesperson, the product advertisement, a company spokesperson, or some other form of corporate communication. Our car owner would be very dissatisfied with 30 mpg's if an over-zealous sales rep suggested that the car "might get as much as 40 mpg's on the road." BMW recently had to retract an advertising claim it made about the rigorous tests that its engines supposedly endured during product testing. Had the consumers believed and adopted their advertising claim as a performance standard, it might have resulted in dissatisfaction with products that could not achieve the advertised level of performance. Clearly a product or service provider's promotional communication should be realistically tied to performance. According to satisfaction theory, "overselling" is a recipe for dissatisfaction. The risk of a customer adopting marketer promises as a comparison standard may especially result in problems for organizations with little control over what their salespersons say (especially those under pressure to meet sales quotas).

Industry Norms. Finally, industry norms might be the basis for comparison standards. Customers with considerable experience in a product category (across companies and brands) or access to industry standards might develop a "modal," or average, level of performance as their standard. This industry norm may, in fact, be different than the comparison standard represented by any individual competing brand. Our car owner may, for instance, know that cars in the same category as hers typically get about 30 mpg's.

With these different sources of comparison standards available to customers, it is easy to see how satisfaction judgments can vary significantly, as they are based not upon product performance but upon an adopted standard. Clearly, it is imperative for managers to understand which or how many standards their customers may be using to judge product or service satisfaction.

Managers grappled with this problem at Xerox when they recently decided to hold back a copier introduction. Although the copier jammed less often than their competitors' machines – a performance level that historically would have been sufficient for the product to go to market – the copier's introduction was postponed because Xerox felt that its performance was still below the customers' desired performance level. In other words, while the product's performance would have been judged satisfactory for one standard (that of the competing brand), Xerox managers feared that it would be judged as unsatisfactory given a more stringent and more likely standard (the customer's ideal).[13]

Emotions

There is increasing evidence that it is important for satisfaction measures to capture not just perception (how the customer thinks that the product performed relative to the comparison standard), but the resulting customer emotion.[8] Typically the more customer emotion is generated by products and services (both positive emotions such as delight and happiness, and negative emotions such as frustration and disappointment), the more motivating customer satisfaction will be in terms of future behaviors, such as repeat purchase, word of mouth, and complaints.[14] In fact, many researchers have advocated the use of emotion-based measures of customer satisfaction.[15–18]

Based upon our own research, we believe that when a customer simply says that he or she is "satisfied" with a product, this represents an almost neutral state of evaluation. In the customer's mind, the word "satisfaction" may increasingly be synonymous with "meeting minimum expectations," hardly an outcome that generates emotion. Think of the implications for measurement. It is quite common for customer satisfaction surveys to use a "satisfied" to "not satisfied" scale to measure customer response. Product and service providers that continue to think only in terms of "satisfying" their customers may be gauging their product performance against levels that are not high enough. This may explain the ironic finding that 60 percent of customers who left their suppliers had previously reported that they were "satisfied" with them.[19]

Equally important is a manager's ability to identify emotionally laden product attributes and consequences, or "hot buttons," that have the highest potential for eliciting customer emotion (both positive and negative). These should be some of the most strategically important product dimensions to understand. Managers will want to identify which currently unavailable or even unknown emotion-laden dimensions might be added to future product offerings, to understand how existing hot buttons might be improved (to become "positive" hot buttons) or eliminated (if they are negative), or to understand which hot buttons should be targeted for marketing communications. For example, many companies take advantage of consumers' positive emotional response to products that are "made in America" in their communications aimed at creating product awareness, interest, and brand loyalty.

The Relationship Between Customer Value and Satisfaction

Several issues are important for understanding the relationship between customer value and satisfaction. These are elaborated below.

Customer Satisfaction Is a Reaction to Value Received

As we discussed in Chapter 3, *value (and value hierarchies) capture the relationship between the product, the user, and his or her goals and purposes in a specific use situation.* In describing this three-way relationship, value identifies (1) which product dimensions are central to the customer's ability to attain desired end states, and (2) how these product dimensions are related to each other and to the customer. Value creation, then, is a process for continually aligning an organization's product offerings with the customer's use situation, desired consequences, and end state requirements.

Satisfaction, in contrast, measures a different relationship:

the relationship between the product's actual performance and a performance standard. As such, satisfaction captures the customer's *response* to a particular organizational offering – how the customer feels about the value received. In essence, it is a measure *of how well* an organization's value creation efforts are aligned with its customers' value requirements.

Customer satisfaction is a customer's positive or negative feeling about the value that was received as a result of using a particular organization's offering in specific use situations. This feeling can be a reaction to an immediate use situation or an overall reaction to a series of use situation experiences.[20]

Note that satisfaction and value are related but not synonymous. The relationship between the two is a subtle but important one. In short, "value" tells an organization *what to do* (i.e., gives it direction), while "satisfaction" tells the organization *how it is doing* (i.e., gives it a report card).

For example, an understanding of customer value may indicate that car owners desire "comfort." That is, what car manufacturers should be about is the creation and improvement of comfort. However, different automobiles will vary in their ability to deliver comfort; some companies will be better at it than others. The consumer may feel very satisfied or delighted with the comfort received from one car, only somewhat satisfied with the comfort received from another car, and completely dissatisfied with the comfort received from yet another. It is even possible that the consumer's reaction to the comfort of a particular car may vary across situations. For instance, he or she might be very satisfied with the comfort of the car for short trips in town but dissatisfied with the comfort of the car on more extended outings.

In sum, satisfaction judgments (and satisfaction measures) complement the information of a value hierarchy in a very important capacity: they provide feedback on customers' reactions to value received. (More will be said on this later in the chapter.)

Historical and Future Orientation

Satisfaction has traditionally been conceptualized as a judgment that occurs during and/or after consumption. Because of this orientation, satisfaction measures tend toward a historical perspective; they are a documentation of what previously occurred. (An organization's "current" offering is, in fact, merely the result of many past decisions.) While it is true that comparison standards may be in place prior to product consumption, satisfaction judgments are not typically made until the customer's experienced performance can be compared against that standard. When organizations measure their customers' satisfaction, they are typically asking, "How do you feel about your prior experiences with our product?"

While value hierarchies may be influenced by historical relationships between the product and customer, they are not tied to postconsumption measures. We talked in Chapter 3 about the inherent future orientation of value hierarchies. While the attribute level of the hierarchy will typically be defined by the current market offerings (because of customers limited ability to think beyond them), consequences and desired end states are customer needs and requirements that are indicative of future expectations.

Customers may well have value hierarchies in place *before* the purchase of a product or service. "Ideal" or "desired" hierarchies may indicate preferences for value. For instance, a consumer may have thought about the possibilities for a new automobile and determined that he or she prefers to trade off gas mileage for higher performance levels such as acceleration, power, and speed. Such value hierarchies may serve as guides for consumer decision making (i.e., the consumer will seek out and choose alternatives that maximize value as defined by his/her pre-choice value hierarchy). Or, prior to consumption, the consumer might have "anticipated" value hierarchies representing what he or she is likely to receive from specific products or services (e.g., from reading *Consumer Reports*). While these hierarchies may well be the result of prior experience, word of mouth, advertising, or other sources of information, they express the customer's desires for future product consumption experiences.

Particular Supplier Orientation

An additional distinction between customer value and customer satisfaction concerns what is on the customer's mind. As noted in the previous definition, customer satisfaction is an evaluation related to a particular organization or supplier. In this sense, a customer's satisfaction judgments, by definition, are idiosyncratic to a particular product or service offering. By contrast, customer value is "generic" in the sense that it represents product requirements and needs that are desired across, or regardless of, particular products or suppliers. It is absolutely possible for a customer to have a value hierarchy in mind that is independent of any particular offering that exists in the marketplace.

This distinction has important measurement implications. First, as opposed to customer satisfaction (which must be measured anytime after product consumption), customer value can be measured before, during, or after consumption. In essence, while customer value may be influenced by prior consumption, it exists independent of any particular consumption experience. Secondly, this distinction suggests that customer value can – and should – be measured independently of customer satisfaction. It also suggests that companies that are currently measuring only customer satisfaction probably are not doing a good job of measuring customer value. (We will come back to this point when we lay out the logic for a customer value determination process in Chapter 5.)

To sum up, satisfaction represents a customer's postpurchase evaluations of product performance. In contrast, value hierarchies indicate what the customer *wants* to achieve (in a future orientation) and are not necessarily constrained by what he or she *can* achieve through existing market offerings (i.e., they are independent of particular product offerings and suppliers). These distinctions have important strategic implications. While knowing "how we did" is important for obvious reasons, managers are very often concerned with "what we should do next." While traditional satisfaction measures may be entirely adequate for the former, they are not as useful for the latter.

Table 4.1 summarizes the important definition characteristics of customer satisfaction and its differences from customer value.

Linking Customer Value to Customer Satisfaction

Table 4.1. A Comparison of Customer Value and Satisfaction.

Customer Value Is . . .	Customer Satisfaction Is . . .
1. What the customer desires from the product or service	1. The customer's *reaction to or feeling about* what he or she received – a comparison between the actual performance of the product and a performance standard
2. Exhibits a future orientation; is independent of the timing of the product use/ consumption	2. Tends to exhibit a historical orientation; is a judgment formed during or after product/service use or consumption.
3. Exists independent of any particular product/service offering or supplier organization	3. Is an evaluation directed at a particular product/service offering or supplier organization
4. Provides *direction* for the organization: *what they should do* to create value	4. Provides a *report card* for the organization: *how they are doing (or how they have done)* with their value creation efforts

The Limitations of Customer Satisfaction Measures

We have gone to pains to separate the concepts of customer value and satisfaction, but this effort begs yet another question. If so many organizations are measuring customer satisfaction, how useful is that information?

The answer, of course, is that customer satisfaction measurement has both its benefits and its limitations. We do not wish to make the case here that value measurement is better than satisfaction measures, or that one is "good" and the other "bad." Rather, the point that we want to make is that the two types of information are complementary but inherently different, and it is important to understand these differences. In Chapter 5 we will make the case that a combination of the two measures provides the greatest benefit to organizations. However, let us first examine some of the limitations of customer satisfaction measures as they are traditionally or most commonly practiced today.

Our study of customer satisfaction measurement as practiced today, which crosses many organizations and industries, has led us to conclude that most current customer satisfaction measurement (CSM) processes, or what we term "traditional" CSM processes, are not as effective as they could be. In addition, the managers who are using this information may not fully understand what they are – and are not – getting from satisfaction measures.

First, satisfaction measures generally are focused on the *product or service* – what the organization provided. The questions are often phrased as "how are we doing with respect to . . . (fill in the product or service dimension)?" For instance, the most frequently surveyed dimensions of customer satisfaction measures of fast-food restaurants are attributes such as the speed of service, the friendliness of the staff, the cleanliness of the restrooms, and the quality of the food. In contrast, it should be clear from the previous chapter that a value orientation specifically explores *the interaction between product or service, the user, and the use situation requirements.* Value determination might reveal that consumers have concerns such as "feeding my family a meal that I can feel good about" or "helping me to manage time pressures in my day" (characteristics more descriptive of the *customer*). These types of customer-oriented questions are rarely found on traditional satisfaction surveys.

Second, while value hierarchies consider all levels of the customer's interaction with the product (including attributes, consequences, and end states), most traditional customer satisfaction measures are focused almost exclusively on the attribute level of the value hierarchy. There are obviously several limitations with this type of data, including its orientation toward the short term, its emphasis on incremental or marginal change in the product or service provided, and its historical perspective (what has been offered in the past). In contrast, exploring all levels of the user-product interaction, especially the upper levels of the value hierarchy, assumes an orientation that is much more stable over the long term, that provides opportunity for significant creativity and radical change, and that can provide a future focus for the firm. In addition, because consequences are virtually nonexistent for satisfaction measures, these processes fail to measure the hierarchy at the level where value is critically determined (i.e., at the consequences level).

One fast-food restaurant company that we know about believed that the temperature of its food was a critical variable determining customer satisfaction. Therefore, there was a great deal of pressure placed upon their franchise managers to ensure that customers were served consistently "hot" food in a specified temperature range. The managerial response to this pressure was to standardize the production process to deliver more consistently hot internal food temperatures. Had this organization thought more in terms of consequences, they might have found, for example, that consumers were concerned with "a meal that I can feel good about eating." There might be many other, creative ways to create a meal experience that the consumer can feel good about, not only through heat but through other food characteristics such as nutrition, service, promotion, atmosphere, and the like. Again, the broader nature of consequences opens up more, new, and creative options for delivering value to customers, while an attribute focus tends to lead toward incremental attribute improvement.

Another way to think of this is that consequence level information helps the provider interpret attribute level information in a way that makes it more actionable. For instance, the customers of a particular fast-food restaurant might respond that they are not very satisfied with the "speed" with which the food is delivered (an attribute). In the absence of understanding (and measuring) higher order consequences, it may be difficult to understand what that information means or how management should act upon it. For instance, our fast-food customers may actually be concerned about consequences such as "having to wait while one employee had to do everything to complete an order – gather each sandwich, put french fries in their containers, and pour each drink one at a time." Likewise, the consequences might be "my children are impatient while standing in line," or "I have to pull over in the parking lot because of a special order placed at the drive-through window." All of these consequences suggest that speed is important, but knowing the particular consequence that is desired – or not desired – will provide more action-able data that will indicate what aspects of the operation should be altered to improve service speed (e.g., adding more cash registers, improving the system for special orders in the kitchen, putting in a play corner for children, or adding "self-service" options so that one worker isn't responsible for so many tasks).

To sum up, there are several problems with the way in which customer satisfaction has most commonly been practiced in industry today. Table 4.2 summarizes the differences in the information that is acquired through a customer value focus versus the information that is gathered in traditional customer satisfaction measures.

As we stated earlier, the types of information produced by value and customer satisfaction measures are different but complementary. Going back to our earlier discussion, we think that it is vital for organizations to know both what they need to do (value) and how they are doing (satisfaction); they need both a direction and a report card. The problem is that most organizations are invested in measuring customer satisfaction alone, and their managers are looking to this data for direction about how to better serve their customers. While customer satisfaction information may be helpful in this regard, it is clearly inadequate. Knowing which product attributes customers are currently satisfied or dissatisfied with provides at best only indirect evidence of what organizations might want to consider for future offerings. We do not wonder that many managers increasingly express dissatisfaction with their customer satisfaction data. In fact, they are simply expecting too much from it in its existing form. (One unfortunate result of this dissatisfaction is that, in some instances, managers are beginning to doubt the benefit of *any* customer data. We often see that such information is mistrusted or completely ignored. This may be a difficult bias to overcome in the future.)

Consider, however, the possibility of putting a system in place that could gather both customer value and customer satisfaction data. The previous discussion should make the advantages of such a system obvious. We believe that combining both value and satisfaction measurements together in a customer

Table 4.2. A comparison of the types of information which result from customer value versus traditional customer satisfaction measurements.

Customer Value Orientation	Traditional Customer Satisfaction Orientation
Focuses on the user/product interaction—emphasizes fundamental needs of consumer	Focuses on the product—emphasizes the firm's offering or tactical solution
Considers all levels of the user/product interaction—attributes, consequences, and values	Emphasizes attributes
Higher level focus is inherently more long term and stable, provides greater opportunity for creativity and radical change, and has a future orientation	Attribute level focus is inherently more short term and unstable, leads to incremental or marginal product/service change and improvement, and has a historical orientation
Measures the trade-offs which determine value	Typically fails to measure trade-offs which determine value
Provides information that helps to interpret attribute level information in a way that is actionable	Often difficult to interpret in the absence of additional consequence level information

value determination process will provide significantly improved customer feedback for managers than would customer satisfaction alone. Both measures are needed; one is not a substitute for the other. Thus, we are not advocating that organizations throw out the baby with the bath water (their customer satisfaction measurement systems). Instead, we suggest that they augment their existing customer feedback systems to make them more complete. (Exactly how this might be done will be considered in more detail in Chapter 5.)

Summary

This chapter has explored the concept of customer satisfaction. Specifically, it has attempted to show how customer satisfaction is related to, but different from, customer value. Customer satisfaction has been defined in terms of the expectancy-disconfirmation model, comparison standards, and emotion. Next, we explicitly tried to compare and contrast the types of information that result from customer value versus customer satisfaction orientations and measurements. Customer satisfaction measurements are typically product-specific and historical in nature. By contrast, value can be measured independently of specific products and at any point before, during, or after consumption. We discussed how most traditional customer satisfaction measurements are limited by (1) their product versus customer perspective, (2) their attribute rather than whole hierarchy orientation, and (3) their inability to produce actionable data. Finally, we have made the case for an expanded customer feedback process that includes both value and satisfaction measurements. In later chapters, the specifics of this customer value determination process will be discussed. Chapter 5 overviews the entire process, while Chapters 7 through 11 provides a more detailed "how to" perspective for actually implementing such a process in your organization.

References

[1] Michaelson, Gerald A.), "Hyundai Taps Into a 'Hidden Sales Force,' " *Marketing Communications,* 13 (October 1988), pp. 45 – 48.

[2.] Honomichl, Jack, "Spending On Satisfaction Measurement Continues to Rise," *Marketing News,* April 12, 1993, p. 17.

[3] Oliver, Richard L., "A Cognitive Model of the Antecedents and Consequences of Satisfaction Decisions," *Journal of Marketing Research,* 17 (November 1980), pp. 460 – 469.

[4] Oliver, Richard L., "Effect of Expectation and Disconfirmation on Post-Exposure Product Evaluations: An Alternative Interpretation," *Journal of Applied Psychology,* 62 (August 1977), pp. 480 – 486.

[5] Swan, John E. and I. Frederick Trawick, "Disconfirmation of Expectation and Satisfaction with a Service," *Journal of Retailing,* 57 (Fall 1981), pp. 49 – 67.

Linking Customer Value to Customer Satisfaction

[6] Churchill, Gilbert A. and Carol Suprenant, "An Investigation Into the Determinants of Consumer Satisfaction," *Journal of Marketing Research*, 19 (November 1982), pp. 491–504.

[7] Woodruff, Robert B., Ernest R. Cadotte, and Roger L. Jenkins, "Modeling Consumer Satisfaction Processes Using Experience-Based Norms," *Journal of Marketing Research*, 20 (August 1983), pp. 296–304.

[8] Schlossberg, Howard, "Satisfying Customers Is a Minimum: You Really Have to 'Delight' Them," *Marketing News*, May 28, 1990, p. 10.

[9] Schlossberg, Howard, "Dawning of the Era of Emotion," *Marketing News*, 27 (February 15, 1993), p. 1.

[10] Oliver, Richard L. and John E. Swan, "Equity and Disconfirmation Perceptions as Influences on Merchant and Product Satisfaction", *Journal of Consumer Research*, 16 (December 1989), pp. 372–383.

[11] Gardial, Sarah Fisher, Robert B. Woodruff, Mary Jane Burns, David W. Schumann and Scott Clemons, "Comparison Standards: Exploring Their Variety and the Circumstances Surrounding Their Use," *Journal of Consumer Satisfaction, Dissatisfaction and Complaining Behavior*, 6 (1993), 63–73..

[12] Treece, James, "Does Chrysler Finally Have the Jeep That It Needs?", *Business Week,* January 20, 1992, pp. 83–85.

[13] Bennett, Amanda and Carol Hymowitz, "For Customers, More Than Lip Service?" *Wall Street Journal,* October 6, 1989, p. B1.

[14] Woodruff, Robert B., "Developing and Applying Consumer Satisfaction Knowledge: Implications for Future Research," *Journal of Consumer Satisfaction, Dissatisfaction and Complaining Behavior*, 6 (1995), 1–11.

[15] Oliver, Richard L., "Processing of the Satisfaction Response in Consumption: A Framework and Research Propositions," *Journal of Consumer Satisfaction, Dissatisfaction and Complaining Behavior*, 2 (1989), pp. 1–6.

[16] Westbrook, Robert A., "A Rating Scale for Measuring Product/Service Satisfaction," *Journal of Marketing*, 44 (Fall 1980), pp. 68–72.

[17] Westbrook, Robert A., "Consumer Satisfaction and the Phenomenology of Emotions During Automobile Ownership and Experiences," *International Fare in Consumer Satisfaction and Complaining Behavior*, eds. Ralph L. Day and H. Keith Hunt, eds., Bloomington, IN: School of Business, Indiana University, 1983 pp. 2–9.

[18] Westbrook, Robert A. and Richard L. Oliver, "The Dimensionality of Consumption Emotion and Patterns of Consumer Satisfaction," *Journal of Consumer Research*, 18 (June 1991), pp. 84–91.

[19] Sellers, Patricia, "Keeping the Buyers You Already Have," *Fortune*, Autumn/Winter 1993, pp. 56–58.

[20] Woodruff, Robert B., David W. Schumann, and Sarah Fisher Gardial, "Understanding Value and Satisfaction From the Customer's Point of View," *Survey of Business*, 28 (Summer/Fall, 1993), 33–40.

CHAPTER 5

KNOW YOUR CUSTOMER THROUGH CUSTOMER VALUE DETERMINATION

IDS Financial Services Inc., a subsidiary of American Express that offers financial planning services and a variety of investment products, faces an increasingly competitive environment. Its management recognized that they needed to reexamine their entire business to search for ways to achieve an advantage. As a cornerstone of that effort, they decided to look at IDS through the eyes of its customers. Qualitative research helped to identify the dimensions of value that customers seek from financial planning services. These dimensions were screened to determine which were most influential. Eventually, IDS settled on seven key value dimensions, including quality of advice, product knowledge, the ability to handle problems, and being easy to do business with.

Management relies on satisfaction measurement to determine how well customers think that IDS's financial products and services deliver value on these dimensions. They especially want to know how customers feel about the way IDS' planners interact with them during financial planning sessions. Follow-up information helps managers explore the reasons behind their customers' ratings on each dimension.

This customer information influences several decisions. The company widely publishes these seven key value dimensions internally, so that everyone knows what customers want. In addition, these data guide managers who develop programs for services that support IDS planners when they interact with customers. Satisfaction data also provide a scorecard for assessing the company's performance in the marketplace. The results have been so successful that IDS continues to look for ways to ensure that customer information influences strategic decisions at the highest levels in the company.[1]

Introduction

Most mangers have opinions about what their customers value and even how satisfied they are. Their experience from working with customers is bound to yield such insights. The fact is that no seller could stay in business for long without some understanding of customer value. But are these opinions accurate and up to date? Our discussion of "mental models" in Chapter 2 should make us cautious about answering too quickly in the affirmative.

In fact, evidence indicates that differences are common between what managers think their customers value and what customers actually value.[1] These differences may be about (1) value dimensions, (2) the preferred performance on value dimensions, (3) the importance of value dimensions, and/or (4) the degree of satisfaction with the value delivered. For example, a hardwood lumber producer's marketing and production managers were asked to list the important value dimensions (both attributes and consequences) they thought their customers wanted.[2] Using the same interviewing procedure, customers also were asked about their value perceptions. The results of the two interviews are shown in Tables 5.1 and 5.2. Take a minute to scan these data.

As you can see, there are important differences between the lists of value dimensions for both attributes and benefit consequences. Some value dimensions (e.g., accurate communication, optimization of yield, and a consistent lumber supply) were mentioned by customers but not by the supplier. Other value dimensions (e.g., constant communication, protective information, and increased product value) were identified by the supplier but not by customers. In a few cases, the supplier and customer interpreted a particular value dimension (e.g., stable prices versus competitive prices) differently. These gaps, when uncovered, can shake a manager's confidence in how well he or she knows the customer. They also encourage organizations to rethink what customer information is really needed and how best to get it.

There is another interesting trend going on. We hear more and more managers talk about "going beyond satisfaction" when

Table 5.1. Hardwood Lumber Company's Management's Versus Customers' Perceptions of Desired Attributes

Customers' desired service attributes	Seller's perception of customers' desired service attributes
Stable price	Competitive prices
Promptness of delivery	Promptness of delivery
Responsive to order	Reliable sales personnel
Availability of grades and species	Constant communication
Supplier's reputation	Provision of stock list
Personal relationship	Provision of kiln-dry lumber
Accurate communication	Good public relations
Trademark	Trademark
Packaging Information	Protective packaging
Protective packaging	Efficient loading and unloading processes
	Packaging Information

serving the customer. They argue that a better business goal is to "delight" customers by exceeding their expectations.[2,3] Others advocate concentrating more on "customer value" than on satisfaction. But are these concepts of satisfaction, delight, and value so different? We think not. As we argued in the previous chapter, these concepts are highly interrelated. However, this questioning of satisfaction and its measurement seems to be another indication that some organizations are reassessing the processes by which they come to know their customers.

In this chapter, we come back to the customer value determination (CVD) process briefly introduced in Chapter 1. We build a case for integrating customer value and satisfaction measurement into a comprehensive and systematic process for knowing your customers. In the next section, we expand on the

Table 5.2. Hardwood Lumber Company's Management's Versus Customers' Desired Benefit Consequences

Customers' desired benefits	Seller's perceptions of customers' desired benefits
To avoid arbitration	Maintain a smooth business atmosphere with customers
To maintain and improve good working relations with the supplier	To meet our customers' product and service specifications
To optimize the yield	To improve productivity
To minimize production cost	To minimize production cost
Improve the product value	Add value to our products
To improve productivity	Be competitive
Maintain supplier loyalty	
Maintain a consistent lumber supply	

relationship between value and satisfaction. Then, we show how CVD takes advantage of this relationship. Finally, we present some issues concerning how to manage the CVD process.

The Customer Value Determination Process

Managing your business toward the goal of highly satisfying or delighting customers requires that you ask the right questions about customers and then apply what you learn from the answers to create and deliver value to them. As we have argued before, being customer-value-oriented is a data-driven way to manage. Our ideas about customer value and satisfaction, presented in Chapters 3 and 4, offer insights into just what these right questions are. For instance, we rely on the following questions when working with organizations on customer value analyses for targeted markets or segments:

1. What are the value dimensions that your customers desire?
2. Out of all these value dimensions, which ones are the most strategically important?
3. How satisfied are customers with your value delivery, particularly on these most important value dimensions?
4. What are the reasons for both high and low satisfaction (again, particularly on important value dimensions)?
5. How will customer value be likely to change in the future?

We made these questions the cornerstone of the customer value determination process first introduced in Chapter 1 and shown again in Figure 5.1. Each activity in this process brings together the methods and data needed to answer one of the previous questions. By sequencing these customer information activities, this process offers a comprehensive and systematic methodology for knowing your customers. Let's see how these CVD activities are linked together.

Identify Customer Value Dimensions

A CVD process requires that you adopt a well-defined concept of customer value. We advocate the customer value hierarchy concept presented in Chapter 3. CVD also presumes that you know which customers are currently or potentially important to your organization. As we discussed in Chapter 2, selecting these customers is based on information activities in a larger market opportunity analysis and for that reason alone CVD should follow the market definition component of a market opportunity analysis (MOA).

Every organization should learn how its targeted customers *currently* perceive value. We believe that you have to interact with customers to discover what the various dimensions of this value are. One way to do this is through direct contact with customers during normal business activities. For instance, when properly trained in information skills, salespersons can be an important source of customer value information. Research can help, too, by rigorously exploring how customers see value.

Customer Value Determination

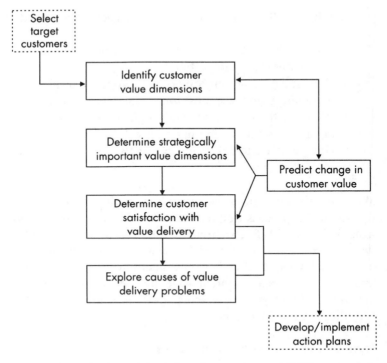

Figure 5.1. The customer value determination (CVD) process.

We have found that customers tend to consider many value dimensions at one time or another as they engage in use situations. The fact is that most customers want a lot from you. For example, in our work with a beverage business unit, we used qualitative personal interviews with 80 consumer users of the product to learn about what they value during active use situations such as while riding a bicycle, running a race, or playing soccer. The data analysis revealed more than 140 attributes and consequence value dimensions, some associated with product and others with services.

The data from this first CVD step should help you learn about as many different value dimensions as possible. Clearly, we do not want to overlook any dimensions that customers believe are important. Fortunately, qualitative customer value research techniques are very good at uncovering a wide range of customer value dimensions. (In Chapters 7 and 8, we discuss several techniques for developing this wide-ranging under-standing of customer value.)

Determine Strategically Important Value Dimensions

Few organizations could work on improving value delivery on so many dimensions at once. But which ones should we work on? The next CVD step tackles this issue. Essentially, you must implement a screening activity to determine which value dimen-sions, identified in the previous step, are most important. At the heart of this activity are the criteria that you use to guide this screening. Each criterion treats "importance" in a different way. For instance, "importance" might mean the extent to which customers desire a value dimension for meeting their needs. Or it might mean something else as well, such as the degree to which a value dimension, if delivered, would provide an advantage over competitors in the minds of customers.

The entire screening activity is only as good as the criteria employed. The fact is that different criteria may well lead to selecting different value dimensions as being important. We know of one case where a hospital applied a competitor-based criterion. Analysis from the larger MOA revealed that custom-ers believed that a key competitor hospital did not perform well on a particular value dimension. The hospital administra-tors felt they could take advantage of this competitor's weakness by improving its own corresponding value delivery process. Interestingly, if the hospital had not used the competitor-based selection criterion, this value dimension would not have been singled out for special attention. We expand on the techniques for accomplishing this step in the CVD process in Chapter 10 and Appendix III.

Determine Customer Satisfaction with Value Delivery

Obtaining actionable customer satisfaction data depends almost entirely on a sound understanding of customer value. It does little good to know that your customers are satisfied with something that is not important to them. In contrast, obtaining satisfaction data on important value dimensions will help you focus your improvement efforts on those things that will make the most difference to your customers. Suppose you ask how satisfied your customers are with your organization's performances on such dimensions as "on-time delivery," "trust in the relationship," or "understands my needs." You want to be confident that your performances on these dimensions are most likely to influence customer behavior toward your organization.

The source of ideas for satisfaction measurement should come from the previous two activities in the CVD process. When designing a satisfaction survey questionnaire, qualitative research and value dimension screening data should guide the development of questions. Even when using other sources of satisfaction data, such as salesperson call reports, it is critical to ensure that the right questions are being asked about your customers' important value dimensions. In general, you can go a long way toward ensuring that your satisfaction data are actionable if customer satisfaction measurement is preceded by sound customer value measurement. (We expand more fully on this point in Chapter 10.)

Explore the Causes of Value Delivery Strengths and Problems

As we argue in the next chapter, one of the most important applications of satisfaction data is to help managers improve the delivery of value to customers. In today's practice, it is common for managers to receive periodic reports that display satisfaction scores or ratings for various value dimensions. These data are supposed to guide improvement efforts. For instance, suppose you get back a report that displays a "5" (on a seven-point scale where 7 is high and 1 is low) for "on-time delivery," a "4" for "trust in the relationship," and a "3" for "understands my needs." These scores are low enough to indicate that there probably is room to improve your performance on these three value dimensions. Satisfaction scores are good at telling you *where* to focus improvement efforts, but they do not provide any clues as to *how* to improve. Exactly what improvement actions should you take?

CVD responds to this dilemma by including a follow-up activity to explore the customers' reasons for their satisfaction ratings. The data from customer satisfaction measurement help you determine for which value dimensions you need further probing. You surely should want to know why you got low scores on important value dimensions in order to stimulate ideas about how to improve. You also may want to know why you got high scores on important value dimensions so you know what to continue doing well. (We discuss techniques for this activity in Chapter 10.)

An illustration of this follow-up qualitative research comes from our work with a pleasure boat manufacturer. A national satisfaction survey was conducted among owners of the company's luxury sport cruisers. The resulting satisfaction scores indicated that customers were quite happy with their cruisers on most attribute and consequence value dimensions. However, the gaps between the sponsoring company's and competitor's scores for two value dimensions indicated problems: (1) "designed with an interior layout that is easy to use the way I want to" and (2) "built so that things are conveniently located for me." (See Figure 5.2) The survey provided no clues as to why customers were relatively less satisfied with the boat's performance on these value dimensions. So we recommended using qualitative studies, specifically focus group interviews, to help managers understand what is causing these low ratings. Improvement efforts can then attack the customer-perceived causes of these problems.

Predict Changes in Customer Value

No one argues with the observation that customer value changes over time. Further, we have yet to come across an organization that would not like more lead time to design and implement changes in its value delivery strategy to respond to value change. Our CVD process recognizes this information need by trying to predict customer value change in the future.

Customer value predictions can benefit from the first two activities in the CVD process. An important source of data is to

Customer Value Determination

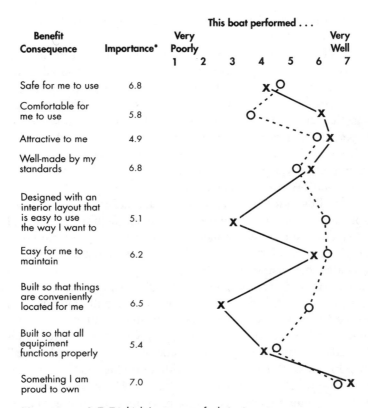

Figure 5.2. A performance profile chart.

note trends in value dimensions or their importance over multiple time periods. In addition, once you have predicted new customer value dimensions, you can feed them back into the rest of the CVD process. For instance, you might want to integrate these value dimensions into value importance studies. After describing what each new value dimension is like, ask your customers to rank or rate its importance relative to current value dimensions in order to see what changes may occur. Which current value dimensions are most likely to decline in importance as the new ones emerge?

Suppose a business school predicts that employers (a high-priority customer segment) are becoming much more interested in new hires having strong leadership skills. A subsequent importance study might reveal that along with the emerging emphasis on leadership, employers want new hires to have stronger communication and interpersonal skills as well. On the other hand, the new hires' computer programming skills may become considerably less important. Findings such as these should lead to significant changes in the business school's curricula.

Coordinate the Phases in a CVD Process

CVD is the means by which you bring your customers' perspective into your organization where it can influence value delivery strategy decisions. Because of the way in which customers evaluate products and services, value and satisfaction are intertwined in customers' minds. You do not have to listen to customers talk about your products and services for long to realize this relationship. That is why we think that, in your organization, customer value measurement and customer satisfaction measurement must be integrated into the same information process. We cannot stress enough that each activity in CVD must be coordinated with the others.

Unfortunately, our experience suggests that this coordination is often lacking. One reason is that no one in the organization may have an overall sense of what is involved throughout a CVD process. Coordination becomes very difficult if, conceptually, you do not fully appreciate how one activity affects the next. For instance, we often see too little effort devoted to learning about the wide range of possible value dimensions that customers perceive and to screening these dimensions for importance before customer satisfaction survey questionnaires are designed.

Another problem is organizational. Different departments may be given responsibility for different CVD activities but not provided with any way of bringing the results together. For instance, product design may do research to find out what customers want while quality assurance conducts satisfaction surveys. If there is little or no coordination between these departments, the two research efforts may not concur on the same value dimensions. Product design may concentrate on some dimensions while quality assurance focuses on others.

These coordination problems are perplexing. It is not enough to bring the right techniques to bear on the right questions individually. Every organization must reach consensus on a CVD process to serve as a guiding framework that everyone understands and can accept. We think that the process in Figure 5.1 provides that framework. In addition, overcoming these coordination problems requires effectively managing the implementation of the entire CVD process. In the next section, we discuss selected implementation issues that organizations face.

Managing a Customer Value Determination Process

The same issues that we discussed in Chapter 2 concerning managing MOA processes also apply to managing CVD processes. After all, CVD is a major component of a larger MOA. In this section, we want to extend that discussion by highlighting three additional issues specific to CVD. We selected these issues based on questions that we are frequently asked about CVD implementation, and they concern (1) designing a CVD process, (2) transforming a CVD process into a system, and (3) applying CVD to internal customers.

Designing a CVD Process

Customer value determination processes can be expensive, though resources used vary extensively across organizations.[4] We know of one company that spent about $35,000 to go through this process one time for selected models in one product line in its product mix; management thought that this expenditure was a bargain. Another company spent nearly $500,000 to learn about customer value and satisfaction across several segments for its major product line. This cost was considered high. In one sense, these costs are the price an organization pays to manage in a customer-value-oriented way. You must know your customers well to be responsive to their needs. Fortunately, effective design of a CVD process can help to ensure that these resources are controlled and justified. We discuss two particularly important issues in this regard: (1) which customers to learn about and (2) how frequently to conduct CVD research.

Which Customers to Learn About. One part of this issue is strategic and reflects prior target market decisions. Many organizations target multiple customer groups at the same time. These groups may be segments within a market for a product or service line or they could be multiple markets across an entire product mix. Ideally, we should know all our customers well, but the resources available for that purpose may be limited. In this case, the question becomes how to allocate CVD resources *across* these markets or segments.

We answer this question in the same way at either the market or segment level. One point of view is that an organization should target only those markets or segments that it can afford to learn about. In other words, the opportunity in a market or segment should be sufficiently great to justify on-going customer value determination. When resources cannot be justified for this purpose, you may want to consider phasing out of that market or segment. Consequently, CVD resources become a factor to consider in your strategic decisions on customer targeting.

Another point of view is that not all targeted markets or segments need the same level of spending on customer value determination, and so resources should be differentially allocated across the organization's targets. In this case, higher priority markets or segments should receive more CVD resources. There may be many reasons explaining why a particular market or segment is designated as high priority, but certainly one ought to be potential for market opportunity. It is probably easier to justify allocating more CVD resources to segments or markets with more potential for opportunity than to those with less opportunity. At the very least, you want to be sure that you are staying current on customer value and satisfaction in the highest priority markets or segments.

Customer Value Determination

A second part of the "which customers" issue is more of a research sampling concern: Which customers *within* a selected market or segment should we select to participate in research? While it is beyond the scope of this chapter to cover sampling in depth, we can offer a few observations. First, how you sample depends on which activity in the CVD process you are in. Qualitative research to identify value dimensions, for instance, typically requires a much smaller number of respondents than do customer satisfaction surveys. For one thing, customers in the same segment are more likely to have similar desired value dimensions than similar satisfaction feelings. And, since satisfaction surveys come after value research has been done, the former can be used to validate the findings from the latter.

Secondly, when customers are businesses, their willingness to participate in a study may be a factor in choosing a sample. You may have to include all those who will cooperate in order to get the research done. In this case, our opinion is that any information probably is better than none, and that you should aggressively gather information wherever it is available. However, you must be cautious about trying to make inferences from these "willing" participants to your larger customer base.

Finally, there may be instances where you will ignore the sampling approach and specify that a particular key customer, such as a large retail operation, participate in the CVD research. That customer may be key because it makes up a significant portion of your sales. Key customers can also be "opinion leaders" whose actions are closely watched and emulated by other customers. Or, some customers may be identified as being "key" not for their present position, but because their strategic impact will be greatly felt in the future. For example, while wholesale clubs may represent a small fraction of current revenue for snack foods, this percentage is likely to become even more substantial in the future.

The "which customers" issue becomes even more complicated when customers are other businesses, whether in the trade or end users. In such cases, you have to consider all the contact points in which your organization is interacting with a customer, such as its purchasing, receiving, billing, and user departments.

The customers' desired value and satisfaction feelings can differ at each of these contact points. If a customer is large enough, such as Wal-Mart is for Frito-Lay, you probably will identify contacts for that customer alone. For smaller customers, you may want to generalize about contact points across customers in the same segment.

In general, there are always a number of factors to consider when deciding which customers to learn about with a CVD process. Some factors are strategic while others are more research-oriented. A professional market researcher can help you with the latter ones. But for the former ones, like target market decisions, you will have to tie CVD into your strategic planning.

How Frequently to Conduct CVD Research. The CVD process should not be done once and forgotten. Inevitably, events will happen that affect what value customers desire as well as how satisfied they are with your value delivery offering. Competitors may innovate, use situations may evolve, the economy may shift, or any of a number of other things may trigger change in customers' perceptions. It is best to think of customer value determination as an ongoing process. So, how often should you apply the CVD process?

This question forces us to consider a number of factors, including cost of research, management's ability to act on the results, the degree of change going on in markets or segments, and the willingness of customers to participate in research. A detailed discussion of each of these is beyond the scope of this chapter. However, we can offer a few observations. Most importantly, the appropriate frequency of research will differ for each activity in the CVD process; change is not likely to happen at the same rate for value versus satisfaction.

Typically, *customer value identification research* for the same market or segment need not be repeated more than once every two or three years. The customers' desired value dimensions probably will not change any more quickly than that. Of course, if you know that an event is happening that will affect value dimensions, then the first two CVD activities should be done regardless of when the last research was conducted. Consider a luxury boat manufacturer facing a macroenvironment event. Recently the U.S. government relaxed the luxury tax on pleasure boats. This event is quite likely to trigger value change, and so it is prudent to initiate customer value research to see what new value dimensions are emerging.

Our experience has been that organizations are more likely to err by not doing customer value research frequently enough than by doing it too often. Perhaps managers tend to think that their customers are less dynamic than they really are. We know of one bank that last conducted a customer value study more then seven years ago. This span of time is too long. If you just think about the major changes that have occurred in banking markets, you can count on the fact that customers have changed during this period. You simply must keep up with what customers' currently want.

Customer value dimension importance research should be done even more frequently. The relative importance of customer value dimensions is likely to change faster than the dimensions themselves. At a minimum, you should go through the entire importance screening every time you repeat a customer value study. You also may want to measure perceived importance of those value dimensions included in a satisfaction survey to see if change is occurring. If so, importance measurement will be repeated as frequently as you do customer satisfaction survey research.

We see great variation in the frequency with which organizations conduct *customer satisfaction research*, ranging from monthly to once every one to two years or more. Optimal timing is not the same for every organization; again, there are many factors to consider, including the frequency of contact with your customers, the consistency of your value delivery processes, and the degree of competition. It also important to be realistic about your organization's ability to respond to problem areas that may be uncovered. If you survey customers about satisfaction, they will expect some action. So it may not be prudent to do satisfaction research if you cannot act on what you find out.

If you decide to repeat satisfaction research, then you have to think about the proper timing. Suppose that you decide to conduct satisfaction research twice a year. Do you space the research evenly during the year, say one survey every six months? Or is there some other timing that makes sense? Consider a seasonal product manufacturer such as a snow ski manufacturer. This company may want to conduct its satisfaction research before and during the skiing season rather than, say, at the middle and end of the year.

You also may want to consider trigger events, particularly if they happen at predictable times. Such events lead to change in satisfaction, and satisfaction surveys can be spaced to catch customers at these particular times. For example, a large university knows that sometime during the first few months after arriving on campus incoming freshmen are likely to experience the reality of being away from home and on their own. Some students get overwhelmed by the adjustments that they have to make. Since the university wants to retain these students, a satisfaction survey can be most helpful if it comes during this critical period. Services intended to help these students can be evaluated and unhappy students identified. This information can guide decisions on how best to ensure that these students receive the help that they need.

Finally, some organizations monitor or track selected customer variables over time, such as consumption frequency, use applications, brands purchased, and intentions to repurchase. It makes sense to monitor satisfaction as well, by including several bellwether satisfaction questions in the tracking questionnaire. These questions can be used to determine when a larger satisfaction survey should be conducted. For example, a downward trend in a bellwether satisfaction item may signal the need for a survey to see what is happening in a targeted market.

Satisfaction cause research usually is needed frequently— maybe even continuously. Every satisfaction survey is likely to uncover at least some value dimensions for which your organization's offering falls short as well as some for which there is very high satisfaction. These dimensions should be put on a list and prioritized for action. It is not unusual for this list to be longer than management can deal with at one time. You may have to schedule research to explore causes according to this priority. This scheduling can make this research virtually ongoing.

Customer Value Determination

Customer value prediction research probably should be frequent as well. You can never relax your vigil in trying to anticipate what customers will want in the future. The quicker you can see value change coming, the more lead time you have to respond to their new demands on you. At a minimum, information from this CVD phase should be a regular part of your organization's annual strategy planning process.

Transforming CVD from a Process into a System

So far we have talked about CVD as a measurement process. However, we believe that ultimately organizations should think about CVD as a system for continuously learning about its customers. Systems thinking goes well beyond designing and implementing CVD measurement and analysis of primary research data. It requires that an organization delve into such activities as (1) building databases, (2) linking databases to managers, and (3) designing analyses and reports to facilitate using data for decisions.

This transformation from process to system begins when management decides to integrate all available sources of customer value and satisfaction data into a database. While it is beyond the scope of this book to examine database design, we offer the following guidelines:

- The database should integrate data on customer value and satisfaction coming from all the different sources available.
- The database should be disaggregated so that is can be organized by product, market, segment, individual customer, and individual customer value dimension.
- The database should be organized to show trends from repeated research.
- The database should be integrated with other data from an MOA (e.g., macroenvironmental, market definitions, and competitor data).

Periodically, an organization's CVD database should be evaluated for completeness, among other things. You can benchmark your database against the databases of truly excellent customer-value-oriented companies. If "holes" are found, additional data sources may be requested. However, new data has a cost, and so criteria must be established to evaluate these data requests; actionability should be one of those criteria. You must be able to show that requested data, to be worth the added expense, can improve the way managers make decisions. Otherwise, new customer data will not add any value to your organization.

Systems thinking also requires identifying which managers have access to customer data and information. Advertising, product design, product/brand management, sales, quality assurance, and customer service logistics managers are just some of the possibilities (see Figure 5.3). This systems design issue is complicated by the fact that each type of manager will have some unique data needs to which the CVD system must respond. Consequently, you have to anticipate users' questions in order to ensure that they can be answered with the database.

Finally, a CVD system must convert data into actionable information and present them in report formats that are easy for managers to use. There is little question that the form in which data are presented is a factor in gaining managers' support for using a CVD system. In Chapters 8 and 11, we suggest "user-friendly" ways to present CVD data. There are other formats available as well, and the personal preferences of individual managers should be considered.

Applying CVD to Internal Customers

Throughout this book we focus on customer value determination as a way to learn about external customers. CVD is a versatile approach for knowing business or consumer end users as well as trade customers. We believe that CVD is just as applicable to knowing your internal customers inside an organization. The concept of internal customers is appealing. Most employees require some input from one or more other groups (e.g., functions, departments, or teams) in the company. There is no reason why one internal group cannot study another to learn about their value perceptions and satisfaction feelings. The same techniques and processes should apply equally well, no matter who the target customers are. For instance, we have already suggested

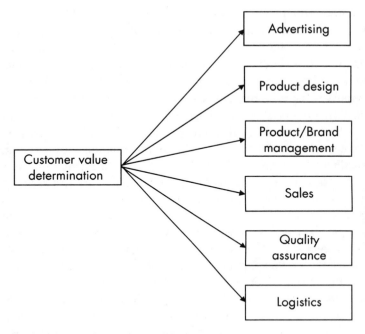

Figure 5.3. Sharing customer value determination data.

above that those responsible for designing an external customer CVD process or system should thoroughly understand the information needs of those managers who are users (i.e., the process or system's internal customers).[5]

Summary

There is growing evidence that managing toward customers is a successful way to do business, and customer information is a key to making this approach work.[6,7] That fact alone is incentive for every organization to periodically reassess how effective its process or system is for knowing its customers. In this chapter, we presented a customer value determination process that can serve as a framework or benchmark for this purpose. CVD is designed to answer key questions that managers should ask if they really want to manage toward customers.

Answers to these questions enable an organization to link its value delivery processes to important customer value dimensions as well as to continuously improve these processes.

We recommended that organizations integrate both customer value and satisfaction into the same CVD process, which consists of five interrelated activities. The initial two activities identify customer value dimensions and determine which are most important. The next two activities bring satisfaction into the process. We have to know how customers feel about our value delivery performance and what is causing both our strengths and problems with this delivery. The fifth activity looks ahead to predict how value dimensions are likely to change in the future.

Finally, we feel strongly that every organization should effectively manage its CVD process or system. Knowing your customers requires a coordinated effort. We have found that several key issues arise when CVD processes are implemented, and we discussed three of them: (1) designing a CVD process, (2) transforming a CVD process into a system, and (3) applying CVD to internal customers. Decisions on these issues can make a significant difference in how actionable CVD processes are for customer value delivery strategy decisions.

References

[1] Kaarree, James E. and Stephen W. Epley, "IDS Takes a Fresh Look at Customer Satisfaction," *Marketing Research*, 5 (Spring 1993), pp. 7–10.

[2] Dutka, Alan, *AMA Handbook for Customer Satisfaction*. Lincolnwood, IL: NTC Business Books, 1994.

[3] Peterson, Donald E., "Beyond Satisfaction," *Creating Customer Satisfaction*. New York: The Conference Board, Research Report No. 944, 1990, pp. 33–34.

[4] Griffin, Abbie and John R. Hauser, "The Voice of the Customer," *Marketing Science,* 12 (Winter 1993), pp. 1–27.

[5] Woodruff, Robert B., William B. Locander, and David J. Barnaby, "Marketing in a Value-Oriented Organization," in Michael J. Stahl and Gregory M. Bounds, eds., *Competing Globally Through Customer Value*. New York: Quorum Books, 1991, Chapter 23, pp. 566–585.

[6] Kohli, Ajay K. and Bernard J. Jaworski, "Market Orientation: The Construct, Research Propositions, and Management Implications," *The Journal of Marketing*, 54 (April 1990), pp. 1–18.

[7] Narver, John C. and Stanley F. Slater, "The Effect of a Market Orientation on Business Profitability," *The Journal of Marketing*, 54 (October 1990), pp. 20–35.

Notes

1. For example, see Morgan, Leonard A., "The Importance of Quality," in *Perceived Quality,* J. Jacoby and J. Olson, eds. Lexington, MA: Lexington Books, 1985, pp. 61–64; Zeithaml, Valarie A., "Consumer Perceptions of Price, Quality, and Value: A Means-End Model and Synthesis of Evidence," *The Journal of Marketing*, 52 (July 1988), pp. 2–22; Zeithaml, Valarie A., A. Parasuraman, and Leonard H. Berry, "The Gaps Model of Customer Service," *The Journal of Marketing*, 64 (July 1988), pp. 32–45.

2. For more on the research that provided the basis for this example, see J. O. Idassi, T. M. Young, P. M. Winistorfer, D. M. Ostermier, and R. B. Woodruff, "A Customer-Oriented Marketing Method for Hardwood Lumber Companies," *Forest Products Journal*, 44 (July/August 1994), pp. 67–73.

CHAPTER 6

HOW CUSTOMER VALUE DETERMINATION IMPROVES BUSINESS DECISIONS

Over a several month period I experienced a string of negative service encounters with my local car dealer. Because the dealership did not actively seek customer feedback, on several occasions I voluntarily registered my concerns with the manager of the service department, although there was rarely any response.

Later, the dealer's national organization contacted me to conduct an in-depth telephone interview. No doubt my name was selected at random from a list of consumers who had visited their dealerships across the country. "At last," I thought, "Now I'll get some action!" For 30 minutes I responded to numerous scales and questions and recounted specific experiences with my local dealer. Following the interview, I waited for a response. None was forthcoming. After several weeks had passed, I had the occasion to talk to my local dealer. Why, I asked, had there been no response to my interview? The dealer responded that the specific information gathered by the national organization was never shared with the local dealers. In fact, the only information the dealers received were a few summary scales (ranging from one to ten) indicating the customers' overall attitudes towards their dealerships. He then inquired about my comments, and I repeated the information which I had already given to the national organization. Not surprisingly, I never received a response from the local dealer either.

In fact, there was great consistency in the lack of response from the national organization to the local dealer to the service department manager. Clearly, the service providers at the local level were following the lead of their national organization. While customer information was sometimes gathered (formally or informally), it was not clear what, if anything, was done with it. Unfortunately, this inability to turn customer feedback into useful management information is all too common in many organizations.

Introduction

Previous chapters have explored the concepts of customer value and satisfaction and have made a case for why both should be integrated into a customer value determination (CVD) process. These chapters have focused on the types of customer information that managers should gather in order to respond more effectively to their customers' needs and requirements.

However, as the previous anecdote illustrates, gathering information is only part of the story. In fact, if customer responses are not actively and purposefully incorporated into the decision-making processes of managers, then even the most brilliant information-gathering activities are for naught. Several business managers have candidly told us that although their companys' market research departments gather a great deal of customer information, it was not clear who gets it or what is done with it. One Fortune 100 vice president admitted that his company's product managers purposely do not access their customer research because they are certain that they already understand what the customer is thinking. To be sure, gathering good data is a critical first step. But it is only the first step. Subsequent steps require that managers take action based upon what is learned from the information.

Managers today frequently speak of the need for "actionable" data – that is, data that can form the basis for action plans and strategic decisions. There are basically two characteristics that define whether data is actionable. First, the data must be potentially useful; that is, the data must be *relevant* to the decisions that managers must make. In this regard, all customer data are not created equal. Actionable data must provide answers, direction, and purpose. The preceding chapters have hopefully explained why a combined customer value and satisfaction measurement system is important for managers who want to take action; managers need to know both what to do (value) and how they are doing (satisfaction).

A second characteristic of actionable data is related to how – or whether – that information is actually used after it is gathered. It is this second aspect that will be elaborated in this chapter. In some ways, this is a much larger problem, as it encompasses a variety of issues. Managers must determine which decisions within the organization will benefit from customer value and satisfaction information (i.e., to what specific departments, functions, activities, individuals, or systems this information should be communicated). Managers must also consider the various organizational processes, policies, and politics that can facilitate and/or inhibit the dissemination of data within the organization. How information is used is often a function of eliminating barriers to information flow.

This chapter discusses how information from the CVD process can and should be used to affect organizational change. First, we discuss the need to specifically link CVD data to value delivery and the importance of top-down leadership to ensure this linkage. The following sections highlight specific areas of strategic decision making (e.g., new product development and customer service) in order to show how CVD can and should influence these specific decisions. In addition, we suggest how CVD can become a unifying theme for interfunctional coordination within organizations. Finally, we address broader organizational behavior and culture issues associated with the dissemination of data. Although such topics are complex and well beyond the scope of this chapter, we feel that it is important to draw attention to them, as they are critical to the success of a value determination process.

Linking Customer Value Determination to Value Delivery

It is safe to say that CVD will have its greatest impact when the organization's value delivery systems are explicitly linked to the resulting information. A value delivery system coordinates all those internal activities and processes that are necessary to provide a particular value or bundle of values to the firm's customers. One example of a value delivery system is the computerized tracking process used by Federal Express. This service attribute is Federal Express' response to the fact that customers do not want to worry and wonder about where their package is, or when and whether it has been delivered. (The service thus seeks to eliminate or reduce negative customer consequences.) Advertising further enhances this value dimension by creatively informing customers about the positive consequences (e.g., no worries, a sense of control) that the customer will experience due to its offering.

In addition, linking customer value data with value delivery systems suggests that managers should measure and evaluate the effectiveness of their value delivery systems. For instance, Federal Express understands that its customers want to know the location of their package when they make in inquiry. This dictates a very short window for getting this information – perhaps a few minutes. Internal measures can be put into place to measure (in minutes? seconds?) the response time between a customer request and the response to that request.

Finally, organizational operations and flexibility are becoming increasingly related to customer responsiveness. Organizations are already implementing flexible manufacturing and just-in-time delivery to move in that direction. More recently, new notions of distributed leadership, information networks, flexible work forces, and interorganizational partnerships are being used to attain the degree of flexibility needed to compete in today's and tomorrow's markets.[1] However, all of these developments are dependent on having timely and actionable customer value and satisfaction information to ensure that *customers* have a voice in how organizations structure their value delivery systems. Flexibility alone will not help, if there is no customer understanding to serve as your "north star."

Customer Value from the Top Down

Putting the concerns of the customer at the center of an organization's decision-making process is not a new idea. A customer-based decision model was advocated in the 1950s by the proponents of the marketing concept, and this concept was picked up with renewed enthusiasm by advocates of the quality movement some thirty years later. Between the 1950s and the 1980s, however, came the realization that it wasn't *just* the marketing department's job to be attuned to the customer. For a customer value orientation to be effective, it must be practiced throughout all aspects of the organization, from top to bottom, and the responsibility for championing the orientation must be placed squarely on the shoulders of senior management. Without leadership at the top, there are significant limits to how far lower level initiatives can go. Senior managers in the organization must leave no question that understanding and delivering customer value is a top priority within the firm, and they must support it as a guiding principal for all decisions.

The following real-life example brings home how it is sometimes quite easy, even for outsiders, to ascertain the priorities of senior management. Recently a friend spent the day with a business owner, an automobile parts wholesaler with customers ranging from Detroit to small retailers. Throughout the day, my friend was impressed by the consistency and urgency with which the owner communicated the importance of creating customer value to his employees. For example, he chastised his sales organization to forget "selling products." Their first priority, he said, was to make sure that they served their customers needs. Throughout the day, this message was repeated, with some variation, to every employee within the organization with which the owner spoke. There was no possibility for mixed signals.

In stark contrast, on the flight home at the end of that same day my friend overheard a conversation between two managers from a manufacturing firm. They complained bitterly that their customers were ordering large quantities of product and disrupting their own firm's manufacturing schedules. In response to this situation, the manufacturing firm's managers decided that their customers would have to alter their ordering procedures. Clearly, management's first priority was to keep their own organization, specifically their production facilities, running smoothly and to bring their customers in line with that priority.

Senior management clearly communicated that the customers' needs were a "problem" that the customers must fix, rather than an opportunity for the manufacturer to respond to the customers' needs and deliver value.

It is clear that a customer value orientation must go beyond simple lip service or a slick public relations message. Senior-level management sends a multitude of signals through the ranks of an organization that spell out their priorities. These signals will be watched with diligence by top-, middle-, and lower-level employees. Eventually, it will become very clear what the *real* priorities of management are (regardless of what management says in public), and the employees' hearts, minds, and behaviors will follow accordingly. If senior management is serious about adopting a customer value orientation, they must make certain that there is consistency in the signals that they send to the organization, and they must constantly reinforce their message.

A customer value orientation must also be carried throughout the strategic planning process, from the loftiest statements out of the corporate headquarters to the most fundamental and minute decisions at the bottom of the corporate hierarchy. It should start with the mission statement, a clear and concise message that delivering customer value is priority one within the firm. From there it should be consciously and meticulously incorporated into the firm's performance objectives (e.g., market share, customer retention, customer satisfaction), into the particular product or service strategies and value delivery systems that it develops (e.g., new product development, logistics, customer service, and corporate communications strategies), into the way support activities are organized and directed (e.g., accounting, purchasing, market research, information systems, and human resources), and into tactical decisions (e.g., performance evaluations, job descriptions, hiring procedures, training programs, and compensation systems).

In summary, we expect that if customer value is to really drive an organization, it must permeate the thinking at all levels of management and of the strategic planning process. Assuming that is the case, we will now look at some specific areas within the firm and how they might orient their strategic decisions around customer value and satisfaction information.

Using Customer Value Data to Orient Strategic Decisions

Chapter 2 discussed how a customer value orientation and adopting a mental model of market opportunity based upon cooperation might underpin a firm's major decisions, helping to determine strategic issues, such as which markets to target and how to provide value to those markets at a competitive advantage. The following section takes the customer value orientation further by addressing how it might be incorporated into other strategic and tactical decisions. While not meant to be exhaustive, in this section we describe some of the most obvious organizational activities and decisions which could – and should – make use of information from the CVD process.

Product Development

Determining an organization's product or service offering should be critically dependent on CVD information. In light of this information, current offerings can be evaluated and improved, and new products can be created.

Evaluating Existing Offerings. There are very few industries today where organizations can be complacent about their product offerings. Intense levels of competition, more challenging global quality standards, and changing customer requirements are among the many reasons why companies must constantly reevaluate their existing offerings. Unfortunately, the solution is rarely just a matter of "adding more" or "improving" the existing offering. While new bells and whistles are always a possibility, such improvements generally come at a financial cost. And these costs must be carefully considered in a business environment where cost consciousness increasingly reigns supreme. In short, many managers are in the double bind of needing to improve products while attempting to keep costs down. For example, a case history of the Chrysler minivan reveals how, despite overwhelming evidence of consumer demand

and a brilliant design, this project was almost scrapped because of the need to conserve resources.[2]

The airline industry is another good example of this dilemma. In the U.S. market, competitors are operating on razor-thin margins (if not losses) in an environment where consumers are extremely price sensitive. However, airlines are also very much a service industry, and they are constantly evaluated on their customer responsiveness relative to competitors. Assuming that there are countless new features or services that could be added to their offering, how are the airlines to decide which are the most important? Larger seats? Better food? More luxurious lounges for business travelers? Competitors in the airline industry must decide which are the critical (or even the minimal) services that they must offer, which ones can provide them with a competitive advantage, and even which ones could be eliminated to reduce costs with the least adverse effect on the company.

Such decisions could benefit greatly from a customer value determination (CVD) process. *First, CVD information would rather quickly reveal differences in the value hierarchies that are representative of unique market segments* (e.g., business versus leisure travel). This might lead the organization to reconsider larger decisions about which markets to target, how to respond differently to different markets, which markets might provide the best match with the company's capabilities, and so forth. (See also Chapter 2 on the MOA process.) This, of course, implies some circularity. While CVD is ideally done *after* an organization determines its market opportunities, it may also encourage the organization to loop back through its MOA process based upon emerging information.

Value hierarchies would be helpful in determining which product features or service activities are most important to the chosen customers. *Identifying the most strategically critical customer consequences would help managers to see what attributes might be used to enhance them.* For instance, if airline customers tell you "not having to wait in lines at the gate makes me feel more relaxed and at ease," how do you go about enhancing that benefit? How might check-in be facilitated or eliminated? Are there alternatives to cuing up at a desk?

By contrast, managers might determine that some attributes are not related to important consumer consequences at all and thus might be targets for elimination. One air carrier recently reported a change from china to plastic dishes that went unmentioned by the customers, much to the airline's surprise. The customers apparently placed little significance on the quality of the serving dishes in enhancing important higher order consequences and end states.

Likewise, customer satisfaction ratings have been used for years to identify "red flags" where product attributes or services are performing at levels below or above customer standards. As stated earlier, satisfaction measures identify areas where organizations can make improvements, although direction on how to do so will often require a complimentary value determination process.

Developing New Products. A more challenging issue for many managers is how value determination data can be used to develop new, unimagined products for the future. Every manager would love to know what customers will want five years from now. Being able to predict future product or service offerings is important not only for competitive purposes, but because cycle times require organizations to make decisions and put resources in place years ahead of actual product delivery.

Earlier, we suggested that managers have trouble identifying future needs because they often ask customers for attribute-level information (e.g., "What size, what flavor, what style will you want?"). We feel that customers are rarely able to answer such questions well. However, they may be better able to articulate what consequences are desired, both in terms of positive consequences desired and negative consequences avoided, as well as what end states are important drivers of their consumption decisions. These tend to be expressed in broad and abstract terms ("I want to feel secure in my car," "No hassles," "I need to provide value to *my* downstream customers."). Remember also that higher levels of the value hierarchy tend to be more stable over time, so they will be less subject to change in the near future. It is, in fact, the identification of consequences and end states (rather than just attributes) that can be most powerful in directing future product or service design initiatives.

This orientation was recently used to completely redesign the MBA offering at the University of Tennessee. For several years MBA programs across the country and, more specifically, their graduates have been sharply criticized by corporate America and the press. Given that most programs are educating 1990s business students based on a 1960s education model, this is hardly surprising. Like many other schools, Tennessee began to explore what the MBA program of the future would look like (a classic example of new product development).

In order to answer this question, the school went to the MBA school's "customers" – business managers who hire MBA graduates and MBA students themselves – to find out what this new product should look like. Knowing very little about academia, curriculums, and pedagogy, these "customers" were ill equipped to provide an attribute-level description of what the new program should be. However, they were quite able to articulate the negative consequences that they experienced as a result of the current offerings (the money spent on retraining, inadequate cross-functional managerial understanding, the lack of familiarity with current industry initiatives, and so forth), as well as the desired consequences that were not being provided (leadership skills, the ability to work in teams, communication skills, consensus building, and the like). It was clear that marginal, attribute-level changes to the existing program (adding one more class) would be insufficient to achieve these ends. Thus, these consequences became the focus for a radical reconfiguration of the MBA program that included a breaking down of the traditional semester class schedule; cross-functional team teaching; a just-in-time, learn-apply rhythm throughout the year; and a much heavier emphasis on interpersonal, managerial skill development. In truth, the resulting "product" was one that might never have been envisioned by the providers (i.e., the educators) without the vision of the customer.

To be sure, understanding higher order consequences and desired end states will not take managers completely off the hook. To them is left the very important job of translating customer requirements into a configuration of attributes and doing so in a way that is creative, effective, efficient, appropriate, and hopefully unique relative to competition. However, these decisions are no longer made in the dark. Customer value understanding guides this translation process.

Customer Service

Customer service is an increasingly important component of an organization's offering. This fact is keenly felt by an organization's logistics staff as it responds to increasing customer demands for more frequent deliveries, smaller inventories, more precise forecasting and information sharing, long-term relationships, and systems flexibility. In a recent survey of logistics and transportation managers, nine out of ten responded that customer service had increased in importance in the last ten years; a majority judged the increase to be "substantial."[3] In addition, respondents said that customer service is now clearly seen as the most important element of the marketing mix, replacing price, which was the single most important element three years ago, and just edging out product features. Organizations are responding to these demands by placing responsibility for customer service at increasingly higher levels of the corporate hierarchy. The trend has been for these responsibilities to move from middle-level managers to vice presidents. According to a spokesperson for Andersen Consulting, "Logistics managers increasingly recognize that a quality product at a competitive price now has to be a given. Customer service is a key differentiator, even for heavily branded products."[3]

However, as with product design, customer service can quickly degenerate into a discussion of which *attributes* to add. EDI? Better on-time delivery? More accurate order filling? The temptation to view customer service in this way often leads to parity, where new offerings are quickly copied by competition.

What the customer may be looking for is a supplier who will provide the optimum combination of positive consequences and/or reduce the negative consequences of transacting business. In fact, it may be far less relevant to customers *how* your organization delivers value (from an attribute sense) than how they benefit from it. In this sense, they may be surprisingly open to new ideas and initiatives, despite their seeming emphasis on competitive parity.

Again, it helps to think in terms of higher order end states and consequences that are being served by a logistics function (e.g., profitability, longevity, quality, reduced inventory, higher inventory turns, and so forth). EDI may in fact be an attribute that can help your customer achieve some of these goals. But how might your organization go to the next step? What bundlings of services and technology will allow your customer to better achieve these ends, especially after EDI becomes commonplace among competitors? Again, the answer lies in understanding the entire hierarchy and the linkages within it, rather than myopically focusing on the attribute equivalent of "keeping up with the Joneses."

Price

Price is the variable most frequently associated with "value." That is because value is often narrowly defined from an economic perspective – as the monetary cost associated with exchange. Business publications tend to foster this perspective, most recently by discussing the importance of "value pricing" in the grocery, consumer products, and fast-food industries.[4,5]

We would like to change this perspective from "value pricing" to "pricing as an indicator of value." The former perspective suggests that the price of a product should be driven by costs and, more specifically, by cost reductions. By contrast, the latter perspective suggests that pricing should consider a wider range of factors that result in consequences for the customer and be set accordingly. Stated another way, the price should be a reflection of the value that is created by the product and not vice versa.

In talking with middle- to senior-level managers across a variety of different industries, we have increasingly heard the complaint that the only thing their customers think about is lowering price. Suppliers feel that they are caught in a vice that demands that they squeeze costs to the limit in order to offer the lowest – or at least a competitive – price. Certainly there is the need for organizations to operate in an efficient and lean fashion today. Otherwise, they will not even be in the ball game. However, one way out of this trap is to begin to compete by providing value in ways other than just being the "low cost leader." Even in light of increasing pressures to lower price, both consumers and customers can respond positively to products and service that clearly provide advantages over the competition.

For example, Ritz Carlton, a recent Malcolm Baldrige Award winner, has carved out a competitive niche by competing on service rather than on price in the very competitive hospitality industry. In this case, understanding value requirements helped Ritz Carlton identify which particular consumers (or segments) would respond most positively to the delivery of value at the premium end of the pricing continuum. But "pricing for value" does not always necessitate a premium strategy. Saturn has found ways to be competitive in the moderate price category of the automobile industry. They create value through an emphasis on quality and service, no haggling over the sale price, and their perception as an "alternative," more approachable manufacturer. Their perceived value, and the resulting customer loyalty and positive word of mouth, recently propelled them to the top of the J. D. Powers Customer Satisfaction Survey.[6]

Promotion

Once a strategic decision has been made to provide a particular level of value via the product or service offering, an important consideration is how to communicate that value to current and potential customers. One of the important objectives of promotion should be to help customers understand the value that is created by the consumption of a particular product or service.

First, in putting together promotional campaigns, the provider may want to place special emphasis on the value dimensions that are critical to customers. In this sense, value determination can help to prioritize different elements of the promotional message to target themes that resonate with customers. Consequences, in particular, can serve as effective positioning themes for advertising campaigns – "Wisk eliminates ring around the collar." Delta Airlines, in a recent attempt to actively incorporate its customers into its advertising theme, has changed from an attribute focus ("Delta Gets You There" and "We Love To Fly and It Shows") to a consequence focus ("You'll Love the Way We Fly"). Understanding use situations, which results from value determination, can also be helpful. Advertisements can show the product responding to the requirements of important use situations. For instance, a large boat manufacturer recently discovered that its products were being used as a way to keep the family together (a desired end state) and changed its advertising to show more examples of family outings.

We also believe that companies that wish to build brand equity will be more successful by appealing to higher level requirements of the value hierarchy. In contrast to an attribute focus, a consequence or desired end state focus has many advantages: the ability to target customer needs specifically, the ability to be a unifying theme across multiple products, and a longer term stability that will allow continuity and consistency of communications over time.

Prior to purchase, promotion can also help customers identify what performance variables should be used to assess value. For instance, automobile manufacturers are increasingly suggesting that their products' value be judged in terms of their ability to provide safety. Computer manufacturers have, over the years, changed from stressing attributes alone (e.g., memory, RAM, functions, and so forth) to an increasing emphasis on user friendliness (e.g., you don't have to spend a great deal of time learning the system). However, one note of caution should be made here. Managers must also be careful about the potential downside of emphasizing value dimensions on which your product or service cannot deliver. The customer satisfaction model presented in Chapter 4 points out the danger that occurs when product performance cannot live up to the standard implied or promised by promotion.

Promotion will also have an obvious role to play when, as was suggested previously, an organization wishes to price its product or service to reflect superior value. In this case, the arguments for why a higher price is warranted will fall heavily on the promotional tools that are used. Clearly the promotional strategy must be consistent and integrated with all the value that is created by all elements of the marketing mix, including price, distribution channels, service, and the product offering itself.

Finally, it should be noted that promotion, itself, can be used to create value. Promotion to end users has long been considered to add value to channel customers (i.e., distributors and retailers) who require assurances that inventories will turn. Likewise, the nature of the interpersonal relationship that is established between a salesperson and customer can be extremely powerful and can both create and add value for the customer. For the consumer, advertising and other types of promotion (both before and after the sale) can add value by enhancing the reputation of the product as well as the product provider. Cognitive dissonance research, for example, show that consumers may actually read more advertisements for products *after* they have been purchased than before. Clearly some value (e.g., feelings of security, validation of the decision, and dissonance reduction) is being provided by the advertisement in a way that may enhance both the subsequent perceived value of the product as well as repeat purchase.

Distribution

Distribution strategies should be tied to the delivery of value. Among other things, the selection of the distribution channel (e.g., the number and type of channel intermediaries used) can create a tremendous amount of value for end users and therefore should be finely tuned to their needs.

For instance, a value hierarchy may help you understand how important the consequences of convenience and waiting time are for your customers, relative to other value requirements. Knowledge of these consequences has a direct impact on decisions related to the number and location of an organization's distribution outlets. Do your customers look for a high degree of service to be provided by the channel, or are they more price sensitive? Again, different customer targets will answer these questions differently. For instance, the founder of Domino's Pizza pursued a home delivery strategy after he found that a large portion of customers in his restaurants were buying carry out pizzas to eat at home. This distribution strategy offered Domino's a considerable competitive advantage, leaving Pizza Hut and others to play catch up.

Value as a Performance Evaluation Tool

Once a value orientation becomes truly pervasive within an organization, it should find its way into employee evaluation policies and practices. In fact, unless the evaluation and reward systems within organizations are in line with a customer value orientation, they have little hope of encouraging the behaviors that are consistent with this orientation; they may in fact undermine it. This can be seen in a multitude of sales forces where the charge of "customer satisfaction" quickly comes into conflict with performance evaluations based upon attaining quotas, a holdover from the sales orientation that has been pervasive in many corporations.

How should performance evaluation and reward practices be altered to be consistent with customer value? To address this question, let us use one aspect of the business as an example. Because of their unique interface position, the sales representatives are typically the first and most frequent employees of an organization to come in contact with customers. An examination of existing sales force evaluation procedures and reward practices can quickly reveal the priorities of the firm (or at least what the salespersons understand the priorities of the firm to be). To be sure, there should be some attention to productivity and sales. No one would discount their importance. But are these the sole or primary considerations? What about issues such as customer satisfaction, customer retention, increased volume with existing customers, selection by the customer as a sole or preferred supplier, the amount and type of contact between sales reps and customers? *A customer value orientation will, at a minimum, begin to broaden the types of behaviors and activities that are considered in performance evaluations beyond traditional bottom-line considerations.*

Another interesting aspect to examine is whether all of the measures of sales force performance are at the attribute level (e.g., the number of errors in paper work, the timely return of calls, and the number of presentations made), or whether sales force evaluations also include consideration of customers' higher order consequences and desired end states (e.g., the customers' evaluations of the ease of transactions, the extent to which the customer's firm operates more smoothly as a result of the relationship, the extent to which the relationship allows the customer to more effectively serve its customer base, how satisfactorily customer complaints are handled, and so forth). *Performance evaluations which reflect a customer value orientation will include both attribute level and consequence level evaluation dimensions.*

One thing that immediately becomes apparent when one begins to include *customer* consequences in performance evaluations is that it is difficult, if not impossible, to measure them without input from the customer. This is another dead giveaway about the orientation of an evaluation system. *If the evaluation system is driven by internally generated data, then it probably does not reflect a customer value orientation. The former requires feedback, which only the customer can supply.* Andersen Consulting suggests that for managers attempting to upgrade their organization's customer service, it is imperative to establish performance objectives based on input from customers. This might include random surveys, focus groups, benchmarking, or surveys done on a random transaction basis.[3]

Customer value can and should be applied to any employee of the firm who is responsive to the customer. This could impact any number of areas of the firm including but not limited to accounts payable, logistics, customer service technicians, new product development, sales, and marketing.

Value and Hiring Criteria

If an organization seriously considers and orients its performance evaluations around a customer value focus, then it stands to reason that these same performance indicators should shape hiring criteria. From the outset, managers will want to identify individuals possessing interpersonal and technical skills that will enhance customer needs and value requirements. In some cases, this may require a translation process in order to define the specific skills, job experience, training, background, and personality most conducive to meeting the customer's value requirements. However, the "downstream" benefits of reconsidering these hiring qualifications could be significant.

Value as a Training Tool

Finally, a value orientation will very likely influence corporate training initiatives. Understanding the customer, how the customer defines value, and getting employees oriented toward the delivery of that value should be a primary objective of the organization. In order to reinforce the top-down communication that was discussed earlier, training and educating employees are imperative. Such training fosters consistency of thinking among the employees, encourages the incorporation of a value orientation at all levels of the organization, and provides an important feedback mechanism for senior management to ascertain the location of the various areas of the organization on the customer value learning curve.

Using Customer Value Data to Achieve Interfunctional Coordination

Delivering value to customers is an organizationwide responsibility. In one way or another, every department or functional area in an organization has a role to play in internal processes that lead, directly or indirectly, to value being received by customers. Increasingly, organizations are using transfunctional teams comprised of people with various specialties to manage the development of these processes (see Figure 6.1). Customer value data can provide a unifying direction for these teams, promote a common language, and reveal opportunities for improving internal processes and developing competitive advantage. In this respect, customer value data itself creates value for the internal customers of an organization.

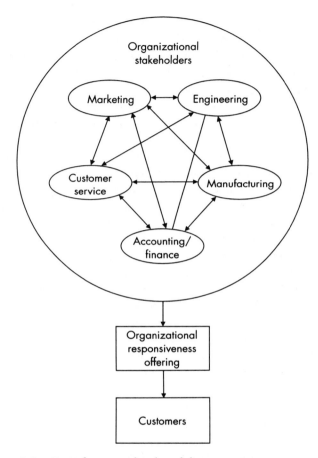

Figure 6.1. Transfunctional value delivery systems.

A case in point is the pleasure boat manufacturer discussed in a previous chapter. In its product development process, design engineers wanted to improve the ease with which customers can use the convertible canvas top that covers the cockpit area. Marketing helped by gathering information from dealers and focus group research that uncovered the problems customers were having with the existing design. Product design used the information to change the mechanism for putting the top up and down. Manufacturing worked with product design and marketing to incorporate the changes into the boat model. Customer service worked with marketing and retail dealers to demonstrate the improved design to customers. All these organization functions worked effectively in a system that delivered improved value, and the success of the product change is a tribute to the cooperation between the functional departments, which all held a common goal in mind: to be responsive to customer needs.

Another good example of this potential interaction is associated with quality function deployment (QFD). QFD is being used in many organizations to translate external customer requirements into physical product characteristics, and the starting point for this process is an understanding of customer requirements from research on end users. A team of people from different functions jointly discuss what product and service specifications are needed to meet these requirements. (While traditionally these requirements have had an almost exclusive attribute focus, they may also be expanded to include higher order consequences.) It is easy to see how customer value data could provide important input for this process.

Which area within the organization should take the leadership role in bringing customer expertise into these cross-functional decision-making teams? The answer to this question will vary across organizations. The marketing department may serve this role because of its unique position as an external interface with the market and customers. However, the research function in many organizations is separate from the marketing function per se. In addition, many organizations have recently added quality managers. It might be a natural fit for any of these areas to play a role in gathering and disseminating customer information across the organization.

Regardless of which individual or area in the organization takes on this role, he or she should possess the following skills:

- Understand the value sought by external customers (both end users and channel customers).
- Understand the information needs of other internal players in the organization's value delivery system.

- Be able to communicate effectively with people from other functions, including education and training. (This requirement suggests the need for a fairly high level of credibility and influence within the organization.)
- Be adept at overcoming possible conflict between functions and reaching grounds for cooperation.[7] Cooperation is more likely to occur when all functions are able to look beyond departmental objectives to what will benefit customers.
- Be committed to treating these activities as ongoing. Some firms may not conduct customer value inquiries until a crisis occurs, and then it may be too late. Management must be committed to regularly studying changes occurring in markets and with targeted customers.

Getting the Most Impact from Value Determination Data

In order to get the maximum benefit from customer value determination data, management must get the data into the right hands and in a timely fashion. In short, a system must be in place that will provide for the dissemination of the customer value information. There are several things that organizations can do to facilitate the dissemination and use of value data. In many ways, these are no different from the suggestions for the use of any market research data. However, because of the emphasis on actionability that was noted previously, the following brief summary of these points is necessary.

1. There should be an action plan for managing the dissemination of the data. This action plan should include:
   a. the assignment of responsibility for dissemination of the data, and
   b. an action plan that includes information about *who* within the organization will receive what *type of data* and *what they are expected to do with it.*
2. Data must be disseminated in a timely fashion.
3. Efforts should be made to link the value determination data to internal processes.

4. Value determination data should be linked to reward systems.
5. Value determination data should be related to critical outcome measures.

Each of these points will be elaborated below.

Managing the Dissemination of Data

One of the first and most critical steps to ensure the use of CVD data is to have a fully developed action plan for its dissemination. Ideally, this plan should be developed *prior* to the gathering of customer value determination data.[8] A thorough understanding of how these data will be disseminated throughout the firm, i.e., understanding who will be using the information for what decisions, can even shape what kind of information is gathered in the first place.

Assigning responsibility for the dissemination of this information is critical. This will help ensure that the data do not "slip between the cracks." However, it is important to consider who within the organization will be assigned this responsibility, as this decision will send a strong signal to employees. Clearly, more importance will be attributed to individuals at higher levels in the corporate hierarchy and, to a lesser extent, to line versus staff positions. Most importantly, the assignment of this responsibility will signal whether management sees such information as simply a "report card" or whether their attitude is more proactive (e.g., whether management will assign a "change agent" who is charged with helping the organization to *act on* the information).[8]

The action plan for dissemination should also include a discussion of who within the organization will receive different elements of the CVD data and what they are expected to do with it. For each phase of the consumer research they conduct, South Central Bell has generated a grid that lays out the type of research that will be done, its objectives, and how the results will be used. For example, the results of their customer satisfaction studies "are presented at company and state levels" and they are "reviewed by an interdepartmental team for opportunities to improve service and address concerns."[9]

Getting the Data to the Right Managers

Getting the data into the right hands is an important issue to consider in the action plan. The anecdote at the beginning of this chapter was an example of how not to do this. A great deal of customer information was gathered by the car manufacturer, but it never got back to the level where that data could become actionable – the local dealer. In contrast, the Promus Organization, representing Hampton Inns and Homewood Suites, provides a more positive example. After contacting customers about their stays at Promus facilities, this information is immediately routed to the manager of the facility in question so that they can conduct any follow up that may be required.

Another positive example is found in Andersen Consulting's "Five Step Customer-Service Action Plan" for logistics functions. Andersen suggests that performance reports be distributed "to all levels in the company. In warehouses (or distribution centers), post the performance results on activities assigned to these specific workers (e.g., order-picking accuracy and percentage of damaged orders)."[3] Andersen also suggests putting the customers themselves on the routing list for the data. They suggest that sharing performance data with key customers is a way to both improve services and get closer to key accounts.[3]

One of the most important reasons why dissemination responsibility must be assigned and action plans developed is the expectations of the customer. When you ask your customers to take the time to provide feedback, there is an implied promise that your organization will do something with that information. One of the most damaging things an organization can do is to undermine customer trust by not responding to customer feedback. In fact, considering the negative customer backlash that can result, it might be better not to have gathered customer feedback at all. Chrysler is known for actively soliciting and incorporating customer feedback into the design changes of their minivans. They have set an expectation that they will respond, and this expectation is reflected in a comment by one of their customers who stated, "I guess I trusted Lee Iacocca to follow through with customer suggestions."[10]

The Timeliness of Data

Timely dissemination of the data is also critical. Product and service offerings can change quickly, as can the competitive environment and customer attitudes. The more quickly data are utilized, the more effective they will be. Likewise, data that is allowed to languish in the research department or in reports that do not get circulated in a timely fashion will be less actionable. What if the manager of a Promus facility found out three months after the fact that a customer had a bad experience at his hotel? By that time, the customer would have come to feel a great deal of ill will against the hotel and its management. It is questionable if any remedial action would be effective. Fortunately, Promus' customer feedback system is set up so that managers get information from their customers within just a few days of their stay.

Another reason to process information in a timely fashion is, again, that management must be mindful of the signals that are sent. If data are allowed to languish, to not be disseminated and used, then the clear message to employees is that management does not perceive this information to be very important. In turn, it suggests that employees should have little urgency about responding to it. In contrast, feedback that is swiftly processed and disseminated suggests a high priority, and employees are more likely to respond accordingly.

Linking Value Data to Internal Processes

As stated earlier, it is important to tie customer value data to the internal processes of the firm.[8] It is only by making these links explicit that customer value information can be translated into action and solutions. For example, customer feedback from Xerox customers indicated that they were experiencing repair delays, and thus becoming dissatisfied. To make the link back to value delivery, these experiences were analyzed by a team of Xerox employees to determine the most appropriate response.

They eventually rejected conventional wisdom, which was simply to put more parts on repair trucks, and were able to use delivery services such as Federal Express to rush the correct parts to customers at less expense. By understanding and acting on their customer problems, they were able to find a solution that created customer value.[11]

Linking Value Data to Reward Systems

It was suggested previously that performance evaluations should be closely tied to CVD data. Many organizations, including Xerox and Promus, already use customer satisfaction data to influence employee compensation. Allen Paison, president of Walker Customer Satisfaction Measurements, estimates that a third to one half of his clients link compensation to satisfaction in some way.[12] IBM recently reported a change in their sales force compensation that ties 40 percent of the commission to customer satisfaction.[13] Again, when it comes to sending signals, such a practice does much to get the appropriate "share of mind" of an organization's employees. It should, however, be noted that there are many who are skeptical of this practice, believing that it is rife with potential for the abuse and misuse of data and employees.[12] Probably the most compelling response to such critics is that customer feedback should serve as an *aid* to management judgment about employee performance, and not as a *substitute* for it.

Linking Value Determination to Outcome Measures

Finally, feedback from customers can and should be linked with a firm's bottom line. It has been suggested that firms more directly link strategic analysis and decisions with shareholder value.[14,15] Bridging customer value and financial analysis can be understandably difficult as the two perspectives "use different conceptions of value, focus on different constituencies (customers versus shareholders), pertain to different markets, use different levels of analysis, address different decision variables, and emphasize different measures."[14] However, firms must begin to see the two perspectives as being complementary rather than in conflict. While financial outcomes engender a necessary accountability and reality check for strategy decisions, articulating the assumptions upon which strategy decisions are based (e.g., customer value objectives) can help increase the precision of financial analyses, especially those using forecasts.

Harris Corporation has traditionally tied its customer satisfaction feedback to performance measures such as return on equity, sales, and income for various divisions.[16] Over the years they have been able to demonstrate a positive relationship between customer satisfaction and performance. Customer retention rates and share of customer purchases might also be considered to gauge the success of customer value determination and delivery processes.[17]

Managers should not shrink from bottom-line issues. In fact, strategies to create and deliver superior value should lead to marketplace success and in turn create shareholder value. Therefore, financial measures may be important for evaluating both the forecasted and historical success of a firm's customer value orientation. However, a note of caution is needed. Companies with an unsatisfactory bottom-line situation may need to look to a variety of reasons for this problem; its customer value orientation is only one potential cause.

Summary

In this chapter we have attempted to highlight issues that can enhance the actionability of CVD information. First, we discussed the importance of linking value determination with value delivery. Next, we addressed the need for top-down leadership for fostering a value orientation within firms. We then highlighted several strategic decisions within firms and discussed how they might benefit from the value determination process. Finally, we broached some of the organizational and process issues that can facilitate and inhibit the dissemination of value determination data.

Clearly, a single chapter is not sufficient for a thorough discussion of these issues. How to use CVD information could well be the subject of an entire book. A complete discourse on the dissemination and use of customer data also quickly leads into the complexities of how organizations are structured, managerial leadership styles, and the much larger realm of organizational psychology. Such topics are obviously beyond the scope of this book. Hopefully, however, this chapter has served to raise some of the critical issues that must be wrestled with in order to turn customer feedback into meaningful input for managerial decisions.

References

[1] Hey, John, "The New Post-Heroic Leadership," *Fortune,* February 21, 1994, pp. 42–50.

[2] Taylor, Alex III, "Iacocca's Minivan," *Fortune,* May 30, 1994, pp. 56– 66.

[3] "Customer Service: The Great Differentiator," *Traffic Management,* 31 (November 1992), pp. 40 – 44.

[4] Power, Christopher, Walecia Knorad, Alice Cuneo, and James Treece, "Value Marketing," *Business Week,* November 11, 1991, pp. 132–140.

[5] Oster, Patrick, Gabrielle Saveri, and John Templeman, "Procter and Gamble Hits Back," *Business Week,* July 19, 1993, pp. 20–22.

[6] Woodruff, David, James B. Treece, and Sunita Wadekar, "Saturn: GM Finally Has a Real Winner. But Success Is Bringing a Fresh Batch of Problems," *Business Week,* August 17, 1992, pp. 86–91.

[7] Reizenstein, Richard C., Joyce E. A. Russell, Joseph O. Rentz, Tammy D. Allen, and Barbara Dyer, "Cross-Functional Conflict: The Case of the Brand/Sales Interface," Working Paper, University of Tennessee, Knoxville, TN 37996-0530, 1994.

[8] Maginnis, Corinne, "The Numbers Are In: Now What Do You Do With Them?", *Marketing News,* April 12, 1993, p. 9.

[9] Marketing Research Matrix of Surveys, *Perspective,* South Central Bell Telephone Company Employee Publications, 600 North 19th Street, Birmingham, AL, September 29, 1989.

[10] Treece, James B., "The Streetwise Makeover of Chrysler's Minivans," *Business Week,* September 24, 1990, pp. 110–113.

[11] Mathews, Jay and Peter Katel, "The Cost of Quality," *Newsweek,* Sept. 7, 1992, pp. 48 – 49.

[12] Donath, Bob, "Satisfaction Measurement Sometimes Goes Too Far," *Marketing News,* March 15, 1993, p. 9.

[13] Sager, Ira, Gary McWilliams and Robert D. Hof, "IBM Leans On Its Sales Force," *Business Week,* February 7, 1994, p. 110.

[14] Day, George S. and Liam Fahey, "Putting Strategy Into Shareholder Value Analysis," *Harvard Business Review*, 68 (March-April 1990), 156–162

[15] Barwise, Patrick, Paul R. Marsh, and Robin Wensley, "Must Finance and Strategy Clash?" *Harvard Business Review*, 67 (September-October 1989), pp. 85–90.

[16] "Linking Total Quality and Business Success," A Presentation by the Harris Corporation to the Manufacturers' Alliance for Productivity and Innovation Council on Quality, November 9–10, 1992, Washington, DC.

[17] Reichheld, Frederick F., "Loyalty-Based Management," *Harvard Business Review*, 71 (March-April 1993), pp. 64–73.

Section III

CUSTOMER VALUE
DETERMINATION TECHNIQUES

CHAPTER 7

MEASURING CUSTOMER VALUE

There is an enormous difference between understanding a product and understanding the user's relationship to that product. Most design engineers understand their products quite well – how they are made, their performance potential, their limitations, and so forth. However, these same people may not as clearly understand the product user's experience.

This point was demonstrated in research that we recently conducted for a manufacturer of luxury cruise boats. In a series of interviews and focus groups with their customers, we used a method called "grand tour" (described later in this chapter) to allow the owners to walk us through their experiences operating and using their boats. One insight was particularly revealing. The grand tours indicated that it is very common for two individuals to pilot a boat, with one actually driving the vessel and a second navigating. However, the instrument panel on the boat was designed so that it could only be easily viewed by a single driver. As a result, this placement made the instruments very difficult for the navigator to read. Traditional attribute-level measures are less likely to uncover such insights. However, this is precisely the type of rich information that can emerge when measurement methods are used that directly pursue the product-user-situation interaction, which is fundamental to the understanding of value.

Introduction

Convincing managers of the need to understand customer value is only a first step. Having committed to the "religion" of customer value, you have to consider the types of customer information that your organization needs to make strategic decisions. In short, you have to bring that commitment down to an operational level of how best to measure customer value.

As we discussed in Chapter 4, there is a difference between customer value and customer satisfaction. Not surprisingly, the methods by which organizations have traditionally measured customer satisfaction are not entirely adequate for measuring customer value. Therefore, managers must consider alternative measurement methods, which are described in this chapter.

This chapter focuses on the first step in the customer value determination (CVD) process: measuring customer value. We begin with a brief discussion of the differences between quantitative and qualitative methods, the latter of which are particularly useful for customer value measurement. Next, we introduce a framework for conducting qualitative research. This includes issues such as identifying which customers to interview, deciding who should conduct the interviews (e.g., in-house versus contract researchers), and weighing the pros and cons of several methods, including observation, focus groups, and in-depth interviews. We conclude with some general measurement issues, including establishing rapport with customers, effectively using probes, and planning and timing customer interviews.

It is important to note at the outset that the basic methods described in the following sections (in-depth interviews, focus groups, and observations) are commonly used for many types of customer research. Their use in CVD differs from their more traditional usage, however. First, we offer specific suggestions about when and in what types of circumstances these methods might best be employed. More important, we also address how to use these techniques to more effectively capture customer value. Here we offer some interviewing techniques – laddering and grand tour – that have been specifically used and created to capture value hierarchy dimensions.

Qualitative versus Quantitative Measures

Measuring customer value is rooted in the use of qualitative data-gathering techniques. For some managers this will not be a problem. But for others who are steeped in the tradition of quantitative techniques (e.g., large-scale surveys that are scanned and analyzed by computers) this may be an uncomfortable change. Qualitative research techniques are inherently less structured, more open-ended, and more subject to interpretation. The resulting data are more likely to be presented as profiles, descriptions, and summaries than as mean scores, standard deviations, and p values. In short, qualitative techniques and the data they produce are often considered by managers to be "soft." Why is this type of research method needed? What are its advantages over quantitative techniques? A brief comparison of two typical data-gathering methods, surveys and depth interviews, highlights some of the fundamental differences between quantitative and qualitative techniques, respectively.

Consider the characteristics of surveys (whether conducted by mail, telephone, or in person). On the positive side, they are generally quick and economical to administer. Their data typically consist of numbered responses to scaled items that can easily be reduced to means, bar charts, and other quantitative analyses that can, in turn, be easily digested by managers and manipulated by computers. However, there are some significant limitations to surveys. Surveys are by nature more highly structured, and as such they are somewhat constrained by the amount and type of data that they can generate. They are most appropriately used when the feedback required of customers can be reduced to a finite number of questions (not too many) with identifiable content (the important issues to be measured can be determined a priori) and in a limited format (customers respond to evaluation or performance-based scales, such as Likert or semantic differential). Although such instruments often contain some open-ended questions ("Do you have anything else you would like to say?"), these are typically few in number and customer response to them is generally limited.

In contrast, one way to think about customer value is to imagine an onion with many layers. Beginning with the surface, each of these layers must be peeled back to expose new surfaces beneath until the heart of the onion is reached. Understanding customer value requires such a "peeling back" process and much more flexibility in the amount and type of customer information gathered than is typically represented by surveys. Depth interviews provide this needed flexibility.

When first asked to discuss their relationship to product or service offerings, most customers will begin with the most obvious and objective issues – attributes. They will talk about "what is," and the researcher should pay close attention to customers' perspectives on this level of the value hierarchy. However, the researcher must also encourage customers to explore their relationship with the product at deeper (higher value hierarchy) levels. He or she must probe and explore and encourage the customer to discuss important outcomes of product or service use, such as positive and negative consequences, and the researcher must dig deeply to allow deep-seated desired end states to come to the surface. Most importantly, he or she must let the customer lead the interview to issues that *the customer* feels are important. (In fact, it is helpful if the researcher maintains a naive posture throughout the interview and thus avoid interjecting any a priori biases about what product issues he or she thinks are important to the customer.) It is often impossible to know where such an interview might lead or what new insights might be discovered when the customer dictates the direction of the interview.

Such a "peeling back" process is much more conducive to – or even dependent on – open-ended, loosely structured questions. Qualitative techniques are uniquely suited to this task. Such techniques allow the customers to use their own words and experiences to describe product performance rather than predetermined criteria that may be unnatural or even inappropriate for the customer. On the downside, qualitative techniques typically make considerable time demands on customers and are more costly to conduct in terms of both time and money for the firm; the resulting data are often more cumbersome to analyze and present. However, in balance, the benefits derived from qualitative techniques in terms of the depth of customer understanding far outweigh their costs.

The following are the critical questions that should be considered when conducting qualitative research.

1. Who should conduct the research?
2. Who should be interviewed? (Identifying a customer sample)
3. How should the pros and cons of the different qualitative methods be weighed?
   a. Observation.
   b. Focus groups.
   c. In-depth interviews using laddering or grand tours.
4. What are some general issues for conducting a qualitative interview?
   a. Getting started and establishing rapport.
   b. The use of probes.
   c. Planning and timing the interview.

In this chapter different measurement methods and techniques will be described and their pros and cons evaluated. However, it is important to note at the outset that we will not recommend any one "best" method for measuring customer value. Organizations wishing to conduct qualitative research will need to weigh the merits of many methods and determine which is best suited to their information needs, their resources, their customers, and their own preferences.

Who Should Conduct the Research?

One of the first questions that must be determined is "Who should conduct the research?" This generally entails a choice between either using one's own employees or outsourcing this task to third parties, such as a research or consulting firm. It is important to make this decision early, because the manner in which it is resolved can have implications for subsequent decisions. For instance, a decision to use in-house employees might dictate which customers to interview. Customers with which your firm does not have good rapport may be uncooperative or defensive if confronted by your own employees. As stated earlier, there is no "best" answer to this question. However, we can lay out some of the issues, pro and con, that need to be considered.

At the outset, we assume that whomever does the qualitative research, whether an employee of your organization or not, is adequately qualified and trained. And hiring someone from an outside research firm is not always necessary to ensure adequate interviewing skills. In fact, in many organizations there are individuals who are quite capable of carrying out qualitative research, either because of their existing skills or because of their ability to be trained at a nominal cost. These people might be found in market research, human resources, or even in sales departments. Generally, you should look for employees who can easily establish rapport with customers in an uninhibiting manner. In addition, some specific training in observation, focus group moderation, or in-depth interviewing may be warranted. Obviously, the assumption about third-party researchers is that they already come equipped with these required skills.

Individual skill levels being equal, there are several issues that speak for and against in-house versus third-party researchers. Let's begin with using your own employees. There are several advantages to going this route. Most important is the fact that your own people should be closer to the problem. They should be familiar with the conduct of business, with the players, with the jargon, and with the history of the relationship between the customer and your firm. This background can be an important advantage in an interview setting. Such an individual is much more likely to know which issues to probe, where the sensitive issues or political booby traps are hidden, and simply how to talk with the customer. Using your own people is a particularly good idea if you have established a good rapport with your customers, and it may also engender goodwill for your firm.

The main advantage of an in-house interviewer – proximity – can also be a strong disadvantage, however. Sometimes your own people can be too close to the problem. They may be biased or subjective. They may be too defensive to really listen to what the customer is saying. And, in cases where rapport has not been established, your customers may be less than honest with your own employees. This might be especially true if the relationship between your firm and the customer is strained. It may be difficult for your customer to look you in the eye and say you are not doing a good job.

Third-party researchers from consulting or research firms provide the opposite set of problems. On the positive side, these people may be more objective, they may be more sensitive to your customer, they are more likely to be objective in their questions and in their responses, and customers may be more honest and candid with them. The main disadvantages of these individuals, in addition to the expense (which can be considerable), is that they may simply lack the necessary understanding of a complex situation to be able to interview effectively. They may require extensive "background" training on the way business is done in your industry and on jargon that is unfamiliar to them. Their lack of knowledge of the relationship between your firm and customers may also limit their ability to pick up on important strategic issues and they may fail to probe where it would be useful.

In short, there are pros and cons to whichever solution your firm selects. Most likely this decision will be made on the basis of resource availability (both personnel and money), personal preferences, and the nature of the relationships that exist between your organization and your customers.

Who Should Be Interviewed? Identifying a Customer Sample

The second question that your firm will need to answer is which of your customers should be interviewed. Again, subsequent research decisions will flow from the answer to this question, such as what data-gathering techniques are best to use. For instance, it is possible that a particular customer group might be a better candidate for, say, conducting focus groups than for in-depth interviews. Observation techniques may be a possibility for some customers but not all of them. In this regard, the choice of which customers to interview should definitely dictate the appropriate research method, and not vice versa.

Sample Size Issues

A few words must be said about the sample size. As mentioned earlier, qualitative data gathering is typically done on a small scale. The time and cost associated with these techniques makes it virtually prohibitive to conduct them on large numbers of customers. Unless your firm is in the unique position of having a very small, identifiable customer base, it is unlikely that you can gather qualitative information from more than a small subset of your total customers. In addition, it is unlikely that you will be able to generate a statistically representative sample. This is a point of great discomfort for many managers who are used to conducting surveys on a large scale using sophisticated sampling techniques.

In contrast, qualitative techniques typically use a convenience sample. While some researchers are dubious about the merits of convenience samples, if the participants are selected carefully, a wealth of information can be gathered. (More will be said on this later.) The important thing to keep in mind is that convenience samples must be selected so that they maximize information about (1) strategically critical customers and (2) the differences which may exist between various customer groups. In addition, it is helpful to remember that the results from this qualitative stage will be verified in later stages of the CVD process through the use of quantitative techniques and a larger, more representative sample.

In selecting participants for your convenience sample, you must first make sure that strategically important customers or customer groups are represented, even if this means that they are disproportionately represented. It is important to ask "Who are the customers or customer groups that we absolutely must understand?" This may entail prioritizing customers as to their relative importance to the firm. You will also want to sample so that differences between groups are captured, especially if you know or suspect that there is significant variance in customer characteristics and needs. Keeping these two selection criteria in mind will allow you to maximize the information from your convenience sample.

Which Customers to Include

Which specific customers should be included in the value measurement stage? This is actually a question that must be asked at multiple levels. At the first level, you must consider which *segment or segments* to include. If your organization is serving multiple customer segments, you may not be able to adequately sample them all. In such cases you may need to decide which segments need to be understood first. This is an important question that has implications far beyond customer value measurement. In fact, this decision should already be determined by the strategic orientation of your firm and by the larger MOA process (see Chapter 2). For now, we assume that you know who your important segments are.

Managers must next decide which *customer firms* (for a business to business market) or which *households* (for a consumer market) to include in the sample. Again, there are no right answers to these questions. However, it is helpful to return to the previous criteria for convenience sampling. Customers or households should be selected that are either (1) strategically significant or (2) are representative of important differences among the user base. Again, you will want to select customers/households that will maximize your knowledge.

Finally, for both customer organizations and households, you must consider which *individuals* should participate in the sample. Within both customer organizations and consumer households, there are often multiple individuals who participate in the selection, use, and disposal of the product or service. We sometimes speak of these as different "role players." These role players may have different (and even conflicting) perspectives on value, all of which may need to be taken into consideration by your firm.

It may help to think in terms of three broad categories of role players. The first, and most obvious, are the *product users* or *"direct contact" customers*. These are the individuals who have hands-on experience with your offering. In consumer households, they are the individuals who actually eat, wear, drive, watch, or use your product. In a business-to-business setting, these are the assembly line workers, the project managers, or those who use your product or service to perform their job. These individuals will have a very important perspective on whether – or how – your product provides value.

For a potentially different perspective, you may also want to talk with *decision makers* and *decision influencers*. We often refer to these as the individuals responsible for *"supplier determination."* These are the individuals who determine the selection criteria for the product and supplier. They may negotiate the terms of exchange, specify the product specs or requirements, and determine supplier qualifications. All the while, they may never have any (or very little) direct hands-on experience with the product itself. In the business-to-business setting, these individuals may be purchasing agents or managers. In the consumer household, these may be the "chief financial officers" who determine the shopping parameters (e.g., budget constraints, what type of store – discount versus department store – will be patronized, performance requirements, and so forth). Obviously, your firm will have to respond to the value hierarchies of these individuals as well as the product users. It would not be surprising if their perceived consequences were quite different from those of product users. For instance, decision makers may place a higher priority on meeting financial objectives or on the stability and reputation of the supplier, while specific performance criteria may be of higher concern to the product user.

Finally, the third category of relevant individuals for your sample are *facilitators* or *"indirect contact" customers*. These individuals serve a support function to those who are using the product. These individuals facilitate the flow of goods or services into the organization or household. Within business-to-business firms, these persons might be in accounts payable, receiving, warehouse management, quality control, and so forth. In consumer households, these might be the actual product purchasers who may neither consume nor select the product, like a mother who buys the breakfast cereal that her children request and consume. Again, the value hierarchies represented by facilitators may represent a different set of concerns from either product users or decision makers.

Your organization may, in fact, be getting very confusing

signals from different role players in your customers' organizations or your consumers' households. Trying to understand how each of these players perceives the value provided by your firm's offering can be a very enlightening process for both your firm and for your customers. Obviously it would be in everyone's interest to understand and resolve any potential conflicts that result from different role player's perspectives.

In summary, the goal of qualitative interviews should be to maximally expose your organization to the different value hierarchies that exist across your customer base. When determining who to talk to, one must identify the segments to target (see Chapter 2) and the specific customers or households to target, as well as the specific individuals or role players who will participate.

Weighing the Pros and Cons of Various Qualitative Research Methods

Next, managers must weigh the pros and cons of the different qualitative research methods. We have found three types of qualitative data-gathering techniques to be particularly helpful in the initial phases of the value determination process: observation, focus groups, and in-depth interviews. Each will be described separately in the following paragraphs. This discussion is meant to provide an overview of the key issues involved in deciding between and implementing each method. It is not, however, meant to provide a detailed "how-to" explanation. For those wishing further information, there are many available sources on how to conduct qualitative research, some of which will be referenced in this section.

Observation, focus groups, and in-depth interviews all represent viable methods for qualitatively exploring customer value. Each is valuable in its own respect and can provide information that is quite complementary to other methods. This decision need not be an "either/or" situation. In some cases, managers may be able to use multiple qualitative techniques. More likely, however, time and money considerations will dictate that only one technique is chosen. Selecting the most appropriate qualitative method may be a matter of preference, resource limitations, practicality, the willingness of customers to participate, or the information requirements of the organization.

Observation

If a picture is worth a thousand words, a few hours of observation may be worth a thousand survey responses. There are many reasons why customers might have difficulty in articulating their relationship to products or services. First, customers are not always in touch with their experiences and needs at a conscious level. Second, interviewing techniques themselves can be inhibiting, time consuming, and biased by the perspective of the interviewer. Third, there is always the potential for customers to be less than truthful. Social desirability biases often influence customers to provide "correct" responses rather than answers that reflect reality. Finally, there may be instances where the customer has a behavior associated with the use of the product (e.g., the operation of a laptop computer) that may be difficult to articulate. In short, there are many factors that keep customers from providing clear and straightforward answers about their product experiences.

Sometimes the best way to deal with these problems is to bypass them altogether by using direct observation. Customer value measurement ultimately attempts to determine how the product is used by the customer, what the positive and negative outcomes of that use are, and how the specific use situation requirements affect the value of a product offering. Much of this can be explored through simple observation.

Many companies have used this data-gathering method to their advantage. We already mentioned in Chapter 3 how Apple used observational techniques to redesign their laptop computers. In another example, Procter and Gamble mounted video cameras in kitchens to record consumers' use of liquid dishwashing detergents. Interestingly, they found that dishwashing habits had changed over the years. Gone were the days when sinks full of suds were expected to hold up through the washing of many dishes. Instead, a small amount of dish washing detergent was applied directly to each dirty dish, one at a time. This change in use has significant implications for many elements of the product offering: the concentration of the soap that is needed, the effects of the soap on skin, the product positioning that should be used to sell the product ("washes a sink full for pennies" versus "tough on grease"), and so forth.

When Black and Decker set out to redesign their Quantum power tool line to meet the changing demands of the market-place, they used observation extensively.[2] Among other things, its marketing executives spent time in customers' homes and workshops to observe how they used their tools and cleaned up afterwards. They even tagged along on shopping trips to monitor what their customers bought and how much they spent. These observations weren't completely unobtrusive; they also included some interviewing. However, getting Black and Decker executives into their consumers' use and purchase contexts allowed them to observe and ask about issues that may not have even come up in a standard survey. These observations ulti-mately resulted in significant changes in the product line. For example, a mini vacuum was added to some of the tools to keep sawdust from flying all over the work area and, therefore, to decrease one of the negative consequences of power tool use (difficult clean up).

Observational techniques can be used with industrial cus-tomers as well as with consumers, especially when a firm has a good rapport, a partnership, or an alliance with its customers. Ideally, you could get permission to become a "fly on the wall" in various areas of your customer's organization. As a result, you might be able to (1) actually observe the use or consumption of your product or service, (2) watch the reactions of individuals within your customer's firm as they manage the procurement, use, and disposal of your product or service, (3) see how your product fits into the larger mission and objectives of your cus-tomer's organization, and (4) understand the criteria that are being used by decision makers and influencers to select suppliers.

At 3M's medical and surgical products division, observation is used extensively in a low-tech program called Pulse. "All 750 employees, from production-line workers to senior executives, meet face to face with customers, mostly doctors and nurses, at three area hospitals. Employees don scrubs and go into the operating rooms to watch their surgical tapes, drapes, and prep solutions in action. Says Gary Borgstadt (a manufacturing engineer who designed the program), 'We get to feel the pulse of our customers. We see their problems and frustrations up close.' The work teams observed that some packaging was difficult to open, and others, designed for reuse, could not be easily closed. They suggested to 3M's product development people that a Zip-lock-type opening and closure would make their customers' jobs easier. . . . Says Valerie Smidt, staff education coordinator for the operating room at Sioux Valley Hospital in Sioux Falls, South Dakota: 'The 3M people give us pointers on how to better utilize some items, and we in turn suggest how to make some of their products more user friendly.' "[3]

Observation techniques are varied. They can be formal, planned observations by trained researchers. Or they may be informally conducted by sales representatives, service providers, repair technicians, or others who have regular, direct contact with customers in the product or service use context. Observation can be conducted unobtrusively, especially when it is feared that knowledge of observation might inhibit or bias the customer's behavior. Or it can be obtrusive, as in the Black and Decker example. Often the latter is unavoidable or is even desirable in order to enlist the participation of the customer. In short, there is a great deal of flexibility in how observation is to be conducted. Other books offer additional details on how to conduct observation research.[4– 6] In general, however, we suggest the following steps and techniques.

Select a sample of relevant customers. See "Who Should Be Interviewed? Identifying a Customer Sample" on page 163.

Determine the type of observation to be used. Depending on whether obtrusive or unobtrusive observation is being used, the following are possibilities:

1. Videotape. (The ethical considerations of the particular situation may require that the customer's permission is obtained prior to recording.)
2. Personal observation.

Determine who will do the observing. If personal observation is being used, it is advisable to have at least two observers. This will (1) allow the observers to compare notes for consensus and (2) ensure the completeness of the data. Two pairs of eyes are better than one. If videotaping is to be used, you need have only one person available to record the behaviors. Multiple "observers" can watch the videotape at a later time.

Determine the relevant situation. This might include any and all of the following:

1. Purchase situation (e.g., in a store).
2. Use situation (e.g., preparation, use, and/or disposal of the product or service).
3. After-use contact situation (e.g., complaint, repair, and so forth).

Record observations within relevant situations. This should be done both during and after observation. These field notes should include the following:

1. A sequential listing or breakdown of the various behaviors that the user displayed during the product or service interaction.
2. For each sequential behavior, a description of what was going on, including
   - What the user was doing.
   - Which particular aspects of the product or service played an important role.
   - Any problems or frustrations the user seemed to have.
   - Any positive outcomes of the interaction with the product.
   - Displays of emotion by the user when using the product or service.
   - The amount of time expended.
   - Any other situational factors that significantly contributed to the users' interaction with the product (e.g., the involvement of other individuals and role players

and/or factors related to the physical environment, such as the store layout or the availability of alternatives).

Focus Groups

Focus groups represent a second method for gathering qualitative data that is currently one of the most popular. With this method, a small group of customers (typically 5 to 12) are gathered to discuss their product experiences with the aid of a moderator or facilitator. One of the primary advantages of this method is the potential for synergy among the participants, where one participant's comments may stimulate discussion and a snowballing of ideas among the others. Some participants may also feel more at ease in a group format than a one-on-one format where they are the sole focus of attention. If handled correctly, these discussions can be stimulating for the participants and can serve as catalysts for honesty, sharing, and creativity among the customers.

Focus groups for consumer products typically draw a sample from the target end users. Participants for industrial products focus groups can be drawn from within customer organizations. Such groups attempt to sample key individuals within the customer firm who represent various points of contact between the supplier and the customer (see the discussion of role players in "Who Should Be Interviewed? Identifying a Customer Sample" on page 163). Across-customer focus groups may be used to draw participants from multiple customer firms. Obviously such groups are facilitated if the participating customers do not compete directly with each other.

The role of the moderator is multifaceted. He or she is expected to facilitate the discussion and to make sure that particular topics of interest are adequately addressed. Without stifling the participants or dictating the topics with too heavy a hand, the moderator must occasionally reorient the group if they become sidetracked. He or she must control the dynamics of the group, making sure that all participants get heard and that the discussion is not dominated by one or a few participants. In summary, the moderator must foster an atmosphere that encourages discussion and respect for the responses of all participants.

The moderator will be taking notes during the focus group session. These would include any significant points or observations that he or she might want to remember, as well as noting a particular point or statement that might be used for later probing or for redirecting the discussion. However, given the dynamic nature of focus groups, the multiple participants, and the need for the moderator to continually be attentive to his or her facilitating role, most focus groups are generally video- or audio-taped. This frees the moderator from having to take detailed notes during the exchange. At some later point, these tapes can be both observed and transcribed, facilitating their analysis (see Chapter 8).

Focus groups, like group brainstorming sessions, are a good way to get many issues on the table. Also, there are some time efficiencies relative to individual interviews, as multiple customers are captured simultaneously. Finally, the multiple perspectives in the group provide a basis for uncovering areas of consensus as well as differences.

Conventional wisdom is that focus group participants should be fairly homogenous in nature. This perspective might dictate multiple focus groups, representing product users, decision makers and so forth. However, think about the possibility of gathering the following role players from a customer's organization for a within-customer focus group: product users (such as assembly line workers or product designers), decision makers (such as purchasing agents or upper level management), and facilitators (such as accounts receivable and warehouse managers). Such a focus group could help to identify conflict and value trade-offs within the customer's organization, thus providing critical insights for the supplier as well as for the customer. It is not uncommon for different role players within customer firms to be "singing from different sheets of music," either knowingly or unknowingly. Obviously, this creates a great deal of frustration for the supplier. Focus groups are a good way to get these issues onto the table to everyone's benefit.

There are also potential downsides to focus groups. While some participants might find the "safety of numbers" to be liberating, some participants may find focus groups to be inhibiting, especially if their opinion or experience is at variance with the rest of the group or if other participants, such as managers from their organization, stifle their ability to speak openly and honestly. Also, the outcome of focus groups is highly dependent upon the skills of the moderator, and a well-trained focus group facilitator may be costly.

Finally, our experience has been that while focus groups are good at generating a *breadth* of information by getting many issues on the table, they are not always conducive to *depth*. If, for instance, the moderator wished to do additional probing with one participant ("Describe the details of your experience. What were the reactions within your firm? What were the circumstances surrounding the incident?"), this would, for all practical purposes, require shutting down the other participants in the group for a period of time. Because concentrating on any one individual disrupts the flow of the discussion and leads to the potential disengagement of other participants, this is obviously not desirable. Therefore, real depth of inquiry, the peeling back multiple layers of any one customer's experience, is better suited for individual in-depth interviews. Of course, there is always the potential for doing individual follow up interviews with selected focus group participants.

As with observation, there are many reference sources for conducting good focus group research [7,8] in addition to the potential to out-source this activity to research firms.[1]

In-Depth Interviews

The third option for doing qualitative information gathering is the one-on-one or in-depth interview. As suggested above, this is one of the best ways to do extensive probing and "peeling" with your customers. The format, the flexibility, and the amount of time that is spent with an individual customer make it most effective for moving to deeper and deeper layers of the customer's value perceptions.

Another advantage of an in-depth interview is that it places fewer demands on the interviewer. In general, the techniques for depth interviewing do not require the experience and training of a focus group moderator who has to deal with the dynamics of group interaction. In addition, the interpretation of the data can be more straightforward, especially compared to the difficulty of interpreting information from multiple focus group participants. Finally, as indicated above, some participants may feel more free to speak their mind in a one-on-one interview without being inhibited or biased by the presence of others.

The primary downside of in-depth interviews is the time necessary to conduct them. The best information can be gathered if the customer commits a fairly significant amount of time for the interview (ideally 1 to 2 hours). Clearly there may be difficulty in getting the customer's commitment for such a period, especially in the case of business customers. The second time consideration is data collection, which is generally much slower with a series of depth interviews than with focus groups. (One is generally trading off time for in-depth information.) Research has suggested that it takes about four individual depth interviews to elicit the same amount of information that is uncovered in a focus group.[9] A summary comparison of the differences between focus groups and depth interviews is contained in Table 7.1.

There are two ways to record data from in-depth interviews. The first, and obviously most strenuous, is for the interviewer to record the participant's responses as well as any observations. This may be the only alternative if the participant objects to being recorded or if audio or video recording is not an option. However, there are obvious downsides to this arrangement, including (1) the enormous demands on the interviewer, who must record while presumably both listening and planning ahead and (2) the possibility that the interviewer might miss something. For these reasons, whenever possible we either use audio or video recorders during such interviews. These recordings can later be transcribed in order to facilitate their analysis. We also feel that there is considerable merit in examining the participant's body language and facial expressions (in the case of video recordings) and levels of emotion (in the case of both audio and

Table 7.1. A Comparison of Focus Groups versus In-Depth Interviews

Focus Groups	In-Depth Interviews
Considerable training needed for moderator	Interviewing techniques more easily learned and trained
Data collection costs in time and money are generally lower	Greater time and money costs for data collection
Interpretation of data is more difficult due to multiple respondents	Interpretation of an individual's response is less difficult
Good for generating "breadth" of issues	Better for probing "depth" of issues
Group dynamics can both enourage (synergism and snowballing) and discourage (inhibiting participants) participation	No interference of group dynamics; however, the respondent may feel more self-conscious
Ability to contrast multiple (and even conflicting) perspectives, e.g., "within organization" focus groups	Only single perspectives can be explored within one interview
Mistaken tendency to generalize from 1–2 focus groups	Less tendency to generalize from only a few interviews

video recordings). These very telling pieces of information will often be lost if recordings are not made.

Finally, as will be discussed further in Chapter 8, we place a premium on being able to use the customer's exact words and descriptions during data analysis. Clearly these are lost if the customer's responses are filtered through the notes of the interviewer. While using a second researcher to take notes resolves some of these concerns, they do not resolve all of them. In addition, such a person may be an inhibiting factor for the customer.

The two most important issues to consider in depth interviewing are (1) the degree of structure that is desired and (2) determining what types of questions to ask in order to elicit value hierarchies. We address each of these issues in the following sections.

Degree of Structure.   Degree of structure is the extent to which interview questions and ordering are thoroughly (and rigidly) specified prior to the interview. Although the degree of structure in an in-depth interview is a matter of preference, there are a few points that should be made. As suggested above, one of the advantages of in-depth interviews is the degree to which they can be unstructured (i.e., they can be flexible enough to follow the thoughts and concerns of the customer). Of course, it is probably undesirable for an interview to be completely unstructured – there will always be certain types of information that you will want to draw out of each interview, and the customer cannot be left to wander too far from the topic of interest. So we are really talking about a matter of degree here. The question really is *how* unstructured the interview should be.

Some in-depth interviews can be highly structured, with a list of questions to be asked in a systematic fashion. Even though probes might be used to generate depth for particular responses, there may be little deviation from such an agenda, either in terms of topics or order; the interviewer is clearly in control of the exchange. While such interviews greatly facilitate the comparison of responses across interviews (because everyone answers more or less the same questions), they require the interviewer to have fairly exhaustive foreknowledge of all issues to be explored during the exchange.

With unstructured interviews, the agenda is more loosely defined. In this case, the interviewer might have a set of questions or issues to be covered. However, he or she can freely move between questions, taking topics out of order as the customer addresses them, following the customer's lead, probing, pursuing pertinent issues not on the original agenda, and so forth. In such interviews, there is more of a sense of joint control between the interviewer and the customer. The "art" of conducting an unstructured interview is to keep a general focus and move the respondent along topics of interest while at the same time allowing a free flow of issues. Even with unstructured interviews, however, good planning is important (see "Planning and Timing the Interview" later in this chapter).

What Types of Questions? The goals of the interview will dictate the types of questions that are asked. Clearly, this is an area where there can be a great deal of "customization," given the concerns of the firm conducting the research. The goal of understanding customer value is sufficiently broad that a number of questions can be asked that all yield roughly the same kinds of information. However, in our research, we have found two types of questioning techniques, laddering and grand tours, to be very valuable at uncovering customer value hierarchies. Each of these will be described in the following paragraphs.

Laddering is a moderately structured interviewing method that is specifically designed to measure the means-end association (between attributes, consequences, and end states) that customers have toward products or services. This method has been rather widely used in conducting research, and the details of its implementation, analysis, and interpretation are available elsewhere.[10] However, an overview of the basic method is given here.

Beginning at the bottom of the value hierarchy, the interviewer must first get the customer to identify all of the attributes that he or she believes are useful to describe or distinguish different brands or products in the category of interest. Several types of questions may be used to elicit this information. One method is to ask the participant to consider two or three products or brands and then to discuss what the differences are between them. "You said you would consider drinking water or a sports drink while running. In what ways are these two drinks similar? In what ways are they different?"

Another method asks the respondent to identify a preferred brand or supplier and to then discuss the reasons for this preference. "You stated that you had switched to supplier B after using supplier A for several years. Why do you prefer supplier B?"

It is also helpful to place the participant in a particular context, such as purchasing or using the product or service. As opposed to discussing products in the abstract, these contexts often help cue the participant to recall important product dimensions. "Think about being in a dealer's showroom. What do you look for in a car?" "Think about driving your car on a long trip. What are the things about your car that you like the most? The least?"

Although these initial questions may uncover consequences and desired end states in addition to attributes, our experience is that product users typically answer these questions at the attribute level, and it is only through more thorough laddering that the higher levels in the hierarchy emerge.

Once the customer has identified product or service attributes, the interviewer will want to separate important from relatively unimportant ones. There is generally not enough time to pursue ladders for all product attributes, and understanding the most important ones is clearly more strategically critical than pursuing ladders for relatively unimportant attributes. This subgroup of "important attributes" then becomes the basis for the laddering.

Beginning one attribute at a time, the interviewer asks a series of probing questions to determine the relationship between the attribute and higher order consequences and desired end states. "Why is that important to you?" "What does that mean to you?" "What does it mean when a product has (or doesn't have) that particular attribute?" The interviewer continues to ask these questions until the participant has worked his or her way up the ladder from attributes to consequences to end states. (Or, in the case where the customer started the ladder in the middle by identifying consequences, the interviewer can ladder down as well as up.) The result should be the construction of a complete "ladder" for each attribute or product feature.

For example, the participant might state that she considered the location of instruments on the dashboard when comparing the cars in her prepurchase consideration set. The following value hierarchy might emerge as a result of laddering.

"I was concerned about the location of the instruments."
"Why was that important to you?"
"Because I don't want to have to search around for them."
"What happens when you have to search?"

"It makes me feel uncomfortable."
"And when you feel uncomfortable?"
"It distracts me from paying attention to the road."
"Why is that important?"
"Because I don't want to endanger myself and my family."
"Why is that important to you?"
"Because I want my family to be safe."
"And why is family safety important?"
"Because I love my family."

A ladder derived from these responses is shown in Figure 7.1. As you can see from this example, the end goal of laddering is not only to get the product user to discuss issues at each level of the value hierarchy, but to explicitly make the connections between them for the interviewer.

One of the difficulties in using laddering is asking repetitive questions to which the answers often seem obvious. There is also the potential for respondent fatigue. Great care must be used in setting up laddering in a way which establishes naiveté on the part of the interviewer and allows the customer to indulge the interviewer's questions even when the answers seem obvious. Customers must be convinced that they are the experts and that their opinions are valued (see "Getting Started – Establishing Rapport" later in this chapter). In addition, with laddering the customers may fairly quickly figure out what kinds of information the interviewer is after. This can potentially lead to social desirability biases or even to the participant making up ladders.

As you might guess, the ability to analyze and summarize laddering data across several interviews is often the most difficult aspect of using laddering. Each participant can generate a significant number of ladders, and these must be summarized across multiple participants. These issues will be discussed later under data analysis techniques in Chapter 8. However, laddering is clearly one of the most direct and established methods for measuring means-end hierarchies.

Our research has led us to devise an alternative technique for measuring customer value which we call the *grand tour*. This technique attempts to understand the value hierarchy indirectly

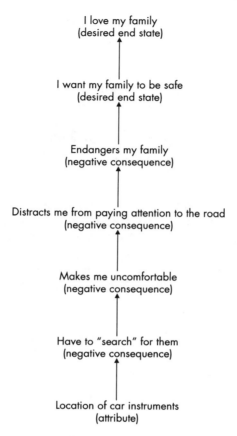

I love my family
(desired end state)

I want my family to be safe
(desired end state)

Endangers my family
(negative consequence)

Distracts me from paying attention to the road
(negative consequence)

Makes me uncomfortable
(negative consequence)

Have to "search" for them
(negative consequence)

Location of car instruments
(attribute)

Figure 7.1. A sample ladder.

by exploring in detail how the product or service is experienced by the customer in a particular context.

To begin the grand tour, the interviewer asks the participant to imagine him- or herself in a typical, real-life situation. This situation should be one that typifies a point in the consumption context (e.g., prepurchase, purchase, use, or disposal) and a context in which the customer normally or regularly interacts with the product. The interviewer then asks the participant to describe, in as much detail as possible, what is going on in that situation. In essence, the objective is to get the participant to walk you through his or her typical experiences with the product. The interviewer might begin with a statement like the following:

> "Tell us about a typical workout that you have at the fitness center. Begin with when you pull up in the parking lot and walk me through what happens, step by step. I want you to tell me what you are doing, what is going on around you, what you are thinking about, and what you are feeling. No detail is insignificant."

As the participant talks through his or her grand tour, the interviewer is free to probe for additional details and meaning. Probes should especially be used to add clarification, to get deeper meaning, to identify what feelings or emotions might be present, to get a better understanding of the connections between value hierarchy levels, or to get a sense of the importance or intensity associated with particular statements. The following are two samples of probing questions:

> "You said that you always like to go to the same locker. How important is that to you?"
> "What are you thinking about or feeling at this point in your workout?"

Unlike laddering, the grand tour does not directly pursue value hierarchies. If the connections between hierarchy levels are not made during the participant's response (and they frequently are not), they must be inferred from the context of his or her response. On the positive side, we have found that, compared to laddering interviews, grand tours tend to yield much richer information about value hierarchies. One research project that involved a direct comparison of the two techniques showed that grand tours produced three times the number of value hierarchy dimensions than did laddering techniques. Relative to laddering interviews, grand tours also yield significantly more information about use situations and their associated product requirements, and about customers' reactions to products, both in terms of evaluation and emotion.

A grand tour interview is less structured than laddering and can be somewhat longer to complete. In addition, its lack of structure calls for a great deal of interviewer skill to move the customer along to relevant issues, to probe for value hierarchy linkages and meaning, to pick up on important issues for additional probing, and so forth.

Laddering and grand tour interviews are both very useful albeit different methods for gathering value hierarchy information. While we generally prefer grand tours, we find the information resulting from the two techniques to be complementary. The pros and cons of both interview methods are summarized in Table 7.2.

General Issues for Gathering Qualitative Customer Data

Finally, almost all methods for gathering qualitative customer data (the only exception being unobtrusive observation) require attention to some general issues. These are (1) establishing rapport, (2) using probes, and (3) planning and timing the interview.

Establishing Rapport

To a great extent, the quality of the information you get from your customer depends on the ability of the interviewer to establish rapport. Stated more succinctly, the customer must feel comfortable. An absence of rapport can lead to the customer not being completely forthcoming, intentionally shortcutting the interview process, being uncooperative, providing only socially desirable responses, or even falsifying his or her responses. While it is true that some interviewers will be innately better able to establish rapport than others, there are some things that all interviewers can do to improve rapport.

First, the interviewers must establish that the customer – not the interviewer – is the expert. Many customers may think that they are being tested or that the interviewer is looking for a "right" or a "wrong" answer. At the outset of the interaction, interviewers must let the customers know that there are no right or wrong answers and that whatever the customers experi-

Table 7.2. A Comparison of the Pros and Cons for Laddering and Grand Tour Interviewing Techniques

LADDERING	GRAND TOUR
Pros	Pros
Structured interview which eases moderator's task	In-depth understanding of customer's situations and product/service-related activities
Reasonably short time frame— about 45 minutes to 1 hour	Yields significantly more information about all levels of the value hierarchy vs. laddering
Connections between attributes, consequences, and desired end states are explicitly made	Yields tremendous insights on product/service use; can uncover strategic opportunities
Cons	Cons
Respondent fatigue may lead to omission of some information	Generally longer to conduct (approximately 1–2 hours)
Respondents catch on to what you are looking for; can lead to social desirability responses and the "creation" of linkages that don't really exist	Needs greater interviewer skill because of the lack of structure and need for probing
Doesn't reveal much about how use situations and other activities may influence product/service value	The connections between levels of the hierarchy are rarely explicit, and must be inferred from the responses

ence, feel, believe, or perceive is, in fact, "right." The interviewers must stress that the customers' responses are of the utmost interest and that every thought they have, no matter how insignificant they think it might be, is important. Granting your customer anonymity (if this is possible or advisable) may be an important factor in facilitating this openness.

In addition, the interviewers must be able to establish themselves as being relatively naive about the topic. This will obviously be easier to do for third-party interviewers. However, even if the interviewers are employees of your organization, they can legitimately claim a naiveté about your customers' experience. ("We know how to make the product, but we don't know nearly as much about what our customers do with it.")

In establishing the customers as the experts, it is also necessary to explain that some questions may be asked that may seem silly or obvious to the customers (e.g., the "why" probes). Again, however, your customers must understand your need to clearly and absolutely understand their responses, as well as your desire to make no assumptions or inferences.

Finally, a rapport must also be established through the interviewers' demeanor. They must be an interested, active listener and must encourage participant response by head nodding and body language that is open and receptive. And most importantly, interviewers must remain a neutral party in the dialogue. The quickest way to destroy rapport is for interviewers to judge the participant's responses, to show preference for particular types of responses, or to be defensive and critical.

The following are some additional tips about which questions are the best (and worst) to lead with when establishing rapport early in an interview.

Use setup questions to put the participant in the right frame of mind. How you begin the interview has a great bearing on how much you ultimately get out of it. You want to begin in a way that:

- Is nonthreatening
- Gets the customer talking about something that he or she knows a lot about
- Makes it easy for him or her to discuss

Start the interview in the proper fashion. This can include asking:

- Questions about the participant (e.g., "Tell me about the last time you went to the store to buy . . .")

- Questions that put the participant in a particular frame of mind, such as asking about the decision or choice contexts or the comparison between two different products and services and/or product or service use context.

Stay away from inappropriate questions. These might include:

- Questions that immediately require making a judgment (e.g., "What do you think about our product?")
- Questions that too quickly push the participant into the higher levels of the value hierarchy (e.g., "What personal desired end states influence your purchase?")

Using Probes

Regardless of whether you use laddering, grand tours, focus groups, or observation combined with interviews, the probes that you use are arguably the most important questions that you ask. Probing is essential to "peel back the layers" of your customer's experience with your product and to get into the higher levels of the value hierarchy. Probing is also necessary for clarification and for understanding how important or significant an issue is to the participant.

For example, in describing an encounter with a car salesman, a consumer might state, "He used pressure tactics on me." Probes should be used here to explore exactly what happened and how strongly the consumer felt about this experience. In fact, a series of probes might be helpful. "Tell me more about that." "What does 'pressure tactics' mean to you?" "How did that make you feel?" "Did that affect your feelings about buying the car? How?" "What usually happens when someone uses pressure tactics on you?" "What happened in this situation?"

As these examples illustrate, the most important characteristic of probes is that they are nondirective. They should simply ask participants to elaborate on what they said without drawing conclusions or biasing the responses. For example, one would never want to probe with a question such as, "Did that make you mad?" Sometimes simple head nodding, some occasional "uh huhs," and other types of verbal and nonverbal positive reinforcement are enough to encourage the respondent to provide more depth. Clarification probes should heavily emphasize issues of how, what, when, who, and where. When using laddering to get to higher levels of the value hierarchy and to understand connections between levels, your probes should be heavily oriented towards "why." "Why does that matter to you?" "Why is that important?" "Why" questions are critical to get at the underlying concerns (consequences and desired end states) of the product user. The following is a list of tips on how to best use probes.

- *Use probes liberally.* The more probing you do, the more information you will get. The only caution is to watch out for potential frustration on the part of your customer. You don't want the customer to feel badgered. The best defense against this is to adopt the "naive interviewer" role at the outset. (See "Establishing Rapport" in this chapter.)
- *Probes should be nondirective.* They should be as neutral as possible (why, how, when, what, and so forth). They should never lead the customer (e.g., "Did that make you mad?").
- *Use probes for clarification.* For example:
  - "Tell me more about that."
  - "What does that mean?"
  - "What is your typical response when that happens?"
  - "How would your company typically make that decision?"
  - "What other individuals were involved?"
  - "When does that typically happen?"
  - "Where are you?"
- *Use probes to explore higher levels of the value hierarchy.* For example:
  - "Why is that important to you?"
  - "Why does the product need to have (a particular value dimension)?"
  - "What are the downsides of using that supplier?"
  - "What would happen if the product didn't have (value dimension)?"

- *Probe for emotion.* For example:
  - "How did that make you feel?"
  - "What were you feeling when that happened?"
  - "Did that effect your feelings? If so, how?"

Planning and Timing the Interview

Finally, as you can tell from the above descriptions, any time you are interviewing customers it is important for the interviewer to maintain some sense of control while at the same time allowing for flexibility and responsiveness to the participant's ideas. This is a delicate balance that can best be achieved by going into the interview with a fair amount of planning.

First, the interviewer should have a list of issues or questions in hand. These will be more structured for some interviews than others. However, even when the interview is to be relatively unstructured (e.g., a grand tour) the interviewer should think about the different topics to be discussed during the interview. Each of these topics can then serve as a different section in the interview. For instance, our interview structure for customers using a fitness center included:

- Arriving at the center
- Checking in and being greeted by the receptionist
- Using the locker room on arrival
- Doing the workout
- Doing postworkout activities and routines
- Using the locker room at departure
- Leaving the facility

Once the sections of the interview have been determined, the interviewer should identify potential lead-in questions for each section and specific probes that might be used.

It is also important for the interviewer to estimate the approximate amount of time that will be spent on each section of the interview, allowing for some flexibility to accommodate the concerns of the customer. This is necessary to ensure that all important aspects of the product experience are given sufficient attention and to guard against certain aspects of consumption becoming disproportionately represented in the interviews.

This "roughing out" of the interview structure can greatly facilitate the flow and effectiveness of the interview. Remember that in many cases you might be talking to the customer for an hour or even two. It is very easy to lose direction in that amount of time. Preinterview planning and timing will prevent this from occurring.

Summary

This chapter has touched on many issues related to measuring customer value through qualitative research methods. Our experience and research has led us to believe that there is no substitute for beginning the CVD process with such methods. Doing it slowly, peeling back the layers, and doing it properly in the initial stages is critical to the success of the entire CVD process. Perhaps an analogy can reinforce this point.

Scientists have long known, and puzzled over the fact, that Amish farmers using simple, "low tech" farming practices are able to get a higher yield per acre than are farmers who employ the most modern techniques. The Amish farmer walks along behind his horse and plow, one row at a time, uses no industrial chemicals, and employs no expensive machinery. In contrast, modern farmers employ a variety of innovations that allow them to sweep over large tracts of land, sitting high above the soil on their combines, chemically and mechanically stimulating the soil. How can the Amish farmers, using such "backward" techniques, produce higher yields? The answer has come to be known as "slow knowledge." The very techniques that the Amish farmers use allow them to be literally closer to the soil, to notice changes in its color and moisture, to note how it responds to different types and rotations of plantings. This "slow knowledge" allows the Amish farmers to be more attentive to subtle changes in soil and plant and to respond more precisely to these changes. They develop a much deeper and more intuitive understanding about how nature and their own actions affect the crops. In short, their senses are more finely tuned to the needs of the land.

There is no doubt that the qualitative research that we described in this chapter takes time and money. And as you will see in Chapter 8, the analysis of the resulting data is complex in its own right. However, we believe that there is no substitute for this "slow knowledge" about your customer. It is absolutely worth the investment, and the downstream yield that you will realize from this effort is tremendous.

References

[1] Abbott, John, "A Star Is Born," *Fortune*, November 29, 1993, pp. 44–47.

[2] Rice, Faye, "The New Rules of Superlative Service," *Fortune*, Autumn/Winter, 1993, pp. 50–53.

[3] Webb, Eugene J., Donald T. Campbell, Richard D. Schwartz, Lee Sechrest, and Janet Belew Grove, *Nonreactive Measures in the Social Sciences*, Boston, MA: Houghton Mifflin Company, 1981.

[4] Taylor, Steven J. and Robert Bogdan, *Introduction to Qualitative Research Methods: A Phenomenological Approach to the Social Sciences*, New York: Wiley-Interscience, 1975, Chapter Two.

[5] Denzin, Norman K., *The Research Act: A Theoretical Introduction to Sociological Methods*, Third Edition, Englewood Cliffs, NJ: Prentice-Hall, 1989, Chapter Nine.

[6] Greenbaum, Thomas L, *The Practical Handbook and Guide To Focus Group Research*, Lexington, MA: Lexington Books, 1988.

[7] Morgan, David L., *Focus Groups As Qualitative Research*, Newbury Park, CA: Sage Publications, 1988.

[8] Griffin, Abbie and John R. Houser, "The Voice of the Customer," *Marketing Science*, 12 (Winter 1993), pp. 1–27.

[9] Reynolds, Thomas J. and Jonathan Gutman, "Laddering Theory, Method, Analysis, and Interpretation," *Journal of Advertising Research*, 28 (February/March 1988), 11–31.

Note

1. See *Marketing News*, March 14, 1994, for a complete directory of firms that conduct focus group research.

CHAPTER **8**

ANALYZING CUSTOMER VALUE DATA

The analysis of customer data is generally considered to be a "scientific" endeavor. Once the data start rolling in, they are typically handed over to highly trained persons who, with the help of their computers, perform all manner of sophisticated statistical manipulations on them – conjoint analysis, regression, clustering algorithms, discriminant analysis, factor analysis. Only well-educated "quant jocks" dare to assume that they understand the mathematical underpinnings of these analyses. Managers, who are often humbled by the complexity of the procedures, are typically only privy to outputs that have been translated with great effort into understandable reports. And typically somewhere along the way, the customer's words, experiences, and opinions are translated into numerical data that stand as testament to the precision and the validity of the analysis.

Qualitative data analysis, while demanding the same level of rigor and thoughtfulness, tends to be a little more user friendly. One of the chief advantages of qualitative research is to truly get close to the customer – to capture his or her words, sentiments, and experiences. In fact, the goal in analyzing these data is to be more restrained about the amount of transformation and translation that goes on between the customer's words and the reports that managers actually see – to reduce the volume of data but not their essence. With this in mind, we offer several suggestions for analyzing qualitative data, ranging from the moderately complex to the very simple. None, however, are beyond the capabilities or understanding of a business manager. More to the point, these different techniques provide multiple opportunities for managers to "muck around in the data" – to immerse themselves in their meanings. Finally, our research projects typically include many "passes through the data" in order to capture their rich implications. For all these reasons, we like to think of qualitative data analysis as a symbiotic relationship between "art" and "science."

Introduction

In Chapter 7 we discussed different qualitative methods for gathering customer value information. Having dutifully followed our recommendations, a manager will probably find him- or herself at this point with a rather unwieldy mass of data. Depending on what techniques were used and what recording devices were enlisted, the outcomes of customer value measurement may include field notes, interviewer notes, interview transcripts, and audio or video recordings. As discussed earlier, qualitative techniques don't yield neat, concise, easily manipulated data sets. Qualitative data, though decidedly rich and worth the effort, are messy.

This information must be summarized, analyzed, and interpreted in such a way that the essence and insights from the data can be reported in a fairly concise manner. However, this is not a straightforward task. In fact, the rich, dense data that result from qualitative methods can be "sliced" in many different ways to yield different perspectives and levels of interpretation. Determining which analysis techniques are most appropriate depends on a number of factors, including what methods were used to initially gather the data, resource considerations, and your organization's information requirements.

The plan for this chapter is to explore several techniques for analyzing customer value data. First, an overall process will be introduced. Then several analysis techniques will be discussed, including the quantitative as well as qualitative analyses that should be considered. Finally, we consider how these data may be used as input into other types of analyses, including importance ratings and customer satisfaction surveys.

A Process for Analyzing Customer Value Data

Figure 8.1 shows a process for analyzing qualitative data. There

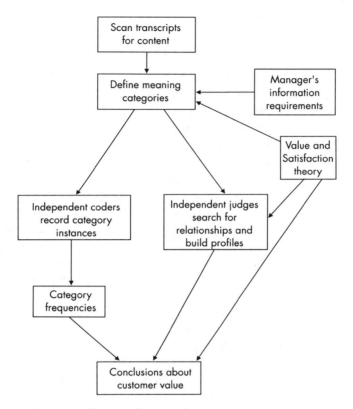

Figure 8.1. Qualitative data analysis.

are two branches or paths from which to choose. The path on the right side of the figure represents qualitative analyses. Pursuing this path leads to the formation of customer "profiles" that summarize critical elements of customers' product or service experiences. The path on the left side of the figure represents a more quantitative approach to data analysis. Using coding schemes and laddering analysis techniques, the data are categorized and transformed into frequency counts that can in turn provide the basis for further quantitative or statistical analysis. These two paths provide useful and, we feel, complementary approaches.

Preparing the Data for Analysis

Both paths begin with the assumption that the qualitative data-gathering methods have resulted in "transcripts." If the focus groups or individual in-depth interviews have been recorded, either with audio- or video-tape, it is generally advisable to have these tapes transcribed into verbatim transcripts to facilitate their analysis. Depending upon the number and length of the tapes, this can be a fairly expensive and time-consuming proposition. However, the following disadvantages of working directly from tapes make transcription well worth the effort:

- Working directly from tapes can be tedious and difficult, given the need to continually start, stop, and rewind the tapes in small increments.
- Working from the tapes may increase the likelihood of overlooking something during analysis, as the presentation pace is difficult for the researcher to control.
- Finally, researchers needing to reference specific points in the data will find it easier to refer to "page 12, lines 5–6," rather than to search for a point on a tape.

Having said that, a supplemental review of the "raw" tapes themselves can also be valuable. The tapes often contain valuable information that generally does not make its way onto transcripts, such as the customer's demeanor at specific points in the interview and his or her tone or emotion. Valuable insights can be gathered from body language, facial expressions, gestures, and other forms of nonverbal communications. These observations can greatly enhance and compliment the interpretation of the transcripts.

While seeming insignificant or obvious, some hints about the transcription process should be briefly mentioned. First, invest in good quality recording devices. This will facilitate the transcription process, decrease the likelihood of losing valuable information, and generally save the sanity of your transcribers. In addition, you will want to identify competent, conscientious transcribers. Their job will be to transcribe, verbatim, the responses of both the interviewer and the customer, including "ums," "ahs," pauses, and repetitions. The transcripts should not be "cleaned up," but should be as accurate a reproduction of the verbalizations as possible. Finally, to facilitate the coding process described later in this chapter, the transcripts should be formatted so that the page can be quickly scanned and so that customer responses can be easily distinguished from interviewer questions and probes. The transcripts should be double spaced to accommodate margin notes.

There may be situations where tapes and verbatim transcripts are not available. In many instances, interviews or observations may instead result in field notes. However, if the field notes are thorough, capturing the detail which we suggested in the section on "Observation" in Chapter 7, they can be analyzed just as effectively as verbatim transcripts. For the remainder of this discussion, we will use the term "transcripts" broadly to refer to the data that are contained in either transcripts or field notes.

Assuming that the verbatim transcriptions or field notes are now in a legible form, different types of analyses may be conducted. Because we often use multiple analysis techniques, we sometimes talk about different "passes through the data." Several analysis options are described in the following sections.

Quantitative Analyses – The Grand Tour Method

If you used the grand tour method described in Chapter 7 to have the customer talk you through a product experience, or if the actual experience was observed and captured in field notes, then both qualitative and quantitative analyses are possible. The quantitative analysis is rooted in the tradition of protocol analysis that has been used extensively in consumer information processing research.[1–3] Basically, this method entails breaking down the transcript into discrete units and using a coding scheme to classify the content of each unit. These codes can then be summarized to yield frequency counts, compute means, and calculate percentages, all of which can be used to compare responses across individuals or groups of individuals (e.g., males versus females) using statistical tests. Three basic steps in this process will be described in the following sections: (1) creating a coding scheme, (2) applying the coding scheme, and (3) building a data set.

Creating a Coding Scheme

You will notice in Figure 8.1 that the second step in the quantitative analysis process is to define meaning categories. In other words, prior to analyzing the transcripts, you must determine what you are looking for in them and define categories to capture that information. A good analogy is a scuba diving expedition. While there are many varieties of fish in the ocean, all are not equally worthy of the diver's attention. Therefore, the diver may determine the fish he or she is most interested in and actively seek them out. Likewise, before coding a transcript, the researcher should attempt to determine the different types of information that he or she wants to watch out for.

Knowing the most important information to "fish out" of the transcripts can draw upon expertise from two areas. First, current theories about customer value and customer satisfaction provide some indication of what to look for. For instance, you would clearly want to code examples of all levels of the value hierarchy, including the customer's mention of attributes, consequences, and desired end states (this comes from the value theory). Likewise, you may want to identify any comparison standards that the customer uses (from satisfaction theory). For this reason, a thorough understanding of the theories underlying customer value and satisfaction is desirable prior to data analysis and collection. These theory-based coding categories may be considered "generic" in that they will probably be useful across a number of different customers, industries, and research projects. However, you also may "customize" the coding scheme in ways that are particular to your organization. The second source of expertise that shapes the coding scheme comes from the unique experiences and information requirements of your organization's managers. Certain types of information specific to your organization, industry, or customer base may be considered strategically important and should be included in the coding scheme. For instance, one company with which we worked was particularly concerned with the process by which vendors or suppliers are qualified to participate in the bidding process for government projects. Clearly, knowing the ins and outs of this process and how it might differ across states and between state departments is vital information if you intend to become a supplier. The coding scheme could easily be customized to capture that type of information. A sample coding scheme is shown in Appendix I.

Applying the Coding Scheme

Details of the process by which the coding scheme is applied have been included in Appendix I. An overview of the process is offered here.

In order to apply the coding scheme, the transcript must first be subdivided into units of analysis (which we simply call "thoughts"). Each unit represents a discrete thought, idea, or behavior that the customer verbalized (in the transcript) or experienced (in the field notes). Coders then analyze each thought to determine which of the codes (or combination of codes) best capture its meaning. Typically, a minimum of two coders analyze each transcript, and their interpretations of each thought must be reconciled so that there is full agreement upon the final codes that are assigned to each thought. This is important because the coding of transcripts is fairly subjective, and it is helpful to have intercoder reliability. It enhances the confidence in the transcript interpretation.

Building a Data Set

Once the coders have analyzed each thought and agreed upon its corresponding codes, it is easy to enter these codes into a data set for computer analysis. At a minimum, one would want to do frequency counts for each type of code in the coding scheme – how often did particular types of codes, such as consequences, appear? In addition, one can look for combinations of codes (e.g., how often a particular attribute was mentioned in connection with a particular consequence).

Finally, by adding some basic demographic information to

the data set for sorting purposes, these codes can be compared across different customer groups. For example, you may want to see how the codes and value hierarchies differ by role players (e.g., product users versus decision makers), by type of customer or consumer (e.g., heavy versus light user, male versus female, private industry versus government, or grocery chain versus convenience store), or by other variables that might be strategically meaningful (e.g., new versus existing customers or geographic location). While such a data set can be built and analyzed with any standard statistical software package, some new software packages have been developed specifically for this purpose.

Table 8.1 illustrates the outcome of a coding process. This table summarizes, by subgroups (indicated across the top, horizontal axis), the *percent* of transcripts that contained reference to a particular response code (listed on the vertical axis). Raw frequency counts or mean responses may be calculated as well as percentages. It is then possible to statistically compare these subgroup responses to identify similarities and differences in their product/service requirements and concerns. Finally, it may be important to collect these data over time so that longitudinal comparisons can be made.

Quantitative Analyses – Ladders

Chapter 7 included an overview of an interviewing technique known as "laddering." One of the chief appeals of laddering interviews is the ability to take qualitative information and transform it into a quantitative analysis.

You will recall that laddering interviews first identify the set of important attributes associated with a product or service. Then, through a series of probes, the participants reveal the higher order consequences and end states that they associate with each attribute, as well as the interconnections between them. These interviews generate a number of ladders (attribute/consequence/desired end states) for each customer interview (such as Figure 7.1). The next step is to quantitatively analyze these ladders.

In general, this is done by first breaking down the individual ladders into their component parts (linkages) and, secondly, by

Table 8.1. Analysis of Coding Category Responses by Subgroup Expressed as a Percentage of Participants Who Mentioned Each Category

Coding Categories	Usage Rates			Use Situations			Segment A	Segment B	Segment C
	Heavy User	Light User	Non-User	At Home	At Work	On Vacation	Teens	Families	Females
Saltiness	43	23	7	25	28	29	68	44	23
Convenience	36	19	11	11	54	67	22	46	31
Availability	71	19	28	18	71	63	56	34	27
Fills Me Up	42	12	9	38	58	34	61	39	13
Good Nutrition	25	7	5	43	34	27	29	33	45
Satisfies My Hunger	61	21	10	28	61	24	47	28	37
Share With Others	15	44	4	47	9	59	36	53	42
Get Tired Of it	54	5	8	32	15	15	39	31	28
Etc.									

using these disaggregate linkages to rebuild a map that summarizes the ladders across the customers. While this analysis will be overviewed below, more detail is available by referring to the original authors, Reynolds and Gutman.[4]

Breaking Down the Ladders

The first step in breaking down the ladders that were produced during the interviews is to develop a set of *summary codes* that reflect the content of the interview ladders. This can generally be done by developing a master list of all of the attributes, consequences, and end states that were mentioned by the customers. Because customers may verbalize the same thought in different ways, this master list will have to include broad categories into which similar content can be collapsed. For example, an "easy to use" code might be developed to account for customers who variously said, "It's so easy to work," "It wasn't hard to figure out how to operate it," and "It's not as difficult as some others I have tried." These codes should be broad enough to allow a meaningful summation of the product characteristics that were mentioned and yet not so broad that details from the ladders are lost. These codes should also stay close as possible to the customers' own words. Once these codes are identified, each is assigned a number. Figure 8.2 shows an example of what these numbered codes might look like.

The next step is to use these summary codes to develop a *score matrix* (see Table 8.2). The score matrix effectively translates each ladder into a string of equivalent codes. For example, a ladder expressed as "expensive - impress others - belonging" can now be expressed as a string of numbers, 3 - 18 - 22. The score matrix is simply a summary of all the ladder codes and contains one row for each ladder which was expressed (note that each customer will have multiple rows, or ladders, in the matrix), and the number of columns in the matrix will be dictated by the longest ladder which was contained in the interviews.

Aggregating the Data

Once the ladders are recorded in the score matrix, the objective

Values

(20) Accomplishment
(21) Family
(22) Belonging
(23) Self-esteem

Consequences

(8) Quality
(9) Filling
(10) Refreshing
(11) Consume less
(12) Thirst-quenching
(13) More feminine
(14) Avoid negatives
(15) Avoid waste
(16) Reward
(17) Sophisticated
(18) Impress others
(19) Socialize

Attributes

(1) Carbonation
(2) Crisp
(3) Expensive
(4) Label
(5) Bottle shape
(6) Less alcohol
(7) Smaller

Figure 8.2. Summary content codes for a hypothetical wine cooler example.

Source: Thomas Reynolds and Jonathan Gutman, "Laddering Theory, Methods, Analysis and Interpretation," *Journal of Advertising Research*, Feb/March, 1988, 11 – 31. [4]

is to aggregate the data so that patterns can be detected across all of the customer interviews. This is done in two steps.

First, a *summary implication matrix* is developed (see Table 8.3). The purpose of this matrix is to capture all of the *linkages* (or combinations of codes) which appeared in the score matrix. To do this, a square matrix is developed (much like a correlation matrix), where the horizontal and vertical axes contain all of the

Table 8.2. Raw Data from Hypothetical Wine Cooler Data

Respondent number	Content codes					
1	1	10	12	16	20	0
2	1	10	16	0	0	0
3	1	10	12	16	16	23
4	3	6	20	0	0	0
5	4	17	20	0	0	0
6	2	10	12	16	18	22
7	1	12	16	20	0	0
8	3	8	20	0	0	0
9	1	12	16	18	23	0
10	1	10	16	0	0	0
11	3	8	20	0	0	0
12	2	10	12	16	18	22
13	1	12	16	20	0	0
14	1	12	16	18	23	0
15	1	10	12	16	20	0
16	3	16	20	0	0	0
17	1	10	12	16	20	0
18	2	10	12	16	18	22
19	1	10	12	16	18	23
20	1	10	16	0	0	0
21	2	10	12	16	18	22
22	3	20	0	0	0	0
23	1	10	12	16	20	0
24	1	10	16	0	0	0
25	3	6	16	20	0	0
26	3	6	16	18	23	0
27	3	8	18	20	0	0
28	3	18	23	0	0	0
29	3	16	23	0	0	0
30	3	8	18	22	0	0
31	3	8	17	18	23	0
32	3	17	18	23	0	0
33	4	13	17	18	23	0
34	4	13	17	18	22	0
35	5	13	17	23	0	0

Source: Thomas Reynolds and Jonathan Gutman, "Laddering Theory, Methods, Analysis and Interpretation," *Journal of Advertising Research*, Feb/March, 1988, 11–31.

Table 8.3. Summary Implication Matrix*

	8	9	10	11	12	13	14	15	16	17	18	19	20	21	22	23	
1 Carbonation	1.00		10.00		4.06			.01	.14	.03	.04		.06		.07	.04	1
2 Crisp	3.00		4.00		.04				.04	1.01	.04	.01			.05	.05	2
3 Expensive	12.00								2.04	1.01	1.09		1.06		.02	.03	3
4 Label	2.00					2.02				2.04	.02		.01		.02	.03	4
5 Bottle shape	1.00		1.00			2.02				1.03					.02	.03	5
6 Less alcohol			1.00		1.00		5.00		.01		.01	1.01		.04	.01		6
7 Smaller				1.00			.01	3.00				.01		.02	.01		7
8 Quality						3.00		1.00	4.00	4.03	4.04		3.02		.09	.04	8
9 Filling				4.00			.04					.01	1.03		.03	.02	9
10 Refreshing						1.00			5.10	.01	.06				.05	.02	10
11 Consume less					10.00							.04	.04	.02	.03		11
12 Thirst-quenching							5.00									.04	12
13 More feminine									14.00						.04	.04	13
14 Avoid negatives										7.00	.08		.06		1.03		14
15 Avoid waste											.02	5.00		4.01	.04		15
16 Reward											1.00		8.00	2.00	.06	1.05	16
17 Sophisticated											11.00		1.00		4.02	5.03	17
18 Impress others												1.00	1.00		10.00	9.00	18
19 Socialize											4.00		3.00		5.00		19
20 Accomplishment																	20
21 Family																	21
22 Belonging																	22
23 Self-esteem																	23

* No relations exist between the attribute elements.

Source: Thomas Reynolds and Jonathan Gutman, "Laddering Theory, Methods, Analysis and Interpretation," *Journal of Advertising Research*, Feb/March, 1988, 11–31.

summary codes (1 to n). The cells of the matrix then are used to represent how many times pairs of codes occurred within the ladders of the score matrix.

The numbers in each cell are fractions that summarize, across all of the ladders, how often codes were directly or indirectly linked by customers. The left-hand side of the decimal shows the number of times that two codes were directly linked, or placed adjacent to each other, in a ladder (such as "expensive" and "impress others" from the example above). The right-hand side indicates the number of indirect links, where the codes appeared in the same ladder, but were not directly adjacent to each other (such as "expensive" and "belonging" from the example above). For example, Table 8.3 shows that "carbonation" and "thirst-quenching" were linked four times directly and six times indirectly across all of the customers' ladders.

Obviously, some of the cells in the matrix will be empty where linkages did not occur (e.g., between "carbonation" and "more feminine"). On the other hand, it is easy to look at this matrix and identify which linkages were most frequently considered by customers. For instance, in Table 8.3 "thirst quenching" is directly linked fourteen times with "reward."

This summary implications matrix can then be used to rebuild a *hierarchical value map* that summarizes the most frequently mentioned linkages across all the interviews. An example of this is included in Figure 8.3. This map simply takes the most frequently mentioned direct and indirect linkages, and aggregates them into a summary hierarchy. Determining the minimum number of times a direct or indirect linkage must be mentioned to be included in the hierarchical value map is essentially a subjective judgment.

Qualitative Analyses

The quantitative techniques described above can provide managers with a level of comfort in the data and in the conclusions that are drawn from them. However, as can be seen, these methods can also be quite effortful, time consuming, and expen-

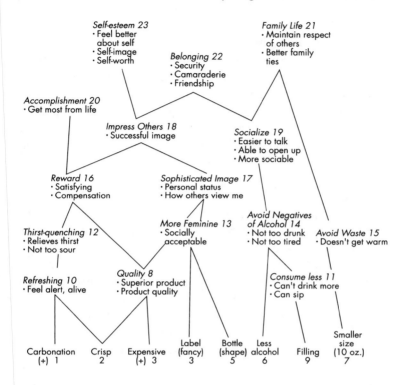

Figure 8.3. A hypothetical hierarchical value map of the wine cooler category.

Source: Thomas Reynolds and Jonathan Gutman, "Laddering Theory, Methods, Analysis and Interpretation," *Journal of Advertising Research*, Feb/March, 1988, 11 – 31. [4]

sive. Some may reject these analyses because they consider the costs to be unreasonable, because they don't feel they have the expertise or ability to conduct the analyses, or because they simply would prefer less strenuous techniques to analyze the interviews. In fact, we have developed some qualitative methods that shortcut much of the complexities of quantitative analyses while preserving the significant insights from the value data. These will be described in the following sections.

Situation Analyses

Some of the more interesting insights that come out of the qualitative methods (whether they be observations, focus groups, or interviews) will be the different product or service performance requirements that are expected in various use situations. In Chapter 3 we noted the importance of use situation in influencing the value hierarchy. One type of analysis that should be conducted is a profiling of the various situations in which the product is used, as well as the important product considerations associated with each situation.

Figure 8.4 shows a template for extracting situation profiles from the qualitative data. For each customer, several of these templates may be completed, one for each of the use situations that he or she discusses during the interview.

Column One: Customer Needs, Behaviors, and Triggers. In this column, you should note information that describes the customer, his or her behaviors in the situation, any particular needs he or she has, and any "triggers" that were noted (see Chapter 3). In this column, be careful to make observations about the *user* and not about the product. You want to describe, as specifically as possible, what the customer is experiencing, feeling, and thinking. For example, for a consumer describing the situation of "drinking a sports beverage after the league basketball game," this column might note:

- Heart rate is up
- Feeling fatigued and worn down
- Sweaty
- Needs to have thirst quenched quickly
- Children are with the user and are impatient to leave

Column Two: Product Specific Use Behaviors. In this column you should note specific *behaviors* related to purchasing, acquiring, using, and/or disposing of the product. In addition, you will want to note any *attitudes* and/or *opinions* about the product that the consumer expresses as well as any value dimensions (attributes, consequences, or desired end states). As opposed to

Consumer Name: _____ **Number:** _____

Use situation type or subtype: _____

Consumer needs, behaviors, and triggers	Product specific use behaviors	Comparison standards and characteristics	Important influences (influential orgs. and persons)

Figure 8.4. Consumption situation analysis.

column one, which focused on the customer, this column specifically characterizes *the product* and the interaction of the customer with the product. For instance, considering our basketball player above, we might note in column two:

- Gets sports drink from team cooler
- Selects a 16-ounce glass container
- Drinks the beverage quickly in a few gulps while standing
- Throws the empty container in trash can
- Likes the citrus taste
- Prefers the glass container, says cans leave a "metallic" taste
- Wishes a wider variety of flavors were available
- Likes the wide mouth on the container
- Makes him feel refreshed and invigorated
- Hydrates
- Feels like he is doing something good for his body – good medicine

Column Three: Comparison Standards and Characteristics. This column is used to note any other products (or alternatives) that were mentioned, as well as how they compared to the selected product. These are essentially comparison standards against which the product is being considered. For instance:

- Doesn't drink water at the fountain because there is usually a line
- Avoids the soft drinks in the machines because they leave him thirstier than before

Column Four: Important Influences (Influential Organizations or Persons). This column notes the extent to which other individuals (e.g., other product users, decision makers, or facilitators) or prior product experiences might have an influence or role in the product use. For example:

- Each week someone is designated to bring the cooler with the drinks
- The coach prefers sports drinks to other alternatives (e.g., juice and water)

In this way, an analysis is prepared for each situation in which the customer participates. It is easy to see how, once these templates are completed, they can be combined, grouped, and sorted in ways that can provide insight to managers. You should also be able to collapse information across the templates of several customers to prepare summary profiles of product use by different situation types.

It is very important that the entries on the templates reflect, as much as possible, the actual words and phrases that the customer used in describing his or her experience. Obviously there is the need to condense the comments from the transcripts. But try to do so in a way that stays close to the customers' expressions, sentiments, and jargon. The more rewording and interpretation that occurs, the more likely the real flavor of the user's perspective will be lost.

Finally, it is possible, if desired, to use the data recorded on these summary sheets to perform the quantitative protocol analysis described above. The only difference would be that the "unit of analysis" would be the phrases recorded on the summary sheets, rather than verbatim responses from the transcripts. In this way, one could derive the benefit of both qualitative and quantitative analysis.

One of the more critical questions, surprisingly enough, is how to define a "use situation." For instance, in talking to consumers of sports beverages, we might distinguish use situations by the *location* where the beverage is consumed. For instance, this might be "at the gym after a basketball game," "at the fitness center," "after jogging," "while driving," and so forth. Differentiating use situations by physical location is probably the easiest, most straightforward way to define them.

However, you may find it desirable to devise a second level of classifications by distinguishing events within these larger situations. For instance, for individuals working out at the fitness center, there may be a variety of activities that are experienced, such as "getting ready in the locker room," "playing racquetball," "using the weight machines," "jogging," and the like. You may want to break situations down into finer categories if you suspect that the product users have different product needs and experiences as they move between these events.

A different possibility for defining situations is not by physical location or activity but in terms of a *time line or a consumption cycle.* Considering the customer's entire experience with a product (from prepurchase, to actually purchasing and obtaining the product, to consuming the product, to disposing of the product), it is easy to imagine that the importance of particular product dimensions and the value they create may vary across the consumption cycle. Therefore, you might want to consider a situational typology that incorporates not only physical location but the point in the consumption cycle at which the user finds him- or herself (e.g., cleaning up/disposing of the product after a meal at home).

Obviously, to come to some agreement about the appropriate classifications of use situations, managers will need to consider unique aspects of their products, their customers, and their industry. Because there is no one prescribed "best" way to define use situations, one recommendation is to read through all of the transcripts and/or notes first, exploring the various types of situations that the customers describe. This is a good way to get a feel for the variety of situations or events that exist in the data, the level of detail that one can expect in each of these situations, and how much variance there is in product requirements across them.

There is clearly a trade-off between underspecifying (in too broad terms) and overspecifying (in too narrow terms) use situations. Obviously, the greater the level of specification, or the more narrow the situation specification, the more complex and time consuming the data analysis will be. However, the more specific the use situation or event (e.g., product consumption while jogging, swimming, lifting weights, or doing aerobics), the richer the understanding of product or service value requirements that will emerge.

Defining use situations at a very broad level facilitates data analysis, as customers can be more efficiently grouped into common situations (e.g., "exercising"). However, this practice may "bury" opportunities for value creation that would emerge in more subtle descriptions of situations or events. It might be important to remember that if use situations have been too narrowly defined, they can relatively easily be aggregated into broader situational contexts. Accomplishing the opposite – breaking down too broad situations into finer units – is much more difficult, possibly requiring a completely new analysis of the data.

Ultimately, there is no right answer to this question. You will simply want to define situations at a level that provides the best understanding of the different opportunities your product has to create value.

Value Hierarchy Analyses

Understanding the value hierarchy is obviously a key objective of customer value measurement. Short of the coding analysis described above, there are two suggestions for helping managers to understand their customers' value perspectives.

Summary Tables.   The first and easiest suggestion is to build a master table which documents all attributes, consequences, and end states which were mentioned by product/service customers, much like was done in the first step of the laddering analysis (see

"Summary Codes" earlier in this chapter). Figure 8.5 illustrates a potential template for this summary, a value hierarchy analysis.

Column One: Product/Service Attributes. This column should be used to note any attribute level features or characteristics that were used to describe the product or service. These would include physical characteristics (e.g., size, packaging, labeling, container type, ingredients, parts, or construction), service characteristics (e.g., delivery, service, availability, order processing, distribution, service provider helpfulness and demeanor, and efficiency), and even features of the "extended" product, including advertising, reputation, brand/company awareness, trade promotions, and the like.

Column Two: Positive Consequences. Entries in this column would describe positive outcomes that the user experienced as a result of buying, owning, using, or disposing of the product or service.

Column Three: Negative Consequences. Entries in this column would be used to describe negative outcomes (e.g., costs, problems, and frustrations) that the user experienced as a result of buying, owning, using, or disposing of the product or service.

Column Four: End States. This column should include any desired end states, values, purposes, or goals that the customer wishes to achieve. As stated earlier, some end states are served relatively directly by the product; that is, product nutrition leads to "good health," family programs at the health and fitness center provide "quality time with my family," and so forth. On the other hand, there are some instances where product consumption indirectly contributes to a desired end state. For example, a consumer may like to play basketball in a local league because it serves a goal of community involvement. In this case, consuming the sports beverage does not directly keep the user involved in community. However, sports beverages are a part of the activity (league basketball) that does achieve that desired end state, so there may be an indirect linkage in the consumer's mind. Both directly and indirectly served end states are important to capture.

There are some important points which must be made about constructing value hierarchy summaries.

Analyzing Customer Value Data

Consumer Name: _____ **Number:** _____

Product/Service Attributes physical product and others, e.g., availability, location, etc.	Positive Consequences Associated with owning, using and consuming the products	Negative Consequences Associated with owning, using and consuming the products	End States Values, purposes and goals of the consumer

* Analysis can be done for an entire product category, for an individual brand/offering, or both.
Attributes describe the product; **Positive Consequences** and **Negative Consequences** describe what happens to the consumer as a result of using the product; **Values** relate to product and larger consumption context, e.g., exercise.

Figure 8.5. Value hierarchy analysis.

- As with situation analyses, it is wise to stay as close as possible to the customers' actual words and phrases. Summarize when necessary, but resist the temptation to translate the customer's words into your own.
- Alongside each attribute, consequence and end state, be sure to enter into the table (1) any evaluations that the user expressed, either positive or negative (e.g., "the citrus taste was *very good*"), (2) any emotion words that appeared with them (e.g., "the size of the bottle *frustrated* me because it wouldn't fit in my cup holder," and/or (3) any indication of the perceived importance of that product dimension (e.g., "the price was what *really made my decision*").
- Be sure to indicate whether the customer's comments refer to a specific brand ("I really like the Brand X's flavor") or whether he or she is referring to the entire product or service category ("Sports beverages have a kind of slimy consistency"). Typically users will talk at both levels, and you will want to separate out comments specific to your product from those that are characteristic of the larger set of competitors. You will ultimately want to capture both, however.

Finally, as with the situational analyses, the data contained in value hierarchy summary tables can also serve as input into a more detailed coding analysis, if desired.

A Value Hierarchy Affinity Exercise. A second, more experiential type of value hierarchy analysis can be very effective. This exercise is ideal for managers to do as a group and can be the source of significant discussion and insights into how customers view their organization's product or service offering. It requires managers to actually "build" a fluid and dynamic value hierarchy.

This exercise requires several packets of post-it notes, a blank wall, and a master list of the attributes, consequences, and end states that have been communicated by the customers. (These can be obtained from ladders, from the value hierarchy table described above, or simply from going through the data and summarizing their contents.) The value dimensions (e.g., attribute, consequence, or end state) are then recorded on post-it notes, one value dimension per note. The managers' job is to use the notes to physically "construct" a value hierarchy by placing and moving the notes on the wall.

At first, a lot of energy will go toward simply separating attributes from consequences from end states – that is, in determining the three levels. This is where the fluidity of this exercise becomes an asset. Individual notes can be moved around the wall and arranged and rearranged to the satisfaction of the managers. The distinction between the three levels is not always clear. For instance, is "fast delivery" an attribute or a consequence? There is much room for debate, but some important insights will occur as the managers grapple with this distinction. (Some rules of thumb might be helpful. We tend to define attributes as dimensions which are clearly associated with the product. These do not vary across situations. Consequences, on the other hand, are defined as *"something that happens to the customer,"* and these tend to be shorter run, specific *outcomes* that are associated with using a product in a particular situation. End states are also descriptions of the customer, but these tend to be *very broad and abstract in nature, longer run, and may be appropriate across any number of products or use situations* (e.g., "love my family," "harmony," or "peace of mind).)

Next, managers will begin to see connections or associations between dimensions in the hierarchy. Again, fluidity is an asset. The managers should begin to rearrange the notes so that they can spatially represent the degree of "connectedness" between the dimensions in the hierarchy. There will need to be some *sorting within levels* (e.g., some attributes may be highly related to each other and should be grouped together within the attribute level). Next, associations *between levels* should be considered, so that attributes and consequences – and consequences and end states – that are strongly connected are placed together. Again, there are some important insights here for managers. Just why is a particular element of our product offering deemed to be important or unimportant? How are the product or service attributes we provide connected with the (potentially many) consequences and end states that the customer desires? Does the customer have any desired consequences or end states that we are currently not serving as well as we could?

The resulting hierarchy is not the most important outcome of this exercise. We find that the discussion that goes on between managers is incredibly valuable. The hierarchy and the exercise provide a format for managers to explore their customer or product interface in a structured and focused way.

Potential variations on this exercise are limited only by the creativity of the managers. For instance, by using different colors of notes, managers can differentiate aspects of the hierarchy where their company is performing well (green) versus areas where they are not performing well (yellow) or not performing at all (red). Such a hierarchy can summarize quickly and visually the strengths and weaknesses of the firm's offering. Or colors may be used to differentiate value dimensions that are associated with different customer groups (yellow equals product user dimensions; green equals decision-maker dimensions), although often it is best to construct completely separate value hierarchies for different customers. Some value dimensions may be more important to customers now, others more important in the future, others less important. Again, using color coding to separate out this distinction could be very revealing.

Finally, one should carefully consider who will participate in this exercise. Think of the benefits, for instance, of having cross-functional teams participate (e.g., managers from new product development, manufacturing, logistics, and marketing). The benefits of doing this exercise are greatly influenced by the make-up of the participating management group.

Additional Analyses

There are two additional types of analyses that complement the techniques just discussed. These are customer value dimension importance analysis and using value dimensions to build satisfaction questionnaires.

Importance Analysis

One of the key pieces of information that managers want to know is customers' perception of the relative importance of the different value dimensions. Of the many things an organization is offering or can consider offering, not all will be equally valued, and it makes sense for managers to pay special attention to those dimensions that are most important to the customer. The primary objective of value determination is to understand value hierarchies and how they are adaptive to specific situation requirements. Where in these analyses might managers find clues to answer the "importance" question?

The answer, in short, is that value analysis provides *indirect* insights to this question. Additional research is typically needed in order to fully understand how customers perceive the importance of value dimensions. A more complete discussion of how to measure importance is included in Chapter 9 and in Appendix II. As you will see the dimensions uncovered during value measurement become the basis for measuring importance in a subsequent research phase. In this sense, customer value measurement is an important prerequisite and input to more thorough research into the measurement of importance.

However, it should be noted that customer value data can yield some initial insights into importance. First, during the interviews or observations, customers will often indicate the relative importance of particular value dimensions. They may explicitly state these importance perspectives (for example, "The real decision finally came down to price"). Or importance may be inferred from behaviors (for example, a customer who reads the nutrition label for the fat content). You can also assume that customers will explicitly mention attributes that are important, and that unmentioned attributes are probably relatively less important. Finally, during the interview itself, the interviewer can and should probe for this information if it is not forthcoming. "How important is that to you?" "Which of those dimensions is most important to you?"

Importance can also be inferred from the presence of emotion. Rarely do customers get emotional (in either a positive or a negative direction) about issues that are unimportant to them. That is why, in the qualitative analyses above, we suggest that any indication of emotion be recorded on the summary tables and that evidence of emotions be identified in tapes.

Finally, a word of caution. Be careful about assuming a positive correlation between importance and the frequency with which product or service dimensions are mentioned in the interviews. There might be a temptation in the laddering analysis, for instance, to impute greater importance to linkages that are frequently mentioned. This may, in fact, be the case. But there are other reasons besides importance that influence frequency of mention. For instance, some product or service characteristics are very fundamental. They are frequently mentioned because they are so elemental to what the product is or does – so basic – that they have to be present. However, this does not necessarily mean that they are the most important dimensions to customers. Many managers, for instance, place a great deal of importance on the price of their product because it is one element that their customers will frequently talk about. This can lead managers to believe that they must compete on price, be a low cost leader, and so forth. However, it may be that price is simply a factor that the customer has to get beyond in order to talk about other, more important things, such as reliability of service. Other dimensions may be mentioned frequently because they represent "the price of admission" for a supplier. These are features that must be available to customers (e.g., JIT delivery) and yet may not be used to determine supplier choice as all competitors must have them.

The other problem of inferring importance from frequency is that product dimensions are often mentioned frequently when all competitors are stressing them. This is especially true in industries where there is a great deal of competitive parity. It may be, however, that a company can gain competitive advantage from pursuing features that are *not* being served by the current competitive offerings and by considering potentially important but relatively unmentioned attributes.

You would obviously only want to go in this direction when the product dimension mentioned less often is – or can be – strongly related to a consequence or end state that you know is highly valued by your customers. In this case, you may actually be able to elevate the perceived importance of the previously unconsidered product dimension. For instance, ten years ago the consumers of toothpaste rarely considered the need for "tartar control." However, there has always been a very strongly held desire (at least for a portion of the customers) for "healthy teeth." In this instance, raising the visibility of tartar control, and the ability of your product to provide it, is obviously a path toward helping your customers achieve healthy teeth.

In summary, value analysis will give the researcher glimpses and insights into where importance lies. However, we suggest that additional research build on the outcomes of value measurement to more systematically explore this strategically critical question. It should also be remembered that value measurement typically occurs for only a small portion of your customer base. Even if indications of importance are uncovered, it is typically wise to validate these insights in a large-scale study.

Input into Customer Satisfaction Surveys

We argued in Chapter 4 that there is a distinct difference between customer value measurement and customer satisfaction measurement. In Chapter 5 we suggested that both of these two types of customer research be done as a part of the entire value determination process.

First, there is an important order effect that should be noted. That is, value measurement should *precede* customer satisfaction measurement. In fact, the results of value measurement become the *input* that shapes the content of customer satisfaction surveys. Therefore, the effectiveness of the latter depends on the former. For example, in one recent study the customer value measurement stage uncovered an important value dimension which was not being included in the organization's customer satisfaction questionnaire, the ability of the supplier firm to provide managerial advice to the customer firms. The satisfaction survey was altered to include this dimension, as well as to eliminate some dimensions which were clearly unimportant to customers as indicated by the value measurement study.

In addition, it is important to remember that the findings of value measurement should be validated on a large-scale sample of your customer base. This is most effectively done through customer satisfaction measurement. In this sense, customer satisfaction research is necessary to confirm the findings of value measurement. So we can see that these two measures, though different, are quite complementary and even dependent upon each other.

In sum, these two methods go hand in hand. More is said in Chapter 9 about bringing these two together in the customer value determination process.

Summary

Just as value measurement was described as "peeling away the layers of the onion" in Chapter 7, analyzing value data includes many different possibilities for peeling away the rich meanings and interpretations of these data. Both quantitative and qualitative techniques can be used, sometimes simultaneously. This chapter described a variety of methods that are useful to help draw out the essence of qualitative data, from quantitative techniques such as protocol coding and laddering analysis to other less demanding types of qualitative analyses (e.g., building situational profiles, value hierarchy analyses, and an experiential affinity exercise). Finally, it was noted that the outcomes of these analyses play an important role as input into subsequent importance and satisfaction analyses.

Whichever of these methods is used, managers will quickly begin to realize that the effort needed to "massage" qualitative data is well worth the results. There is simply no way that the subtle, rich, multilevel complexities of a user/product interaction can be as effectively captured in a paper and pencil survey, in a five- or seven-point scale, in a mean, or in a p value. Likewise, there is no substitute for the customer's actual words, phrases, and experiences, which are often lost in other types of customer research. We believe that once managers begin incorporating methods of qualitative value measurement into their customer research efforts, they will become a vital component of their customer feedback systems.

References

[1] Ericsson, K. Anders and Herbert A. Simon, "Verbal Reports as Data," *Psychological Review*, 87 (July 1980), pp. 215-251.

[2] Nisbett, Richard E. and Timothy DeCamp Wilson, "Telling More Than We Can Know: Verbal Reports on Mental Processes," *Psychological Review*, 84 (July 1977), pp. 231-259.

[3] Biehal, Gabriel and Dipankar Chakravarti, "The Effects of Concurrent Verbalization on Choice Processing," *The Journal of Marketing Research*, 26 (February 1989), pp. 84–96.

[4] Reynolds, Thomas J. and Jonathan Gutman, "Laddering Theory, Method, Analysis, and Interpretation," *The Journal of Advertising Research*, 28 (February/March 1988), pp. 11–31.

CHAPTER 9

MEASURING CUSTOMER SATISFACTION

Recently, we got a call from a large bank asking for help with their customer satisfaction measurement (CSM) process. The bank spends significant resources and effort getting feedback from customers. Its research staff conducts an annual customer satisfaction survey, and from the resulting data computes for each of the bank's branches ratings of performance on various attributes and an overall satisfaction score. Based on this report, every branch manager develops an improvement plan for increasing the satisfaction of his or her customers. Unfortunately, a general feeling prevailed throughout the branch organization that CSM resources were being wasted. Branch managers expressed frustration at how little help they got from the CSM report concerning how to improve performance to better meet their customers' needs.

These complaints indicated that there were problems with the CSM's actionability. For one thing, the data measured a branch's performance with very broadly defined attributes, such as "service personnel." If the ratings uncovered a problem with one of these attributes, there were no other data to help a manager decide what to do about it. For instance, the ratings didn't indicate which service personnel were causing the problem, what exactly it was that they were doing that was causing the problem, or what should be done to improve the situation. In addition, very high percentages of responses to the performance and satisfaction questions tended to fall at the high end of the scales. There was seemingly little room for shifting the scores upward, yet the managers' compensation depended on showing improvement in these scores.

Because of their unhappiness with the satisfaction measurement process, some managers began to question whether managing toward customer satisfaction should continue to be a company goal. Before scrapping the entire CSM process, however, the bank decided to thoroughly reevaluate it to see what should be improved.

Introduction

More and more organizations are focusing outward on customers with an eye toward their satisfaction. The costs of a dissatisfied customer are surprisingly high. For instance, Sandy Corporation estimates that the average cost of each lost customer for a firm in a service industry such as banking, hospitality, or transportation is $189 in foregone revenue and the expense of replacing that customer.[1] A large turnover of customers can make this loss add up to quite a significant amount over time. In contrast, keeping customers satisfied about the things that are important to them – the critical value dimensions – increases the odds that they will purchase again from you. They also are more likely to engage in favorable word of mouth and to develop a sense of loyalty to you as a supplier. It is the impact of satisfaction on these important customer behaviors that make a compelling case for setting satisfaction goals.

Organizations that manage toward customer satisfaction quickly find out how much effort goes into keeping their customers highly satisfied. For one thing, managers have to look at their internal processes from the customers' perspectives. Those processes that create and deliver superior value for customers receive the most attention and resources. As one senior executive puts it, "Our customer satisfaction goal is very simple. It is to improve all our work processes that have an effect on customer satisfaction, so that we can achieve our goal of being number one in customer satisfaction in all of our markets."[2]

Operationally, managing toward satisfaction means making a commitment to rely on data about customers and markets to drive decisions. Your customers' perceptions ultimately determine how they respond to your offerings. You have to become adept at using data to track trends in customer satisfaction levels and, most importantly, to understand what drives that satisfaction. When an organization reaches this point in its thinking, CSM becomes a high priority.

221

Measuring Customer Satisfaction

With all the attention given to customer satisfaction as a business goal, it is not surprising that the topic of CSM has become popular in the last decade. Several how-to books have been published to help organizations get started with measurement [3], and a growing number of research firms are supplying much-needed expertise in this area.[1] Many organizations enthusiastically support the role that CSM is playing in efforts to improve their competitiveness. At the same time, CSM requires a significant investment to ensure that it fulfills its promise as an important decision-making tool.

Do most organizations routinely measure customer satisfaction? Apparently, less measurement is going on than you might think. Just because an organization has customer satisfaction goals does not mean that there is a corresponding commitment to CSM. Consider what Sandy Corporation found out from surveying firms in service industries:

- 42 percent do not perform customer surveys.
- 62 percent do not provide customer comment or complaint cards.
- 19 percent do not employ customer monitoring programs of any type.[4]

As was true for the bank described above, a growing number of managers – even in organizations that do measure customer satisfaction – are expressing unhappiness with their organizations' CSM process. They want data that is actionable, and they get upset when the data is not. For instance, some firms find that over time satisfaction data may loose its relationship to performance.[5] Sometimes satisfaction scores level off regardless of improvement programs, or they may remain high while sales growth levels off. What happened in these cases? Quite often, we find that a company did not change its satisfaction measures to keep up with changes in markets and in customer needs. The data becomes outdated. As we explain later, there may be other problems as well. If you commit to CSM, you can never stop looking for ways to make your satisfaction data more actionable.

In this chapter, we focus on how to measure customer

satisfaction. Hopefully, the measurement issues that we discuss will help you evaluate the CSM process that your organization has in place and suggest some ways to improve it. We start by looking at current CSM practices in industry. Organizations rely on many methods to learn about their customers' satisfaction. The heart of any system, however, should be data coming directly from customers. We concentrate on these data by exploring a process for conducting customer satisfaction surveys. Our approach draws heavily on ideas about customer value and satisfaction laid out in Chapters 3, 4, 7, and 8. Most importantly, we stress the point made in Chapter 5 that customer satisfaction measurement must incorporate what we know about customer value.

Learning from Current CSM Practice

In our work, we devote a lot of time to staying abreast of current CSM practices. We observe satisfaction measurement in companies with which we work, attend practitioner conferences on CSM, and read the practitioner literature. One thing stands out from our experience: organizations learn about their customers' satisfaction in many different ways. Companies rely on many different methods for measuring customer satisfaction. For instance, the following methods are used by companies in one industry alone – the hospitality industry [6]:

Direct Methods
- On-site customer comment cards
- Verbal complaints or compliments
- Written complaints or compliments
- Follow-up complaint or compliment calls
- Surveys of known customers
- Personal interviews with customers
- Trade association studies
- Surveys of potential customers

Indirect Methods/Indicators
- The number of repeat customers
- Sales trends

- Market share trends
- Management reports
- Return on investment trends
- Anonymous evaluations of property

Direct and Indirect CSM Methods

To better understand differences between methods, we find it helpful to divide them into two categories: *direct methods* and *indirect methods*. Direct methods measure customers' perceptions as to how well a supplier is delivering value. Comment cards and mail surveys, for example, require customers to write their opinions on questionnaires. The important point is that all of these methods bring feedback directly from customers back into your organization.

By contrast, indirect methods bypass customer opinion to measure various indicators of satisfaction. In one way or another, most of these indicators reflect customer behavior – that is, what customers actually did in the marketplace. For example, "repeat customers" data measure the number of customers who actually purchased again from the same supplier. When using these indicators, you should feel confident that there is a high correlation between customers' perceptions of satisfaction and a particular indicator. In other words, customers behave in a way that is consistent with their level of satisfaction. Consider a company that relies on sales data to take the pulse of its market; these data are good indicators only if customers' satisfaction perceptions are a key factor that motivates customers to buy from one supplier over another.

As you have probably already suspected, some indirect method indicators are more closely associated with customer satisfaction than are others. It depends on what other factors are involved in the relationship. For instance, satisfaction should more highly correlate with sales than with return on investment because the latter indicator includes an unrelated variable – cost or investment. Or anonymous evaluations of customer contact personnel will indicate customer satisfaction only to the extent that these personnel are evaluated on dimensions that are important to customers. The only way to know for sure is to test for the strength of an indicator's relationship to customer satisfaction. Do pilot research before you commit to any particular indicator.

It is all too easy to think that direct and indirect methods for measuring satisfaction compete with each other, and that managers must choose the "best" one. However, we think that these methods are complementary. They measure different things about customers, each of which may be important to know. Let's explore this point further.

Direct CSM Methods. The primary advantage from using direct methods lies in getting feedback from your customers. Again, how they perceive your offering and what it is accomplishing for them are major factors in determining what they will do in the future. When direct methods work well, they provide managers with a kind of early warning system.

Look at Figure 9.1 for a moment. Satisfaction data and sales performance data are plotted over time. Note the relationship between the two curves, particularly at times t_1 and t_2. At t_1, sales are just taking off on a growth spurt, but satisfaction data have been signaling this growth for some time by showing a strong upward trend. At t_2, the rate of sales increase is leveling off and about to decline. Again, satisfaction data predicted this change by showing a downward trend in advance. Paying attention to these satisfaction trends will help you gain lead time in deciding what actions are needed to deal with the coming sales changes. However, to ensure that you get this advance warning, you must periodically check to see whether your satisfaction data are, in fact, providing a leading indication of changes in sales (or other performance measures). Because markets and customers change, you may have to change your satisfaction measures from time to time to retain their leading relationship to performance.

There are different kinds of direct measures, and these, too, are complementary. Each provides a picture of a different aspect of customer satisfaction. For instance, satisfaction surveys of current customers help guide customer retention strategies, while surveys of potential customers influence strategies for acquiring new customers. Complaints data foster responsive-

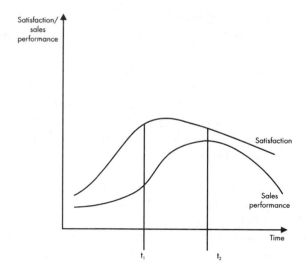

Figure 9.1. Satisfaction as a leading indicator of performance.

ness needed to turn a dissatisfied customer into a satisfied one. In a well-designed CSM system, each kind of data serves a explicitly designated and complementary purpose.

Direct methods are relatively expensive. Using commercial research suppliers, a single customer satisfaction survey may cost from $50,000 to $500,000 or more. The exact amount depends on a number of design considerations, such as the method of questionnaire delivery, the sample size, the number of segments surveyed, the incentives used to get respondents to fill out a questionnaire, and so forth. Each consideration requires making trade-offs that affect costs. For instance, comment cards are much less expensive than surveys, but comment cards are not as likely to get responses from a representative sample of targeted customers. (We have more to say on these design decisions later in this chapter.)

As you think about how to measure customer satisfaction directly, keep one caveat in mind. In the minds of customers, direct methods may well imply a commitment on your part to act on revealed problems. If customers take the time to tell you that they are dissatisfied, they probably expect you to do something about it. As a general rule, you should commit to direct customer satisfaction methods only if you are willing to respond to what customers tell you. Of course, the satisfaction data alone may help convince higher management that a problem exists and should be corrected.

Indirect CSM Methods. Indirect methods offer important advantages as well. Bottom-line performance data, such as sales, repeat customers, market share, and profits, should be readily available from internal records, and consequently are relatively inexpensive compared to satisfaction surveys. Further, managers typically are quite used to relying on performance data for decisions. They often feel more comfortable with these data than with the more subjective or "soft" data measuring customer satisfaction feelings.

Indirect methods keep managers focused on bottom-line performance. On the other hand, indirect methods cannot do everything that direct methods can do. For one thing, performance data may not be sufficiently timely. As we pointed out above, by the time a customer satisfaction problem shows up as a decline in sales or market share, it may be too late; customers may already have been lost to competitors. A product manager in a global consumer products company once commented to one of the authors that he knew of other product managers who were happy as long as sales were going up. They did not look at available satisfaction data, and so they only took corrective action when sales declined, even though satisfaction scores tended to drop off in advance of a sales decline. By not paying attention to satisfaction data, these managers lost valuable lead time and faced periodic crisis situations.

Some indirect methods, such as sales trends, generate summary data and so they cannot pinpoint specific value delivery strengths or problems. Other indirect methods, such as anonymous evaluations, are able to highlight specific performance areas where a company is doing well or poorly assuming, of course, that they correlate with the value dimensions that drive customers' actions. But you have to know these correlations.

Measuring Customer Satisfaction

Suppose a restaurant chain hires "professional customers" to dine in selected stores and to rate performance on such objective aspects of operation as the time it took to be served, the temperature of the food, the cleanliness of premises, and the like. But which of these performances most affects customer satisfaction? Without additional data, you will not know for sure.

Building Systems that Integrate CSM Methods

Which of the variety of CSM methods available should you use in your CSM process? There is no easy answer to this question, but we can offer two opinions. First, we believe that no organization should rely totally on indirect methods for measuring customer satisfaction. Delivering value to customers means giving them what they want, and only customers can tell you whether they got what they wanted. We believe that organizations must listen to customers if they want to set satisfaction as a business goal.[7] Consequently, at least part of CSM should be devoted to direct measures.

Second, an organization should employ more than one method to measure customer satisfaction. It is unlikely that any single method will do everything that managers may need. For instance, a customer satisfaction survey is great for getting customer perceptions of your performance. You can spot areas for improvement quite well. But from time to time it may be prudent to check satisfaction scores against indirect performance indicators, such as sales, to ensure that these scores still measure the drivers of your organization's performance. As another example, satisfaction surveys cannot substitute for having a customer-complaint-gathering process. Complaints may suggest areas and ideas for improvement that would not be evident from quantitative satisfaction survey scores.

The best companies design and implement customer satisfaction measurement *systems*. They bring together data from different methods to meet specific application objectives. They take advantage of the fact that each kind of data, from satisfaction surveys to sales to complaints, tells managers something important about how customers are perceiving and reacting to their offerings. And, these companies continually evaluate their systems, looking for ways to make them even more responsive to their managers' data needs.

Link Customer Satisfaction to Customer Value

In Chapter 3, we introduced the customer value hierarchy concept. This way of looking at customer value helped us think about customer satisfaction measurement as well. We have seen dozens of satisfaction survey questionnaires, and one thing stands out: many companies measure satisfaction only at the attribute level in this hierarchy. Take a minute to look at Figure 9.2. It shows examples of specific attributes used in satisfaction questionnaires by a consumer service organization, a consumer durable manufacturer, and an industrial products manufacturer.

One way to think about these attributes is that they reflect what the supplier offers. So attribute-based satisfaction data measure what customers feel about your offerings. It is like asking the customer, "Here is what I do for you (the attributes), now how do you feel about what I do?" Such satisfaction data can be actionable – they can help you pinpoint strengths and weaknesses in your offering. However, they do not get into your customers' "world" by helping you learn about whether what you do (i.e., your offering) really helps customers accomplish what they want to have happen. Let's explore this important point further.

As indicated by the bank illustration at the beginning of this chapter, some organizations are not entirely happy with their CSM processes or systems. We believe that one cause of this stems from limiting satisfaction measurement to the attribute level in a customer value hierarchy. These data are most useful for helping managers find ways to "tweak" attributes that customers say are important in order to make incremental performance improvements.

Think, however, about two important aspects of this issue. First, there are limits to how much you can improve an established attribute in ways that customers notice. You know this limit is reached when customer satisfaction scores flatten out near the top of your satisfaction scale. Second, most organizations measure satisfaction at the attribute level. So competitors are likely

(1)
Consumer Service (Hotel)

- Friendliness of front desk staff
- Efficiency of front desk staff
- Speed of check-in
- Speed of check-out
- Cleanliness of room during stay
- Food quality
- Speed of service in restaurant
- Speed of service in lounge
- Accuracy of reservation
- Everything in working order

(2)
Consumer Durable (Boats)

- Engine reliability
- Engine performance
- Exterior quality
- Interior quality
- Cabin layout
- Factory-installed options
- Dealer-installed accessories
- Hardware
- Systems
- Radio and electronics
- Canvas
- Fabrics and vinyls
- Overall workmanship

(3)
Industrial Product Manufacturer (Materials)

- Product quality
- Product consistency
- Product line
- Innovation
- Pricing practices
- On-time delivery
- Complete and correct delivery
- Cleanliness of equipment
- Order entry, processing, and invoicing
- Complaints and credits
- Inquiry and request handling
- Technical service
- Technical knowledge and expertise
- Timeliness and reliability
- Technical effectiveness
- Sales representatives' knowledge of our products
- Sales representatives' knowledge of your product and process
- Suppliers' capabilities
- Commodity information
- Integrity
- Timely contact
- Listens to needs
- Accessibility to key personnel

Figure 9.2. Attributes in satisfaction questionnaires.

to be making similar kinds of improvements as you are, since they probably know as much about these attributes as you do. The result can be erosion of competitive advantage for everyone.

We believe that organizations should go beyond attribute satisfaction data if they want to improve CSM actionability.

Ultimately, you should want to know how much value customers feel they get by using your product and services. Satisfaction measured toward customers' desired *consequences* in their value hierarchies are better equipped to provide this insight. To illustrate, examine Figure 9.3, which shows desired benefit consequences taken from questionnaires used by three different companies.

Now compare the items for the boat company given in Figure 9.2 versus those is Figure 9.3 to see how consequence items differ from attribute items for the same product. It is easy to see that you will get quite different data depending on the level in a value hierarchy at which you measure satisfaction. As Figure 9.4 shows, customer satisfaction can be measured at any of the three levels of a customer value hierarchy. Those organizations that break away from solely attribute-based satisfaction data may gain an edge in learning about their customers' satisfaction.

Know Which Satisfaction Concept You Want to Measure

We found that organizations measure many different kinds of phenomena, from attitudes to intentions to repurchase, but call them "satisfaction." All of these measures are related, but the problem is that each so-called satisfaction measure may yield different results. Satisfaction theory can help us better understand what is going on.

Before reading further, please review Figure 4.1 in Chapter 4. Recall that satisfaction theory describes a process whereby customers' product or service performance and disconfirmation perceptions drive customer satisfaction feelings, and satisfaction drives important outcomes such as word of mouth, complaints, commitment or loyalty to a supplier, and intentions to repurchase. In practice, many managers do not distinguish between these concepts or their role in the theoretical disconfirmation process. For example, consider Sandy Corporation's definition of satisfaction: "The intent of a customer to purchase from you again at their next opportunity."[8] According to the model in Figure 4.1, an "intent to purchase" is actually an outcome of a customer's satisfaction feeling and not the feeling

(1)
Consumer Non-Durable
(Beverage)

- Has a variety of flavors so I don't get bored with it
- Doesn't make me feel too full
- Fills that empty feeling I get
- Prevents muscle cramps
- Gives me good nutrition
- Quenches my thirst fast
- Keeps me from getting thirsty
- Feel better fast
- Refuels me
- Helps keep my body from breaking down
- Helps rebuild my body
- Relieves my dehydration
- Easy to get where I play sports or exercise
- Easy to keep on hand for future use
- Affordable enough so I can drink it as much as I want

(2)
Consumer Durable
(Boats)

- Safe for me to use
- Comfortable for me to use
- Attractive to me
- Well-made by my standards
- Easy to use the way I want to
- Easy for me to maintain
- Things are conveniently located for me
- Equipment functions properly
- Something I am proud to own

(3)
Consumer Durable
(Fine Furniture)

- Creates a feeling of warmth in my house
- Creates a feeling of beauty
- Provides a comfortable setting
- Can accommodate both large and small number of guests
- Fits in with my other furniture
- Provides the topic for an interesting story
- Indicates that I care about my home
- Indicates that I am family oriented
- Indicates that I enjoy being around others

Figure 9.3. Desired consequences in satisfaction questionnaires

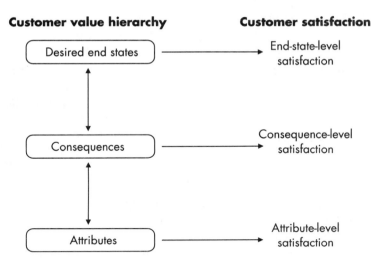

Figure 9.4. How customer value directs satisfaction.

itself. It is an indirect indicator of satisfaction, not a direct measure. This observation may seem insignificant, but it is not.

If you want a measure of "satisfaction," does it make any practical difference if you measure satisfaction itself or some other variable in this satisfaction process? The answer is that it might. Suppose you actually measure the customers' intent to purchase your brand again, but you think that you are measuring how satisfied your customers feel with your brand offering. If there are other factors influencing that intent than just a customer's satisfaction feeling, you can be mislead.

For example, consider a customer who is not highly satisfied with the previous use of your brand but intends to buy your brand again anyway. Maybe this customer thinks that the dissatisfying experience is atypical and wants to give you another chance. Or maybe your competitors' prices or the costs of switching are too high right now. Regardless of the reason, "satisfaction feeling" and "intent to purchase" measures will not give you the same picture of customers' perceptions of your offering. The intent measure suggests that you are performing well – in the short run customers intend to buy from you again. But in the longer run, dissatisfaction among customers will eventually adversely affect your performance. We believe that you must know what concepts you are measuring and what the data tell you.

In general, the current practice in the measurement of satisfaction is moving forward. Organizations are learning how to make CSM better by facing issues and resolving them. In the next section, we explore several of these issues critical to improving customer satisfaction surveys.

Improving Customer Satisfaction Measurement

Customer satisfaction measurement through surveys is an application of survey research. Many of the CSM survey design decisions that you have to make, such as the number of segments to survey, the sample size and composition, the method of questionnaire delivery, the incentives used to get respondents to fill out a questionnaire, the questionnaire format, getting a desired response rate, and the like are typical of survey research in general. It is beyond the scope of this chapter to discuss them all, but there are reference sources that you can consult.[2] Instead, we concentrate on three survey research design issues special to CSM: (1) how to link satisfaction to customer value, (2) how to determine which customer value dimensions are strategically important, and (3) how to translate qualitative data on customer value into a quantitative satisfaction questionnaire.

In Figure 9.5, we lay out key activities in the design of a CSM survey process. The first two activities ensure that we use the results of customer value research to design satisfaction survey questionnaires (issues 1 and 2 above). The third activity applies a satisfaction framework, specifically the model in Figure 4.1, to choose which satisfaction variables to measure (issue 3 above). The remaining two activities are concerned with analyzing satisfaction data, which we cover in Chapter 10.

Start with Value Dimensions that Are Important to Customers

Qualitative customer value research, as we discussed in Chapters 7 and 8, is an excellent means to discover the various value dimensions that your customers want. However, it will not tell

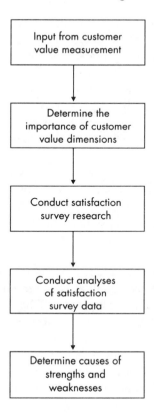

Figure 9.5. The customer satisfaction measurement process.

you much about how satisfied your customers are. Customer value data is, however, essential to guide the design of the content of a satisfaction questionnaire. We want a satisfaction survey to measure customers' feelings about the specific dimensions of value they think are important.

Look back at the list of benefit consequences in Figure 9.3 and find the list of value dimensions for the furniture manufacturer. Each of these value dimensions came from qualitative research. Management wanted to know customers' opinions about how well its furniture delivered these value dimensions, so they were used to develop items (i.e., questions) for a satisfaction questionnaire – for instance, how well or poorly do customers think the manufacturer's furniture helped to "create a feeling of warmth in my home," "create a feeling of beauty," and so forth.

Making the transition from qualitative research to satisfaction questionnaire design can be problematic. Effective customer value research often yields a rather large number of different customer value dimensions. You may not be able to get them all into a satisfaction questionnaire. Further, while customers may want many things from you, they typically do not see them all as equally important. Some value dimensions are crucial to them, while others are not as important. Clearly, a satisfaction survey should concentrate on the most important ones, and so you have to be able to identify which ones these are.

Consider the dilemma faced by a beverage business unit of a large food company. Qualitative research using grand tour interviews (a technique discussed in Chapter 7) yielded more than 140 customer value dimensions related to both product and supporting services. Yet a single questionnaire could not measure satisfaction with all these value dimensions at once. No one wanted to risk getting low-quality data by wearing respondents out. For this reason alone, these 140 dimensions had to be pared down to a more reasonable number. But which ones should be deleted from the list? A good CSM process should be able to answer this question.

To reduce the list of value dimensions down to a manageable number, we need to apply a screening activity. At the heart of this activity are screening criteria to help you identify which value dimensions must be included in the questionnaire. Essentially, these criteria operationally define what you mean by "important." We think that important value dimensions are those that are (1) different from each other, (2) actionable, and (3) perceived by customers as being important in determining overall value they receive from a supplier. You may want to add other criteria, but for now let's examine these criteria more closely. If you would like more details on the entire screening activity, see Appendix II.

The Similarity Criterion. Some customer value dimensions interpreted from qualitative research may appear quite similar to each other. In that case, you may want to select only one of these for the satisfaction questionnaire. For example, suppose a bank learned that customers want to "feel welcome" in the branch and to "feel invited" by employees. These value dimension phrases sound very similar. If the bank were to include both phrases in separate items in its satisfaction questionnaire, respondents may think that these satisfaction questions are repetitious. The similarity criterion requires that you examine the list of value dimensions to eliminate this kind of redundancy.

To implement this criterion, start with the list of value dimensions from the qualitative research. These dimensions already should be phrased in the customer's own words. Then group together the ones that sound similar to each other. You may have to go back to the original data from the qualitative research to be sure about what they mean to customers. For instance, returning to the bank illustration, analysts can reread surrounding passages from transcripts of its customer value interviews to confirm that customers mean the same thing when talking about "feeling welcome" and "feeling invited."[3] Finally, from each grouping, select one or two phrases to represent the underlying common value dimension.

The Actionability Criterion. As we said before, if you know that you cannot act on a particular value dimension regardless of what satisfaction data show, it probably will not do any good to include that dimension in a satisfaction questionnaire. You have a case for dropping such a dimension from your list. Suppose you supply a material used in your customer's manufacturing process. Your customers may want stronger bonding between your material and others used in their product. If you know that there is nothing you can do to your material to help customers with bonding applications in their manufacturing process, why ask about satisfaction with bonding strength consequences? Unless you have some other use in mind, this satisfaction data will not be actionable for you.

Managers who will use the satisfaction data must be

involved in implementing this criterion. Only they know what decisions will depend on the satisfaction data and what can or cannot be done based on the data analysis results.

The Importance-to-Customers Criterion. This criterion brings the "voice of the customer" into the screening activity. Customers can be asked about which value dimensions they feel are most important to them. There are a variety of different techniques available for obtaining customer opinions, and several are presented in Appendix II. Essentially, each alternative uses customer responses to a set of questions to scale customer value dimensions from most to least important based on their ranking or rating. The nature of the questions differ depending on the particular technique. Starting at the top of this scaled list, you then choose from it the value dimensions to include in your satisfaction questionnaire, down to a predetermined cut-off point. Often the maximum allowed length of the questionnaire determines what this cut-off will be. There may be as few as 10 or as many as 25 to 30 value dimension items finally included in the satisfaction questionnaire.

Measuring Customer Satisfaction

Recall from satisfaction theory (Figure 4.1) that there are three major categories of variables: (1) the value dimension performance and disconfirmation drivers of satisfaction, (2) satisfaction feelings, and (3) various behavioral outcomes of satisfaction, such as WOM, commitment or loyalty to the brand, intentions to repurchase, and repeat purchases. Typically, we see corresponding measures from each category included in satisfaction survey questionnaires. Figure 9.6 illustrates questionnaire scale items for selected variables to help you see the differences between them. Take a minute to look at differences in wording and scale anchors.

Satisfaction Drivers. Customers easily express global or overall satisfaction, but we want to know what underlies these feelings. Satisfaction theory tells us that how customers perceive the performance of your product and services determines these

(a)
Performance Perceptions

How well did we perform? Please rate our performance on each of the following items by circling the number that best represents your opinon:

	Excellent						Very Poor
Product quality	1	2	3	4	5	6	7
Product consistency	1	2	3	4	5	6	7
Innovation	1	2	3	4	5	6	7

(b)
Disconfirmation Perceptions

Compared to the performance of your most preferred supplier, how well did we do? Please rate our performance compared to this competitive supplier on the following items by circling the number that best represents your opinion:

	Much Better						Much worse
Product quality	1	2	3	4	5	6	7
Product consistency	1	2	3	4	5	6	7
Innovation	1	2	3	4	5	6	7

(c)
Satisfaction Feelings – Evaluation Overall

Considering everything, how satisfied are you with (name of product/service)?

Very dissatisfied	Somewhat dissatisfied	Slightly dissatisfied	Neither	Slightly satisfied	Somewhat satisfied	Very satisfied
1	2	3	4	5	6	7

(d)
Satisfaction Feelings – Emotion Overall

How do you feel about (name of product/service)?

Delighted	Pleased	Slightly Pleased	Neutral	Slightly Unhappy	Unhappy	Terrible
1	2	3	4	5	6	7

cont'd

Figure 9.6. Measurement scales for satisfaction variables.

(e)
Satisfaction Outcome – WOM

What are the chances that you will:

	No chance						Certain I will
Make *positive* comments to your family/friends about (name of product/service):	1	2	3	4	5	6	7
Make *negative* comments to your family/friends about (name of product/service):	1	2	3	4	5	6	7

(f)
Satisfaction Outcome – Intentions

What are the chances that you will:

	No Chance						Certain I will
Buy another (name of product/service) again the next time:	1	2	3	4	5	6	7

Figure 9.6   Measurement scales for satisfaction variables, *cont'd from previous page.*

global satisfaction feelings. So you can measure either perceived performance or disconfirmation (i.e., perceived performance compared to a standard) on each of the important value dimensions to uncover your strengths and weaknesses on these satisfaction drivers.

Measuring *perceived performance* is relatively easy. This is commonly done by using rating questions. One technique, for instance, is to ask customers to rate a supplier's performance on each of the important value dimensions on a poor-to-excellent scale (see Figure 9.6(a)). These dimensions may be attributes such as friendliness of customer contact personnel, speed of delivery, innovativeness of support personnel, product quality, and the like. Or the dimensions may include benefit consequences such as a customer's confidence in getting a successful repair the first time, a feeling of being valued, a feeling of trust, and a belief that the service is convenient to use.

Measuring *disconfirmation* is a little more complicated. You want to find out whether a customer perceives that your product's performance on each value dimension exceeds (positive disconfirmation), equals (confirmation), or falls below (negative disconfirmation) a comparison standard. The complexity comes from having to select a comparison standard against which respondents are to rate your product's performance.

In current practice, we frequently see "expectations" used as the standard in disconfirmation questions. "Expectations" are customers' predictions of performance that they thought would happen prior to purchasing your product and services. In a questionnaire, we might ask customers, "Compared to your expectations, how well did our product perform for you on each of the following items?" The "items" are the value dimensions derived from qualitative customer value research, and respondents rate each one on, say, a five- or seven-point scale that ranges from "much worse than expected" to "much better than expected."[4]

The problem with limiting disconfirmation measurement to expectations-based ratings is that sometimes customers use other standards in their evaluations.[5] For instance, in one study we found that customers compared a supplier's performance against several different standards.[9] These standards were grouped into six categories: (1) the performance of a competitor's products or brands, (2) prior experiences in other use situations, (3) the experiences of other people, (4) experience with our product on other occasions, (5) marketer-supplied standards (e.g., promises), and (6) internal standards (e.g., ideals, desired end states). So a disconfirmation question could just as well use any one of these standards. For instance, in Figure 9.6(b), the standard is a competitive supplier's brand performance.

The problem we face is selecting from among the several possible standards that customers might use to frame a disconfirmation question. This issue is important because the data results likely will differ depending on which standard you select.

We know of one instance in which a company conducted a test of this difference. It changed the standard used in disconfirmation questions in alternate survey questionnaires. Management was surprised to find out that resulting average scores differed significantly between the test questionnaires – scores summed over value dimensions ranged from the 90s (very high scores) to the 70s (moderate scores), depending on which standard was used. Interestingly, top management felt that the scores in the 70s provided much more impetus for encouraging improvement efforts than did those in the 90s.

Based on our research, we believe that customers are capable of making evaluations based on any one of several standards to which you cue them. Ask your customers how you performed compared to a competitor, and they will give you an answer. Or ask them how you performed compared to what you promised you would do for them, and they will answer that question, too. In each case, customers will see the question as meaningful. The issue you must address concerns which standard to use. We designed a three-step process for determining which comparison standard to use in a particular satisfaction study.

First, analyze the qualitative data from the customer value research to discover the comparison standards that customers mention most often on their own. These standards become the alternatives. Also note the wording that customers use for each one.

Second, decide which of these standards would provide managers with the most actionable data. You have to consider the decisions to be made based on the disconfirmation data. For instance, if the data will be used to assist in the design of a superior product (e.g., as input into a quality function deployment [QFD] exercise), then the "best" standard probably is the "performance of a key competitor." On the other hand, if the data are used to evaluate the effectiveness of advertising, then "seller's promises" might be a better comparison standard. If the data are to have multiple applications, then you must compromise. Which standard has the widest actionability potential?

Finally, you should test how well the standard you want to use in disconfirmation questions actually predicts global satisfaction feelings or satisfaction outcomes. The most stringent test tries out different versions of a satisfaction questionnaire, each of which includes disconfirmation questions using a different standard. Find out which one is most highly correlated with overall satisfaction: an intention to repurchase from you, the likelihood of recommending your product to someone else, or loyalty felt towards you as a supplier. Then choose the standard that is most highly correlated with the customer behaviors that you think are most important to your organization's performance.

Which should you measure, *performance or disconfirmation*? Research sheds some light on this issue. One study found that "performance" is most likely to be the driver for those products or services with which customers feel highly involved (i.e., have high personal relevance to them such as a VCR, car, boat or investment service), while "disconfirmation" plays a more important driver role for products or services that customers are not involved with (e.g., flowers, cereal, or a lawn-fertilizing service).[10] To apply this finding, study how involved your customers are with your offering or the product category in general. Let their involvement level dictate which type of question to use. Or you can conduct tests to find out which measure is more highly correlated with global satisfaction and satisfaction outcome measures.

Satisfaction Feelings. Satisfaction questionnaires also routinely measure customers' overall satisfaction and dissatisfaction feelings. Usually, these measures are intended to find out how customers feel about the entire experience with a supplier and its products and services, considering everything that has happened. Probably the most common type of scaling technique for this measure uses the words "satisfaction" and "dissatisfaction" as anchor phrases at each end of, say, a five, seven, or ten point scale (see Figure 9.6(c)). Intuitively, it may make sense to use these words, but you have to assume that customers interpret them the same way you do. We conducted one research project to find out what customers mean by the words "satisfaction" and "dissatisfaction." We were surprised to learn that consumers do not use these words very much when describing their use experiences with products and services. In addition, we found a tendency for the meaning of these words to be more cognitive (or evaluative) than emotional.[11] In other words, customers can say they are "highly satisfied" without feeling much emotion. Interestingly, this finding supports the intuitive belief of many managers that "delight" (an emotion) is a different phenomenon than "satisfaction."

Another approach to measuring overall satisfaction focuses on the "feelings" content of customers' evaluations, which may range from mild (i.e., pleased) to strong (i.e., angry). These techniques use "feelings" words to encourage customers to express emotional responses. We like to use the D-T scale, which relies on words such as "delighted," "pleased," "unhappy," and "terrible" to capture the range of emotions a customer might feel (see Figure 9.6(d)). There also are other scale techniques that have been used to draw out customers' satisfaction feelings or emotions.[12,13]

How important is it to measure satisfaction as a range of emotional feelings? This issue is related to the current thinking about competitive strategy. In practice, we hear more and more companies say that they want to "delight" their customers. In other words, delight is becoming a specific organizational goal. Donald Petersen, then chairman of the board and CEO of the Ford Motor Company, expressed this point of view when he wrote: "To go the extra step that can build a competitive edge, we must learn to delight the customer, as Colby Chandler, chairman of Eastman Kodak, once suggested – and even more. It is critical to inspire the customer's total emotional response – to reach the customer in a very positive way."[14]

If you subscribe to this strategic point of view, you should ensure that your satisfaction measures allow for a range of emotions to be expressed. That is, your satisfaction scales should measure both the direction (positive versus negative) and the strength (from mild to intense) of the emotion felt by customers in response to experiences with your company or its offering. As Edwards et al. put it, "To continue recording gains in satisfaction, it is time to add new dimensions to satisfaction measurements that provide a more complete picture of your customers' experiences. It is necessary to start measuring your customers' emotional commitment."[5]

Research can help you decide on the best technique for your organization. Test different satisfaction measurement scales to see which ones are most highly correlated with important customer satisfaction outcomes (e.g., word of mouth, intentions to repurchase, and so forth) and/or bottom-line performance indicators (e.g., sales or market share). We know of one company that spent several months and tens of thousands of dollars testing different scales to see which ones best correlated with (i.e., predicted) market share changes over time. Management felt strongly that there ought to be a direct link between satisfaction measures used in CSM and market share performance. The company ultimately selected measures that did predict market share change quite well.

Satisfaction Outcomes. Satisfaction questionnaires typically include selected satisfaction outcomes (see Figure 9.6(e) and (f) for illustrations). In our work, we classify these outcomes into four categories: (1) repurchase intentions, (2) word of mouth (WOM), (3) customer commitment or loyalty, and (4) repeat buying. You may have others that you want to build into your satisfaction questionnaire. As we explained earlier, outcome measures make it possible to periodically test for the importance of various satisfaction drivers and to test alternative satisfaction measures. You also may want to know the correlation between these outcomes and your organization's bottom-line measures to determine which customer outcomes most influence performance. We cannot stress enough that actionable satisfaction-related measures (i.e., performance, disconfirmation, and overall satisfaction) are those that are strongly predictive of important customer behaviors (i.e., the satisfaction outcomes) in your markets.

Other Satisfaction Questionnaire Items. To round out a satisfaction questionnaire, it is common to incorporate several other kinds of items. Demographic questions can help classify respondents to ensure that the sample represents market segments. Similarly, questions about the customer's lifestyle, values, and specific use behaviors (e.g., frequency of use, size or model used, and the like) may be used for the same purpose. Finally, a satisfaction questionnaire should end with a broad, open-ended question asking respondents to write comments about their experience with the products and services. The following offers a suggested satisfaction questionnaire content organized by sections.

Satisfaction Questionnaire Design. We believe that no "standard" questionnaire will be right for every organization. Measuring satisfaction means asking the right questions of your customers, and these questions will differ depending on the organization, its customers, and their use situation. The quality of the data that you get depends heavily on both *what* questions are asked and *how* they are asked. For this reason, we presented the design of a satisfaction questionnaire as a process of making choices in Figure 9.7. You have to work though these choices to determine what is best for your organization.

We laid out important issues in order to encourage you to consider the trade-offs you face during questionnaire design. In doing so, you will go through several iterations before you have a questionnaire ready to send to customers. You can get some help along the way. Get potential users of the satisfaction data involved to consider how actionable resulting data is likely to be. Show versions of your questionnaires to people on your research staff, outside consultants, and research counterparts in noncompeting companies. Their feedback can be invaluable. Also, use pilot research to test alternative formats. This up-front questionnaire design effort can make an important difference in the contribution that surveys make to a CSM system.

Summary

In this chapter, we tackled the complex task of measuring customer satisfaction. We started by linking CSM to an organization's customer satisfaction goals. If you want to manage

1. Background about the product or service use behavior (e.g., frequency of purchase or use, brands purchased, and so forth)

2. Performance or disconfirmation perceptions about customer value dimensions

3. Overall satisfaction

4. Satisfaction outcomes (e.g., word of mouth, intentions, loyalty)

5. Respondent characteristics (e.g., involvement, lifestyle, demographics)

6. Open-ended question asking for comments about the product or service and its uses

Figure 9.7. Content of a satisfaction questionnaire.

toward customers, you need data to tell you how well you are doing, and that, in a nutshell, is the purpose of CSM. It is a process and, like any other process, it must be continuously improved.

Ideas for improving your CSM can come from current practice. We discussed some of the trends occurring in the world of business and drew conclusions from them. For instance, we compared direct and indirect methods for measuring customer satisfaction, and showed how they complement each other. Eventually, you have to think about a CSM system to integrate data describing different aspects of the satisfaction (e.g., drivers, global satisfaction, satisfaction outcomes, complaints, and so forth).

We also argued that satisfaction is interrelated with customer value. Using the customer value hierarchy concept, we showed why the current practice of focusing satisfaction measures on attributes will ultimately limit the actionability of CSM. In contrast, delving into customers' motivations for buying by moving measurement up to the consequence level in this hierarchy can make satisfaction data even more actionable. Managers are more likely to be creative in innovating ways to deliver the consequences that customers want in order to achieve their purposes or goals. In the long run, this approach should lead to more sustainable competitive advantage than just "tweaking" existing attributes.

We devoted a great deal of discussion to three issues pertinent to designing survey questionnaires. For one thing, qualitative customer value research should guide the design. We want to ensure that satisfaction measures provide feedback on how customers feel about the value they received from us. In addition, we want to lock onto the most important of the several value dimensions that customers may want from us. Finally, satisfaction theory tells us that there are three categories of variables that we can measure: satisfaction drivers, global satisfaction feelings, and satisfaction outcomes. Measures of variables from each category help to ensure that we get a complete picture of customer satisfaction on which to base value-delivery decisions.

Measuring satisfaction to get actionable data is only half the CSM process. We have to be skilled at analyzing satisfaction data to draw actionable conclusions. We turn to this activity in the next chapter.

References

[1] Sandy Corporation, *Customer Satisfaction and the Service Industry: A National Study,* 1988, p. 20.

[2] Rickard, Norman E., "Customer Satisfaction = Repeat Business," in *Creating Customer Satisfaction*, Earl L. Bailey, ed. New York: The Conference Board, Research Report No. 944, 1990, p 41.

[3] Hayes, Bob E., *Measuring Customer Satisfaction: Development and Use of Questionnaires*. Milwaukee: SQC Quality Press, 1992.

[4] Sandy Corporation, ibid., p. 11.

[5] Edwards, Daniel, Daniel A. Gorrell, J. Susan Johnson, and Sharon Shedroff, "Typical Definition of 'Satisfaction' Is Too Limited," *Marketing News*, 28 (January 3, 1994), p. 6.

[6] Cadotte, Ernest R. and Norman Turgeon, "Dissatisfiers and Satisfiers: Suggestions from Consumer Complaints and Compliments," *Journal of Consumer Satisfaction, Dissatisfaction and Complaining Behavior*, 1 (1988), pp. 74–79.

[7] Rose, Frank, "Now Quality Means Service Too," *Fortune*, April 22, 1991, pp. 97–110.

[8] Sandy Corporation, ibid., p. 26.

[9] Gardial, Sarah Fisher, Robert B. Woodruff, Mary Jane Burns, David W. Schumann, and D. Scott Clemons, "Comparison Standards: Exploring Their Variety and the Circumstances Surrounding their Use," *Journal of Satisfaction, Dissatisfaction and Complaining Behavior*, 6 (1993), pp. 63–73.

[10] Churchill, Gilbert A. and Carol A. Surprenant, "An Investigation Into the Determinants of Customer Satisfaction," *Journal of Marketing Research*, 19 (November 1982), pp. 491–504.

[11] Gardial, Sarah Fisher, Scott D. Clemons, Robert B. Woodruff, David W. Schumann, and Mary Jane Burns, "Comparing Consumers' Recall of Prepurchase and Postpurchase Evaluation Experiences," *Journal of Consumer Research*, 20 (March 1994), pp. 548–560.

[12] Hausknecht, Douglas R., "Emotion Measures of Satisfaction/Dissatisfaction," *Journal of Consumer Satisfaction, Dissatisfaction and Complaining Behavior*, 1 (1988), pp. 25–33.

[13] _____, "Measurement Scales in Consumer Satisfaction/Dissatisfaction," *Journal of Consumer Satisfaction, Dissatisfaction and Complaining Behavior,* 3 (1990), pp. 1–11.

[14] Peterson, Donald E., "Beyond Satisfaction," in *Creating Customer Satisfaction,* Earl L. Bailey, ed. New York: The Conference Board, Research Report No. 944, 1990, p. 34.

Notes

1. For example, see Dutka, Alan, *AMA Handbook for Customer Satisfaction*. Lincolnwood, IL: NTC Business Books in Association with AMA, 1994; and Naumann, Earl and Kathleen Giel, *Customer Satisfaction Measurement and Management*. Cincinnati, Ohio: Thomson Executive Press, 1995.

2. For more discussion of these survey research issues, see A. Parasuraman, *Marketing Research*. Reading, MA: Addison Wesley Publishing Company, 1991; and Don A. Dillman, *Mail and Telephone Surveys: The Total Design Method*. New York: John Wiley & Sons, 1978.

3. We can approach this analysis more qualitatively using factor analysis to examine similarity in respondents' answers to attitudinal items using all the value dimension phrases. However, this approach would require additional research.

4. For more examples of disconfirmation (and other satisfaction-related) scales, see Hausknecht, Douglas R., "Measurement Scales in Consumer Satisfaction/Dissatisfaction," *Journal of Consumer Satisfaction, Dissatisfaction and Complaining Behavior,* 3 (1990), pp. 1–11.

5. For example, see Woodruff, Robert B., D. Scott Clemons, David W. Schumann, Sarah F. Gardial, and Mary Jane Burns, "The Standards Issue in CS/D Research: A Historical Perspective," *Journal of Consumer Satisfaction, Dissatisfaction and Complaining Behavior*, 4 (1991), pp. 103–109.

CHAPTER 10

ANALYZING CUSTOMER SATISFACTION DATA

Some consumers do not like going to the store to shop for groceries. If you are one of these people and you live in San Francisco or Chicago, Peapod will do your shopping for you. Using their inexpensive software, you can specify how you want grocery items displayed on your computer screen, such as by category (e.g., soft drinks), by brand (e.g., Pepsi, Coke), or by some other preference. Then each time you want groceries, you can call up lists of items and their accompanying prices, and they will be displayed in the manner you specified. After you decide what groceries you want to buy, Peapod does the rest, selecting these items from area stores and delivering your order to the place you specify. There also is a side benefit – Peapod's customers learn to become more proficient shoppers by using coupons more effectively, doing more comparison shopping, and selecting only what they want.

Peapod is committed to learning from its customers. The company asks each customer how well it did after every order. About 35 percent typically respond on a given occasion, and over time most of its customers provide satisfaction feedback at one time or another. In addition, service personnel take calls from customers when they have a problem. Peapod follows up on all these responses to learn more about customers' preferences. Most importantly, these data are carefully analyzed and used to improve the company's responsiveness to its customers. In one case, data analysis led to adding a verification step to the customers' ordering process that significantly reduced the instances of incorrect quantities of items delivered.

The company's commitment to its customers has paid off in very high customer retention rates.[1]

Introduction

Many organizations collect satisfaction data. But how many of

them use these data to make a real difference in their performance? Every organization that spends money and effort on
satisfaction measurement ought to ask itself this question: "Do
our satisfaction data help us make better decisions?" In part, the
answer depends on what is done with the data. It has to be
analyzed, organized into easily interpreted displays, and then
studied by managers to glean key insights about customers. Only
then can the data help drive decisions.

In Peapod's case, managers routinely rely on customer data.
They go well beyond just getting satisfaction ratings; they
integrate multiple kinds of data on customers, devote the time
and effort to learn from all these data, and then use what they
find out to improve the processes for meeting customers' needs.
Peapod never stops learning about its customers, and that is a
secret to its success.

In this chapter, we finish our discussion of the customer
satisfaction measurement process that we laid out in Figure 9.5 in
Chapter 9. We concentrate on the last two activities in that process:
analyzing satisfaction data and doing follow-up research to learn
about the reasons for customer satisfaction and dissatisfaction.
In the next section, we briefly discuss some important preliminary analyses of satisfaction survey data. Then we concentrate
on three core kinds of analyses of these data: (1) satisfaction and
dissatisfaction diagnosis analysis, (2) satisfaction and dissatisfaction cause analysis, and (3) satisfaction score analysis.

Some Preliminary Analyses of Satisfaction Survey Data

As you may recall from Chapter 9, a well-designed customer
satisfaction survey measures several different aspects of satisfaction. For a full range of analyses, we need data on customers'
(1) perceptions of our performance (or disconfirmation) on
selected value dimensions (i.e., attributes and/or consequences),
(2) overall satisfaction, (3) satisfaction outcome behaviors (e.g.,
word of mouth, intentions to repurchase, and so forth), and (4)
customer characteristics and use behaviors (e.g., demographics,
lifestyle, frequency of use, and the like). We like to start the

analyses of these data by addressing two issues, one concerning segmentation and the other dealing with validation of customer value dimensions coming from the qualitative research activity in the customer value determination (CVD) process. (You may want to review the CVD process in Figure 5.1).

Analyze Data at the Segment or Customer Level

Consistent with our discussion in Chapter 2, we think that customer satisfaction data analyses should be done at the segment level. (In some cases the appropriate segment could be an individual customer.) Consider two things. First, customers in different, actionable segments desire different kinds of value. Such differences might show up as customers in one segment wanting entirely different value dimensions (i.e., attributes and consequences in customers' value hierarchies) from those in another segment. For example, from research on small business customers of a bank, we found that small business owners wanted "to be trusted by the bank based on their personal history of meeting commitments." On the other hand, large business customers want to receive the most competitive rates on loans. In other cases, segment differences might lie in the relative importance of value dimensions. For instance, customers in two small business segments may both want trust and flexibility when dealing with a bank. However, one segment's customers may think that trust is the most important value dimension, while another segment places much more emphasis on flexibility.

Second, customers' satisfaction feelings, and the reasons for them, quite likely differ across actionable segments. If you average data across these segments, you are likely to lose a lot of what the data can tell you because of canceling effects. Suppose customers in one of your target segments are dissatisfied with a key part of your service but those in another segment are highly satisfied. After averaging the data from these two segments, you might think that most customers are moderately satisfied. However, this conclusion would not capture what really is going on in either segment.

Organizing satisfaction survey data by segment also allows you to check on the actionability of your current segmentation approach. As a general rule, actionable segments should have noticeable differences between the value dimensions measured for each one. If you do not find these differences, you probably should question your current segmentation. For instance, in research that we did with one company, we could not find differences in customers' value dimension importance or in perceived performance across their current segments. This surprising result brought into question the actionability of the segmentation being used by the company, and so management had to rethink its targeting strategy. On the other hand, finding actionable differences gives you confidence in your segmentation approach.

Validate the Qualitative Customer Value Research Results

As we have said before, we believe that qualitative research is essential to learn about customer value. However, qualitative research is based on small samples, and so you should be concerned about the validity of the results. It is best to conduct validity checks by trying to answer the question. "Are the value dimensions that we discovered from this research the same ones that customers in the target segment want?" Because a satisfaction survey is designed to reach a much larger, representative sample of your customers, it offers a way of addressing this question.

Think back to what we said in Chapter 9 about translating customer value dimensions – the attributes and/or consequences – into items (i.e., questions) for the satisfaction survey. For each important value dimension, you develop one or more items in order to measure how well or poorly customers think that you performed on that dimension. For instance, in a survey for a luxury pleasure boat manufacturer, focus groups research revealed that customers wanted "to be proud of the boat they owned." So we translated that value dimension into a satisfaction questionnaire item by asking, on a seven-point scale ranging from "very poorly" to "very well," how proud the respondent was to own the company's boat. Similarly, each item in the questionnaire operationalizes a particular value dimension.

One validation approach asks customer satisfaction survey respondents to tell you whether these items represent the important value dimensions that they want. (See Appendix II for discussion of techniques for measuring value dimension item importance.) These data enable you to prioritize each value dimension, from most to least important. We assume that the more important an item is perceived by customers, the more likely it is to drive their behavior. So, if you have incorporated valid value dimension items into your satisfaction questionnaire, what should the pattern of importance ordering look like within a segment? They all should range from moderately important to highly important. Suppose customers rate a value dimension item low in importance. It probably is not a driver of customer behavior, and so you may want to exclude that item from your next satisfaction survey.

What if your satisfaction survey questionnaire does not have questions about the importance of the value items? An alternative validation approach takes advantage of the fact that satisfaction surveys typically yield data on the customers' (1) overall satisfaction and/or (2) satisfaction outcomes. We can use these latter data to find out which value performance (or disconfirmation) items are most correlated with the customers' behavior. These items are the behavior drivers. For instance, suppose the boat manufacturer finds out that "being proud of the boat I own" really is an important consequence that customers want. Their perceived performance rating for the boat on this value dimension should correlate highly with their overall satisfaction, intention to repurchase, positive word of mouth, and the like. The stronger the correlation, the more likely that "pride in boat" is a valid behavioral driver for customers in the manufacturer's segment.

In the next sections, we assume that these preliminary analyses have been done. Just remember, analyze satisfaction data separately for each segment and validate the value dimensions selected for the survey. Now let's see what else we can learn from satisfaction data.

Satisfaction and Dissatisfaction Diagnosis Analysis

Organizations that want to manage toward customers have to find out how well their various processes deliver customer value.

Part of that learning comes from analyzing internal data on process performance. These data come from technical measures of quality unique to each individual process. A distribution company, for instance, may measure quality of a customer service process in terms of time to respond to a customer's order, while a phone company wants to know the percent of time a telephone call goes through. However, internal quality measures alone do not say much about the extent to which that process is delivering value perceived by your customers.[2] Your internal data may show that your process is performing well, and yet customers may not think they are getting what *they* want. Customers' perceptions are what count, and so you have to ask, "How well do my customers think that we are performing?"

Customer satisfaction survey data complements internal process quality data by adding the customer's perspective. Through diagnosis analyses of satisfaction data, we can pinpoint where our customers feel we are doing well and where we need to improve. Performance analysis and gaps analysis are two effective ways to draw these conclusions from satisfaction data.

Performance Analysis

As the name suggests, performance analysis focuses on customers' perceptions of a supplier's performance on individual value dimensions. For instance, a pleasure boat manufacturer wanted to know how well or poorly customers thought its sport cruiser performed on benefit consequences like "safe for me to use," "comfortable for me to use," " attractive to me," "something I am proud to own," and several others. From these data, the analysis focused on identifying which dimensions customers believe are the manufacturer's strengths and which ones are perceived as weaknesses.

Before beginning this analysis, you have to define what you mean by performance "strengths" and "weaknesses." In our work, we define a supplier's performance strength as a particular value dimension that (1) customers believe is highly important *and* (2) on which customers think the company is performing well. By contrast, a weakness is a highly important value dimension on which customers think a supplier is not performing well. These definitions dictate which data from a satisfaction survey you will want to use.

To conduct a performance analysis, we draw on two types of data: (1) measures of the relative importance of each value dimension to customers and (2) customers' judgments of the supplier's performance on each of these dimensions.[1] Importance measures can be either direct or indirectly derived (see Appendix II). Both importance data and performance data are summarized over respondents representing the target segment, such as by calculating averages. For example, Figure 10.1 displays importance and performance data from a satisfaction survey conducted by a luxury boat manufacturer for its sport cruiser. (The data represent a single segment.) We call this display *a profile chart*, and we find that managers like its visual effect. It helps them quickly pick out their organization's strengths and weaknesses. Let's take a minute to interpret these data.

Reading from left to right, the first column in Figure 10.1 lists the customers' desired value dimensions – in this case, benefit consequences. The second column displays customers' average importance ratings for the dimensions. These ratings came from items that asked respondents to rate, on a seven-point scale, how much each value dimension contributed to their overall opinion of the total value received from owning and using their sport cruiser. Note that the relative importance of the value dimensions range from moderate (e.g., 4.9, 5.1, 5.4) to very high (e.g., 6.8, 7.0). This pattern helps to validate the selection of these value dimensions for the satisfaction research.

In the next columns, the Xs represent customers' average performance ratings; these express how well or poorly the customers believed the manufacturer's boat provided each benefit consequence. The solid line that connects the Xs reveals a performance profile. As you can see, the customers' opinions varied from "very well" to "moderately poorly" across these value dimensions. This variation in both importance and performance ratings is the basis for distinguishing between strengths and weaknesses.

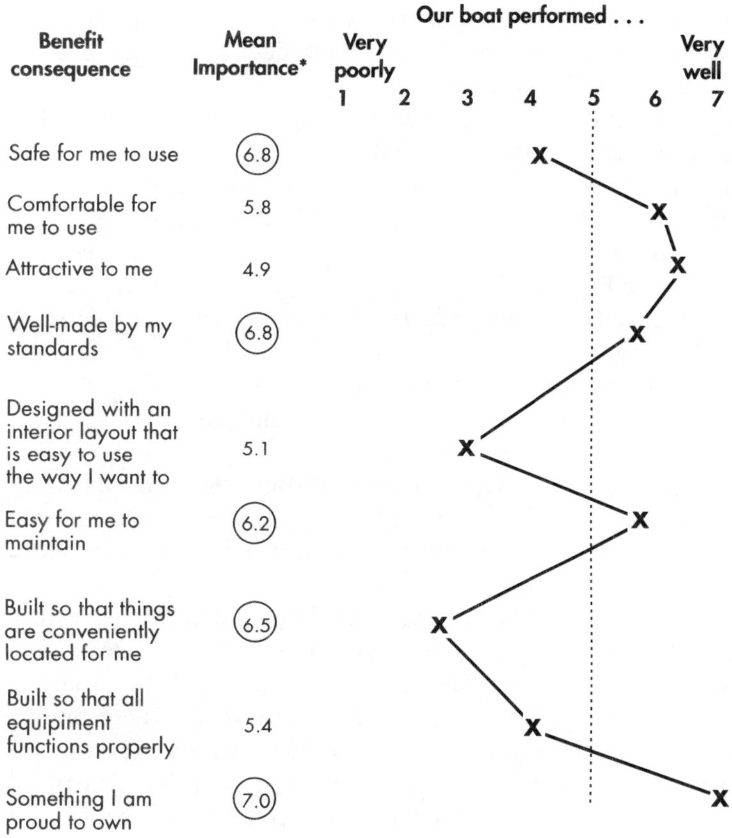

Benefit consequence	Mean Importance*	Our boat performed . . .
Safe for me to use	(6.8)	X near 4
Comfortable for me to use	5.8	X near 6
Attractive to me	4.9	X near 6
Well-made by my standards	(6.8)	X near 5-6
Designed with an interior layout that is easy to use the way I want to	5.1	X near 3
Easy for me to maintain	(6.2)	X near 5-6
Built so that things are conveniently located for me	(6.5)	X near 3
Built so that all equipment functions properly	5.4	X near 4
Something I am proud to own	(7.0)	X near 7

Scale: Very poorly 1 2 3 4 5 6 7 Very well

* Importance scale = 1–7; 7 is high
X = customers' perceptions of sponsoring company

Figure 10.1. Performance profile chart for a boat manufacturer.

Let's interpret this profile chart to find strengths and weaknesses. The analysis process is straightforward. First, determine how you are going to identify which value dimensions are "most" important and which have "high" performance. Operationally, this step requires setting two cutoff ratings, one for "most important" and one for "high performance." Usually, these cutoffs are rather arbitrary, although they should be based on the spread or distribution of the ratings. In this illustration, we settled on those value dimension items with a rating of "6.0" or higher on the value contribution scale as representing "most" important (see the circled "importance" ratings) and those with a"5.0" or higher on the poor-to-excellent scale as denot- ing "high" performance (see vertical dashed line).

Second, look for those value dimensions that are above the importance cutoff criterion. In this case there are five: "Safe for me to use," "Well-made by my standards," "Easy for me to maintain," "Built so that things are conveniently located for me," and "Something I am proud to own." Third, within this set of "most important" value dimensions, look for the ones with performance ratings above the performance cutoff. These repre- sent the product's strengths. As you can see, of the five most important value dimensions, the company has clear strengths on three of them – "Well-made by my standards," "Easy for me to maintain," and "Something I am proud to own."

Finally, find the most serious of the weaknesses. Look again at the high importance benefit consequences in Figure 10.1 and find the ones with below-cutoff performance ratings. In this case, there are two such weaknesses: "Safe for me to use," and "Built so that things are conveniently located for me."

Once you establish the cutoffs, the profile chart makes finding strengths and weaknesses quick and easy. It can handle any number of value dimensions. It also provides an effective graphic for presenting performance analysis in reports and in presentations.

To get the most benefit from a performance analysis, you have to know which internal process delivers each value dimen- sion. Only then will analyses of strengths and weaknesses pin- point where you should take action. Start with the strengths. Your corresponding processes may not need changing, but you can look for ways to reinforce with customers what you are doing well. For instance, the luxury boat manufacturer can use adver- tising to communicate the pride that its current owners have for their boat, perhaps through testimonials. Equally important, you want to pay attention to your weaknesses. Here corresponding processes or outcomes may need improvement. For example, the manufacturer's new product development center should rethink design decisions related to safety and to placement of instruments and equipment to see what improvements are possible.

All other value dimensions are "inbetweeners." They are neither clear strengths nor the most serious of the weaknesses. However, customers think they are at least moderately important and so you cannot ignore them. In terms of priority, they are value dimensions to consider after you have dealt with your strengths and weaknesses. Again, you want to know which of your internal processes link to these dimensions in order to decide if improvement is necessary.

Gap Analysis

In performance analyses, we set arbitrary cutoff points for the importance and performance or disconfirmation ratings in order to identify strengths and weaknesses. These cutoffs are only one of many different comparison bases possible. As you probably suspected, which basis you use will affect conclusions drawn from analyses of satisfaction data.

Please look at Figure 10.2. In this profile chart, we added a second performance profile labeled with "Os" and connected by a dashed line. Suppose this second profile measured customers' average ratings of a key competitor's sport cruiser. Using this competitor's performance as a comparison basis, we can now do a "gaps" analysis to uncover the manufacturer's *comparative* strengths and weaknesses. To consider the effect of comparison bases on diagnosis analyses, let's find the strengths and weaknesses indicated by these data and then see if they differ from those identified by the above performance analysis.

Again, start with the most important value dimensions. To find the manufacturer's strengths, look for the widest difference – or "gap" – between each of these dimension's average performance ratings and those of the competitor. Note that the manufacturer's ratings exceed those of the competitor on two most important benefit consequence dimensions: "Well-made by my standards" and "Something I am proud to own." These

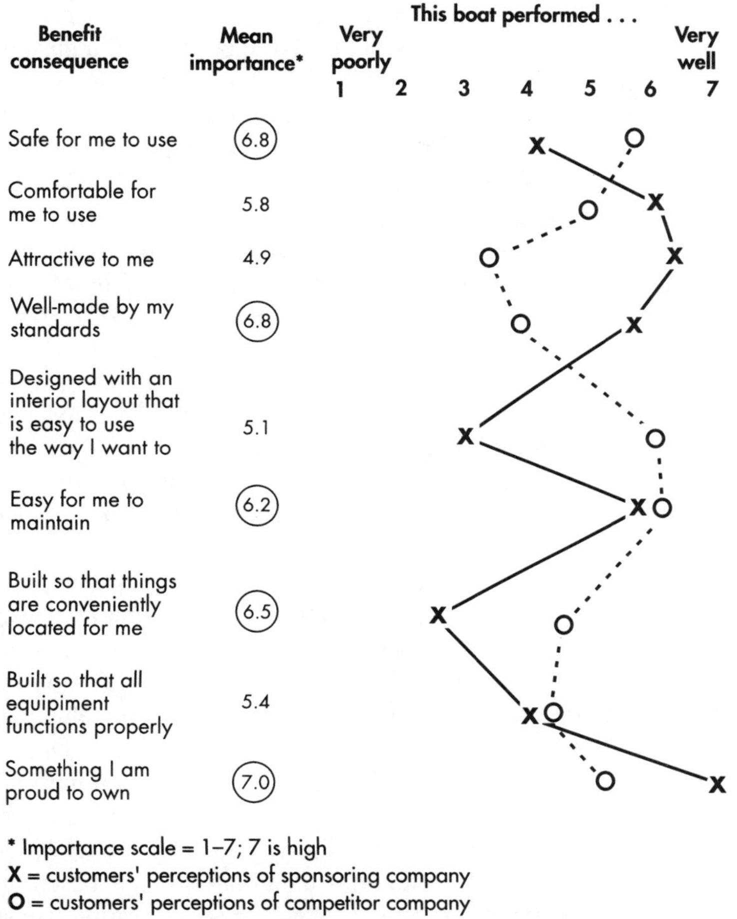

Benefit consequence	Mean importance*	This boat performed . . .

Figure 10.2. A performance profile chart for a boat manufacturer with an additional performance profile.

* Importance scale = 1–7; 7 is high
X = customers' perceptions of sponsoring company
O = customers' perceptions of competitor company

gaps indicate strengths. Similarly, we find the weaknesses by looking for gaps where the competitor's ratings on most important value dimensions are greater than those of the luxury boat manufacturer. Based on this comparison, three weaknesses stand out: "Safe for me to use," "Easy for me to maintain," and "Built so that things are conveniently located for me."

Remember that the only difference between Figure 10.1 and

Figure 10.2 is a change in the comparison basis. However, this difference caused one important customer value dimension, "Safe for me to use," to shift from being a strength (a high performance rating) to a weakness (a negative competitive gap). Instances like this one lead us to believe that diagnosis analyses of perceived performance data are sensitive to the comparison basis that you select.

In order to choose a basis, you have to know the alternatives. In addition to (1) arbitrary cutoffs and (2) a competitor's performance, we have based diagnosis analyses on (3) a preset performance rating goal for each value dimension (what rating do we want to achieve?), (4) a value dimension's rating from previous satisfaction research (did we improve since the last time the research was done?), and (5) customers' ideal or preferred performance ratings for each value dimension (are customers getting what they want?). You may want to consider others.

Unfortunately, we cannot say that any one of these comparison bases is always better than the others. Each one reveals a different type of gap. You must decide to which gaps you want to pay attention. You can make this decision in one of two ways. The first approach requires that you choose one basis to use. In this case, you have to consider which one is "best" for you, and that means doing some more analyses. For instance, you might see which gaps correlate best with customer satisfaction outcome behaviors. Do competitor comparison gaps better "predict" word of mouth or intentions data than do gaps based on comparison to past period ratings? Another consideration is cost of data. How expensive will it be to get data on a particular comparison basis?

A second way to deal with this issue is to rely on several different comparison bases in your diagnosis analyses. Look for consistency across these bases. If your performance on a value dimension shows up as a strength or weakness regardless of the basis, you can confidently decide to focus action on that dimension. Even in those cases where you find inconsistency among different gaps analyses, you may learn something important. For instance, suppose a value dimension shows up as a strength when the customers' average performance rating is compared to your goal but as a weakness when compared to a competitor's rating. You may conclude that your goal was set too low for the level of competitive pressure you face in that segment. Your customers want more from you than you thought.

Displaying Data for Diagnosis Analysis

How you display diagnosis data affects the ease of highlighting your organization's strengths and weaknesses. The profile charts in Figures 10.1 and 10.2 illustrate one way to display these data. Another popular way to display diagnosis data uses a matrix such as the ones shown in Figure 10.3(a) and (b).

Matrices categorize the value dimensions into different cells based on customers' perceptions. The matrix is constructed from value dimension data from the satisfaction survey, such as by perceived importance versus performance ratings as in Figure 10.3(a). Reading across or down the matrix, note that the specific category splits are "high" versus "low." Be sure you know how the "high" and "low" ratings were determined. Some analysts use a median split – those ratings above the median are considered "high," while those below the median are "low." There are other methods. For instance, you might only consider the top third or quarter of the ratings as "high" and the bottom third or quarter as "low." Each cell, then, contains the specific value dimensions that meet the criteria for that category.

Every matrix cell has a different strategic or tactical meaning, depending on how it is set up. In Figure 10.3(a), customer value dimensions are categorized according to both importance and performance ratings. The label for each cell reflects a strategic meaning for the value dimensions in that cell. For instance, those dimensions that represent strengths (i.e., high importance, high performance) are grouped into the lower right-hand cell, while weaknesses are grouped in the lower left-hand cell. Like profile charts, matrices make interpretation of data quick and easy.

The matrix in Figure 10.3(b) reorganizes value dimensions according to importance and competitive comparison gaps. Because the comparison basis used to interpret customers' ratings

(a)
Importance/Performance Matrix

Customer value dimension performance is:

		Low	High
Customer value dimension importance is:	Low	No strategic significance	Potential for cost saving
	High	Seller weaknesses	Seller strengths

(b)
Importance/Competitive Difference Matrix

Competitive difference on value dimension is perceived as:

		Low	High
Customer value dimension importance is:	Low	No strategic significance	Competitive distinctiveness
	High	Competitive standards	Competitive differential advantage

Figure 10.3. Matrix form for presenting results of gaps analyses.

changed from that used in Figure 10.3(a), the strategic and tactical significance labels changed as well. For example, this matrix encourages managers to think about opportunities for building competitive advantage by focusing on the value dimensions categorized into the lower right-hand cell or trying to move a value dimension into the lower right-hand cell.

Which form for displaying diagnosis data do you prefer? We find that some managers prefer the profile chart, while others like the matrix. Personal preference of users of the analyses should rule the decision.

Satisfaction and Dissatisfaction Cause Analysis

Diagnosis analysis pinpoints strengths and weaknesses but says very little about underlying reasons for them. Yet we see many organizations that expect their managers to plan and implement improvement actions based on these data alone. Unfortunately, if you do not fully understand what has caused a low performance rating, you can only guess at what actions might lead to a higher rating the next time. Managers must "shoot in the dark," trying out different actions to see which ones work. This trial-and-error approach can be expensive and frustrating. Worse still, frustration can create a general unhappiness with the whole CSM process.

You are more likely to settle on an appropriate course of action early if you know what is causing the customers' high or low performance ratings. We designed the last step in the satisfaction measurement process to provide this insight (see Figure 9.5). Because satisfaction surveys are limited in their ability to find causes, we turn to other kinds of data for follow-up analyses. To illustrate these analyses, we focus on revealed weaknesses, although we also should understand why customers see other value dimension performance as our strengths. Causes of revealed weaknesses may be discovered from (1) complaints data, (2) customer interaction data, and (3) qualitative research.

Complaints Data

Even when unsolicited, some customers will complain about problems they have with a supplier's offering. These complaints may contain clues to the reasons for weaknesses found in a diagnosis analysis.[2] For instance, suppose that ratings from a supplier's customer satisfaction survey indicate that one model of automobile is "not well-made by my standards." Simultaneously, the company's complaints data reveal that customers frequently complain about squeaks and rattles heard while driving the car. Integrating these findings, through a CSM system, suggests that the likely cause of the poor perceptions on "not well-made by my standards" is excessive squeaks and rattles. This combination of data provides much needed direction for taking action; improving that model's body integrity should lead to improved performance ratings from subsequent satisfaction surveys.

It is common knowledge that most customers who experience problems will not complain. Maybe customers do not want the hassle, or they might perceive that not much will be done anyway. The fact is that you may have to actively solicit complaints data, such as by making it very easy for customers to register complaints. Some companies are spearheading ways to better capture complaints. For example, Whirlpool operates an impressive, easy-to-use 1-800 service function. Customers call the company to talk, person to person, with a service representative who is trained to respond to whatever request is made. The content of each call is fed into a database that can be accessed by other Whirlpool departments, including product design, repair service, marketing, and sales. Other ways to solicit complaints are through surveys, after-the-sale calls to customers, and dealer interviews.

Customer Interactions

Most suppliers have periodic, regular contacts with their customers. Salespersons make calls on customers, engineers visit customer locations, financial managers talk with customers about credit issues, and so forth. In the course of a contact, observations or customer comments can yield insights into reasons for perceived weaknesses. However, if you do not have a reporting activity in place, these insights get lost. No organization should let that happen. To make this activity work, customer contact persons must understand how to report what happened and be motivated to pass that data on to a central location. Part of the motivation comes from everyone, supplier personnel and customers alike, knowing that these data are driving the supplier's actions.

Qualitative Research on Causes

Some organizations do follow-up interviews with satisfaction survey respondents, particularly with the ones who rate performance low on one or more customer value dimensions. Usually, the questions asked are open ended, and they encourage respondents to talk about reasons for their low ratings. These data can provide important insights into causes of a weakness. For instance, look at Figure 10.1. The value dimension "Built so that things are conveniently located for me" has a low mean rating. This rating was perplexing because the manufacturer spends a lot of resources on layout design of its sport cruisers. In one application qualitative research revealed that the instrument panel was easy to read by the boat's driver, but not by someone sitting to the side and helping with navigation. Product design subsequently focused on making the instruments easy to read for both driver and navigator.

A supplier also creates an opportunity to demonstrate responsiveness to its customers by listening to what they say, and, hopefully, correcting the problem. Such responsiveness can lead to subsequent greater overall satisfaction.

The same qualitative research methods discussed in Chapters 7 and 8 on customer value measurement – in-depth interviews, focus groups, and observation – are just as effective in this follow-up research. Only now the focus for the research narrows considerably to concentrate on one or a few related weaknesses or problems. For instance, one company conducts focus group research to learn about the causes of individual problem areas. Respondents are led through a group discussion of their experiences with the product that focuses on the specific value dimension where the satisfaction survey revealed a weakness. Sometimes the focus groups are combined with observations of customers actually using the product in a typical situation. The results of this research are fed to product design engineers and to the sales and advertising departments, who all share the responsibility for improvement actions.

In general, the diagnosis of strengths and weaknesses from satisfaction survey data becomes much more actionable when combined with follow-up cause analyses. You have to be adept at doing the detective work necessary to understand *why* customers are or are not satisfied. The improvement actions that you take are much more likely to succeed if they correct customer-perceived causes.

Satisfaction Score Analysis

A third kind of customer satisfaction data analysis has become popular among many organizations. It uses computed summary scores to measure *overall* customer satisfaction. These scores provide a customer-perception-based measure of performance of selected operating units within the organization, such as an employee (e.g., a customer contact person's satisfaction score), a department (e.g., a sales force satisfaction score), a product or service (e.g., a satisfaction score for a brand), a business (e.g., a satisfaction score for a franchise store), or a geographic area (e.g., a satisfaction score for a region of a country). Before turning to the analyses, let's explore how scores can be used.

Overall customer satisfaction scores usually trigger additional kinds of analyses of operating units. In one application, these scores facilitate improvement efforts by identifying high and low performing units. You can learn a lot about the drivers of performance by looking for those things that differentiate units receiving high versus low customer satisfaction scores. In-depth analysis of customers' perceptions of value dimension performance can help, as can an assessment of internal process performance. For instance, one manufacturer uses dealer satisfaction scores to identify the highest and lowest ranked customer-rated dealers in its distribution network. Further analysis reveals how customers perceive these dealers are doing in delivering specific value dimensions. Managers also look at differences in internal process performance, such as how much is spent on advertising, how advertising dollars are used, the rate of turnover among salespersons, salesperson training, and inventory policy. In effect, performance by the top dealers provides a basis for identifying weaknesses of low performing dealers. The analyses highlight opportunities for improving their performance.

Overall satisfaction scores also may signal where resources should be allocated. In some cases, it may make sense to give more resources to high performers. For instance, some organizations base employee merit raises or bonuses on satisfaction scores. Similarly, departments, products or services, or businesses with highest satisfaction scores may get more resources because of the opportunity for greater returns. Conversely, in other cases it may pay to spend more on low performers in order to bring them up to standards. For example, low-scoring employees may be targeted for more training, and products rated as giving low satisfaction may get more resources for improvements.

When using overall satisfaction scores to reward operating units, keep one caveat in mind. The score should act as an incentive to encourage high levels of responsiveness to customers. Each unit should see that its own performance impacts the score in a consistent way. More responsiveness ought to lead to higher satisfaction scores and vice versa. For instance, suppose a bank computes satisfaction scores for all its branches and allocates branch managers' bonuses based on improvement in these scores. You can be sure that each branch manager will keep track, over time, of the correlation between the branch's actions and changes in the scores. Suppose further that a branch's overall satisfaction scores peak at the top of the scale. Now, nothing the branch does can improve scores, and that creates frustration. We see this scenario happen too often. For score-based incentives to work, you have to be sure that satisfaction scores remain sensitive to the actions of an operating unit, and that requires testing and improvements to satisfaction measurement underlying the calculation of scores.

Finally, if customers are highly satisfied with what you do, why not tell others? You may want to promote how well customers rate your offering overall. Themes built around satisfaction scores communicate a sense that your organization is responsive to its customers. For example, Lexus has advertised for years that its overall customer satisfaction scores place it at the top of the list of automobile companies based on J. D. Powers's annual satisfaction survey. That theme reinforces the company's strategic positioning based on quality and value.

Calculating Satisfaction Scores

Essentially, there are two ways to calculate an overall satisfaction score. The first method takes advantage of the fact that most satisfaction questionnaires include an overall satisfaction question, as illustrated by Figure 9.6(c) and (d). The average rating for this question across a sample of respondents summarizes overall satisfaction (see Figure 10.4(a)). For ease of interpretation, you can convert an average score to a whole number. For example, on a 10-point satisfaction scale, an average rating might be 8.2. Multiplying by 10-converts this number to a whole number, 82, on a 100-point scale.

We sometimes see an organization decide to use a satisfaction outcome measure, such as an intention to repurchase or the likelihood that a customer will recommend a brand to a friend, to indicate overall satisfaction. In this case, the average outcome rating yields an overall satisfaction indicator score (see Figure 10.4(b)). Keep in mind that this score indicates overall satisfaction only to the extent that such outcomes are highly and positively correlated with customers' satisfaction feelings. Occasionally, you may want to test for such correlation.

The second way to calculate a summary satisfaction score is to combine the average ratings from each of the individual customer value dimension items in a satisfaction questionnaire. Please look back to Figures 10.1 and 10.2 for a moment. The rating for each one of these poor-to-excellent scale items can be totaled with the others and averaged to determine a summary score (see Figure 10.4(c)). You can weight the individual value dimension performance scores by the average importance scores to ensure that more important value dimensions affect the average more than less important value dimensions. Again, the result of the calculation is a single score that is usually converted to a whole number.

Because there are different ways to calculate a summary satisfaction score, you have to choose which one to use. How should this decision be made? Most mangers would like to use

(a)

$$\text{Overall satisfaction score} = \frac{\sum\limits_{i=1}^{n} \text{Overall satisfaction rating}_i}{n} \times 10$$

where: $i = i^{th}$ respondent from survey
n = number of respondents

(b)

$$\text{Overall satisfaction indicator score} = \frac{\sum\limits_{i=1}^{n} \text{Intention to repurchase}_i}{n} \times 10$$

where: $i = i^{th}$ respondent from survey
n = number of respondents

(c)

$$\text{Overall satisfaction score} = \frac{\sum\limits_{i=1}^{n}\sum\limits_{j=1}^{m} \text{Value dimension rating}_{ij} \times \text{importance weight}_j}{n} \times 10$$

where: $i = i^{th}$ respondent from survey
$j = j^{th}$ value dimension desired by customers
n = number of respondents
m = number of value dimensions

Figure 10.4. Calculating overall satisfaction scores.

a summary satisfaction score that predicts the kinds of customer-behavior-based performances for which they are accountable. For example, we would look favorably on a satisfaction score if it predicted customer retention rates. You should conduct tests to compare alternative satisfaction scores for predictive capability. Compare the correlations between satisfaction scores calculated in different ways and selected performance indicators such as customer retention, sales, and market share. The "best" calculation method yields scores that consistently are highly correlated with one or more of these outcome performance measures over time.

Analyzing Satisfaction Scores

Suppose we have settled on a method for calculating summary satisfaction scores. What can we do with them? These scores help to evaluate how well operating units (e.g., customer contact personnel, products or services, departments, businesses, and geographic regions) are doing. Let's consider three different kinds of analyses: (1) evaluating a single operating unit, (2) comparing similar operating units, and (3) comparing performance of a single or multiple operating units over time.

Evaluating a Single Operating Unit. By keeping satisfaction data separated by operating unit, you can calculate a score for a single unit for a single time period. For example, you may want to know how well customers perceived the responsiveness of your 1-800-service hotline during a month, a quarter, or a year. If an operating unit has different segments, calculate a separate score for each segment.

A single score for an operating unit, for instance 78, takes on more meaning by comparing it to something else. There are several comparisons possible and each has a different purpose. Suppose you set a satisfaction score goal in advance. Compare the actual satisfaction score with this goal to see whether the unit's performance exceeded, equaled, or fell short of its target. Or compare an operating unit's score with a corresponding score from the immediate past time period. Now you can see how much customers think that the unit improved its performance. As these examples demonstrate, changing the comparison basis yields new insights into customers, and so you may want to make multiple comparisons.

Comparing Similar Operating Units. If you have comparable operating units, then analyses across these units makes sense. Here, each operating unit serves as a comparison standard for the others. For instance, Toyota uses satisfaction scores to compare performance of different dealerships[3], as do many multistore operations, such as banks and restaurants. One purpose is to identify the relative performance of units in order to allocate management time among them. Presumably, the bottom performers need more help. Also, as we saw earlier, comparisons of the practices among top performing units versus those at the bottom helps to pick out those practices that drive high performance. You can then work with low performing units to improve their performance of these practices.

We think that you should be cautious when using satisfaction scores to compare across operating units. Research has shown that satisfaction scores for different categories (e.g., products or services, geographic regions, employees in different departments) are influenced differentially by factors not under an operating unit's control.[3] For instance, it may be easier to get high satisfaction scores for one product category than another due to differences in degree of competitiveness of their corresponding markets. Take these uncontrollable factors into consideration and perhaps even adjust scores accordingly before making cross-category operating unit comparisons.

Comparing Performance Over Time. Finally, you can expand the number of time periods over which you compare operating units to look for trends. Be sure that the scores from period to period are based on comparable data and calculation methods. You want to feel confident that an increase or decrease in satisfaction scores from one period to the next is not due to a change in the way you measured satisfaction. Rather, you want change trends to signal events that drive an operating unit's performance. These events might be market changes such as new competitive practices, or internal performance practices that are doing well or poorly. For example, an automobile dealer may see that satisfaction scores for its service department regularly dip down in the fall quarter of each year. That dip, when correlated with the fact that new car model introductions come at this time of the year, signals that the service department is having problems being responsive to existing customers as well as to the influx of new car customers at the same time. Complaints data from this time period may help management determine which corrective actions to take.

Summary

How much benefit you get from satisfaction data depends on the kinds of analyses you decide to do. In this chapter, we laid out four types of analyses, each of which complements the others. All are needed to help a supplier understand how its customers respond to offerings. We typically begin with preliminary analyses to check for segment actionability and data validity. Then satisfaction diagnosis analysis kicks in to help you identify strengths and weaknesses on individual customer value dimensions. Next, we turn to satisfaction or dissatisfaction cause analysis to help managers learn about the reasons that customers perceive our offering and the value it delivers as they do. We want to direct improvement actions toward these reasons or causes. Finally, satisfaction score analyses allow us to evaluate overall performance of selected operating units and the segments they serve. We want to know where and how to allocate improvement resources as well as reward high customer responsiveness.

Customer satisfaction analyses are intended to facilitate improvements to better meet the customers' needs. These efforts are ongoing, and so you need to repeat satisfaction measurement periodically to keep up with how well you are doing. As one executive puts it, "Unless feedback from customers is obtained regularly, it is impossible to identify trends and reliably determine the impact of continuous improvement on performance quality."[4]

So far, we have been concerned with what your customers value now and how satisfied they are presently. But, what will your customers value in the years to come? Admittedly, that is a tough question to answer. However, we think that you can make some reasonable predictions. In the next chapter, we show how you can go about this challenge.

References

[1] Pine II, B. Joseph, Don Peppers, and Martha Rogers, "Do You Want to Keep Your Customers Forever?" *Harvard Business Review*, 73 (March-April 1995), p. 109.

[2] Kitaeff, Richard, "Customer Satisfaction: An Integrative Approach," *Marketing Research*, 5 (Spring 1993), p. 4.

[3] Bounds, Greg, Lyle York, Mel Adams, and Gipsie Ranney, "Toyota, Part II: Customer Satisfaction Measurement," in *Beyond Total Quality Management: Toward the Emerging Paradigm*. New York: McGraw-Hill, Inc., 1994, p. 642–662.

[4] Lunde, Brian S., "When Being Perfect Is Not Enough," *Marketing Research*, 5 (Winter 1993), pp. 24–28.

Notes

1. Performance analysis, as well as gaps analysis, can be based on either measures of performance or of disconfirmation. As we explained in Chapter 9, the difference between these two kinds of measures depends on whether or not the questionnaire item specifies a comparison standard. Recall that performance measures ask customers to evaluate a supplier's performance on a value dimension without a reference to any comparison standard. Disconfirmation measures ask customers to consider a stated standard, such as expectations, performance of a competitor, or your promises, when evaluating a supplier's performance. The illustrations in this chapter are based on performance ratings, which do not specify a standard, but the analysis is the same when disconfirmation measures are used.

2. For more information on complaint data analysis, see Rust, Roland T., Bala Subramanian, and Mark Wells, "Making Complaints a Management Tool," *Marketing Management*, 1 (2, 1992), pp. 40–45.

3. For example, see Anderson, Eugene W., "Cross-Category Variation in Customer Satisfaction and Retention," *Marketing Letters*, 5 (January 1994), pp. 19–30.

CHAPTER 11

PREDICTING CUSTOMER VALUE CHANGE

It is more than a little perplexing to see great companies lose their dominant positions in apparently opportune markets. IBM built its business by meeting industrial customers' needs for large-capacity computing. Using innovative leasing programs for its mainframe computers, the company grew impressively. Then the market changed as technology opened the door for more personalized computing. New competitors jumped into the fray to meet emerging needs, and IBM was slow to adjust.

Similarly, Sears has had difficulty finding successful ways to maintain competitive advantage. Newer rivals like Kmart, Target, and Wal-Mart helped redefine discounting-based value strategies for both quality store brands and national brands. Consumers responded well to their value positioning.

General Motors also did not adapt quickly enough to the high-quality products offered by Japanese auto manufacturers. The Japanese were astute in meeting consumers' emerging needs for smaller, more economical, and highly reliable cars.

Sometimes even the best will overlook the inevitable. Markets and customers change, and no matter how great the company, it must change too. Loss of competitiveness often results from a company's inability to adjust its internal processes to deliver superior value to customers. The tragedy is that past successes may create an internal culture characterized by invincibility and complacency. Market position may erode so slowly that management has too little incentive or ability to alter strategies or the way decisions are made. New competitors emerge to take advantage of new opportunities. Sometimes, it takes a crisis for a company to begin making internal improvements in processes needed to compete effectively in evolving markets. IBM, Sears, and GM are responding, and clearly the game is not over for them.[1]

Introduction

In the previous four chapters, we concentrated on techniques and procedures for learning about value and satisfaction as your customers *currently* perceive it. We cannot stress enough that it is critical to do these phases in a customer value determination (CVD) process well. As we discussed in Chapter 6, these data can stimulate ideas for improving your value delivery to retain more customers. In addition, how well you execute value delivery strategies affects customer word of mouth, which can be an important factor in acquiring, or losing, new customers. As one executive at Coca-Cola noted, "Consumers who have a good experience with our company tell an average of five other people, but those who have a bad experience tell twice that many."[2]

Our experience suggests, however, that organizations tend to devote their efforts to learning what customers want presently. While it is gratifying to see more and more companies trying harder to know their customers, we must ask whether paying almost exclusive attention to current customer value is enough. Some organizations are coming to the conclusion that it is not.

Customer Value Is Dynamic

We all know that customers' perceptions of value inevitably shift over time. Our research indicates just how complex these changes can be. For example, your customers may change what they value in the interim between the original purchase and the next one. In one research project, we found that consumers consider mostly attributes at the time of purchase, but think more about consequences when evaluating use experiences.[3] Apparently, purchase criteria that customers use during a particular transaction may not be entirely the same value dimensions that drive their later satisfaction feelings.

In another project, we interviewed consumers shortly after they had joined a health and physical fitness center, and then again some nine to ten months later. We learned that trigger events occurred during that period that caused some customers to change their value dimensions. For instance, the center rescinded its policy on free babysitter service and began charging for that service. One customer became very upset because she had not been notified in advance. She showed up for a workout one day and was shocked when asked to pay for babysitting. From that point on, her feeling of trust—something that was not on her mind when she joined the center—became an important value dimension. Unfortunately, she did not evaluate the center very well on this dimension.

Two different aspects of customer value can change. First, a new value dimension may emerge as important. One of the most pervasive value changes going on today, for instance, is customers' desire for assistance from suppliers. Customers want the extras, such as help in learning how to use a product or service, convenient ways to complain about a problem, and faster procedures for responding to their requests. Service companies, such as those in travel, health care, and finance, are reaping the benefits, and there are opportunities for the service side of product companies as well.[4] Second, the relative importance of value dimensions may shift. Product features or price, for instance, may move down a notch or two as customers place more emphasis on services.

Customer value changes create market opportunity for those suppliers who see them coming. Others can get left behind. The difference lies in how well you are able to respond to emerging customer value.

Customer Value Strategies Require Lead Time

The reality is that it takes time to respond to customer value shifts. Some of that time is needed just to go through the process of making decisions on strategies. Consider the new product arena. A phone company may spend two years to design a new phone, a publisher may need three years to design and publish a new textbook, and an auto manufacturer can take four or more years to bring a new model car to market. You can only hope that customer value does not shift again in the meantime.

Even after a decision is made, there may be a long span of

time over which you are committed to a new course of action. Performance outcomes have to be successful for enough time to provide a return for the investment. For example, the U.S. market for sport utility vehicles has been growing impressively. Desires for safety, fun, and image among upscale consumers seem to be driving an unprecedented surge in demand. Seeing an opportunity, Mercedes Benz is building a plant in the U.S. to manufacture its own sport utility vehicle entry. Contracts have been signed, suppliers have been selected, and items have been purchased. The company cannot back out of these commitments quickly or easily. It must bet that the opportunity will continue to be attractive in the future.

Organizations not equipped to recognize changes in customer value risk opening the door to competitors. Further, the longer the lead time that you need to respond to value change once you see it, the higher this risk becomes. Organizations have to find ways to keep that risk at a tolerable level. In this chapter, we focus on an activity for doing that. The next section examines two complementary ways to deal with changes in customer value. Then the remainder of the chapter concentrates on one of them—the difficult task of predicting changes in customer value. We introduce a framework that describes major forces that influence these changes. We use this framework to lay out techniques and procedures for predicting customer value. Finally, we offer some suggestions for designing an ongoing customer value prediction activity.

Responding to Customer Value Change

Organizations can choose among several ways to respond to customer value change. One is to become faster and more flexible by designing and implementing internal processes that enable quick response to customers' needs. Another is to predict customer value change in advance in order to create more lead time for value-delivery decisions. These courses of action are clearly complementary, which creates a third option: to do both simultaneously.

Predicting Customer Value Change

Quick-Response Strategy

We see a lot of skepticism about whether it is possible to predict customer value changes. More than a few managers do not believe it can be done for their customers, at least with sufficient accuracy to help in making important decisions. If you think this way, you have little choice but to become fast and flexible at changing strategies in reaction to shifts in customer value when they become apparent. Perhaps this observation accounts for why many organizations are enamored with "quick-response" strategies. Within the past few years, for instance, AT&T reduced its new telephone product development cycle from two years to one. They significantly increased their odds of beating competitors to market with innovations.[5]

Companies have found many ways to increase flexibility and speed. Electronic data interchange, just-in-time delivery agreements, flexible manufacturing, and strategic alliances are just a few of them. By streamlining or even reengineering internal processes, organizations improve how work gets done. You can reap multiple benefits from this effort, including lower costs, greater capability to respond to customers' needs, and faster response times.

Quick-response strategies may work well when the long-term future is determined by a series of short-run incremental changes in customer value. Fortunately, change commonly happens this way. For instance, the demand for more support services did not reach full bloom over night. Instead, this change evolved over several years. Similarly, American consumers' desire for healthier foods in restaurants has been growing for quite a while. Eventually most suppliers see the trend.

Quick-response strategies depend on fast feedback from markets to make them work. You have to find out which strategy alternatives respond best to emerging customer value. Some organizations capitalize on information technology advances for this purpose. For instance, Kao, the Japanese packaged goods manufacturer, uses its Echo System to gauge consumer reaction to a new product. By combining point-of-sale data with data from focus groups and consumers' calls and letters, managers can quickly determine performance of a new product. One estimate is that within two weeks after introduction, they typically know what market response will be, which is an incredibly short period of time for such feedback. That might help to explain the company's impressive gains in market share in Japanese cosmetics markets over the past several years.[6]

The Kao example illustrates an important point. You cannot entirely eliminate the need for forecasting market behavior. Rather, quick-response strategies simply reduce the length of time for which forecasts must be made. Instead of years into the future, you may only have to predict customer preferences and behavior weeks or months ahead—a much easier task. Furthermore, forecasts focus on customer response to management's decisions and not directly on customer value change itself. The downside is that you may never fully understand what value change is driving customers' reactions to your decisions.

Predicting Customer Value Change

Quick response can take advantage of predicting customer value change. Speed depends as much on when you begin as when you finish a process. We believe that such predictions, by helping managers become aware of value change sooner, can enhance your efforts to become faster at responding to market and customer changes. In fact, by combining competency in predicting customer value change with quick response capabilities, you can exploit a powerful source for sustaining competitive advantage.

The popular business press talks a lot about changing customer perception of value, and it is not hesitant to make predictions.[7,8] Anecdotes suggest how anticipating new value helps organizations become more innovative in meeting customers' needs. For instance, Circuit City Stores is looking ahead to understand the needs of increasingly service-oriented consumers and how to meet them. The CEO sees a computerized information system in the company's future with data on each and every customer. Applications of these data are already on the drawing board. One involves linking the data to appliance repair services to ensure better performance. If a customer calls a service representative about a problem with his or her television, data on the television's make, model, age, and warranty status is sent instantly to the service technician, who then checks whether the likely parts needed are available before going to the customer's residence. Circuit City wants the technician to fix problems on the spot, thereby creating higher satisfaction.[9]

Change in customer value inevitably forces change in organizational value delivery processes. At issue is the timing of the two. Will process change occur as a result of a crisis or because management anticipated new customer wants? Hamel and Prahalad put it well when they wrote:

> Given that change is inevitable, the real issue for managers is whether that change will happen belatedly, in a crisis atmosphere, or with foresight, in a calm and considered manner; whether the transformation agenda will be set by a company's more prescient competitors or by its own point of view; whether transformation will be spasmodic and brutal or continuous and peaceful.[10]

In view of the compelling reasons for predicting customer value change, we have been surprised by our observation that relatively few companies seem to have processes in place for making such predictions. Perhaps one reason is that there is surprisingly little written specifically about *how* to predict customer value change. However, we think that techniques are available, and that organizations can and should be designing and implementing processes that use them.[1] In the next two sections, we show how this activity might be done.

The Sources of Customer Value Change

If you want to know what customers will value in the future, why not just ask them? Some have tried this seemingly simple, direct approach. Focus group research is a popular technique, and it is one way to get customers to speculate about what they might want in the future.[2] However, too often their speculations are not very informative. In most cases, we should not expect that customers are any better at foreseeing the future than anyone else. They cannot always tell you how their own perceptions of value will change.

What consumers in the 1980s could have predicted how value-oriented they would become as shoppers by the time the 1990s rolled around? Economic trends such as slow growth and organizational downsizing and restructuring have had enormous social costs on many consumers who lost jobs or saw their security evaporate. It is not surprising, with hindsight, that consumers would respond by tightening their belts and looking for more value from purchases. Yet during the 1980s most consumers were too caught up in the present to realize that these drastic economic changes were coming or how they would react to them. In short, most consumers could not have told you that their free-spending ways were going to stop within a few years.

If we cannot rely on asking customers directly about value change, what can be done? We think that another option is to employ an indirect process for making these predictions. We can identify and examine what is happening to forces likely to *cause* customer value change and use this learning to make educated guesses. For this approach to work, you must be willing to assume that (1) changes in customer perceptions of value are not random, and (2) that forces causing value change are more predictable than the change itself. We think that these assumptions are quite reasonable.

The Forces Causing Customer Value Change

The first step is to categorize forces that may lead to customer value change. Figure 11.1 brings together major forces that we think are important ones to consider. There may be others, depending on your particular market or segment of interest.

Macroenvironmental Forces. Economic, social, technological, governmental, and natural forces make up a locale's macroenvironment. They combine to create an incredibly complex context for customers, often affecting what they do. Most importantly, each of these forces is in a state of flux, which can affect customers' perceptions of value. Consider the economic

Predicting Customer Value Change

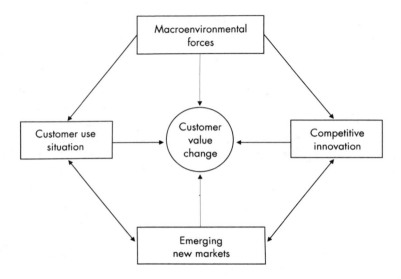

Figure 11.1. Sources of changes in customer value.

changes that are sweeping Eastern Europe. Whole countries are in the process of making a difficult transition from planned to economic systems based more on free enterprise. New businesses are starting up and existing ones are changing to provide more and more products and services. Already consumers are feeling the impact. They are faced with many more alternative offerings in the market place, and so they have to find new ways to make more complicated choices. Consumers with expanding options are bound to develop new notions of value, and both policy makers and business managers must respond to them.

Demographic shifts in a market area also can be profound. As the makeup of a population changes, so will its needs. You can count on customers changing their perceptions of value accordingly. Many businesses in the United States, for instance, target youthful consumers with their product and service offerings. This practice is longstanding. However, the age composition of the U.S. population is shifting rather dramatically. Just consider the following facts:

- Nearly 80 percent of Americans are expected to live past the age of 65.
- In 1983, the number of Americans over 65 became larger than the number of teenagers.
- By the year 2000, the number of Americans over 65 is likely to be nearly one fifth of the total population, about 40 to 45 million.[11]

As consumers get older, their needs change. Consequently, many organizations will have to think long and hard about what these older consumers will demand of them in the next decade. Some predictions are already obvious, including a greater demand for better health care services, wellness education, and retirement homes. Other, less apparent needs will no doubt emerge as well. Those companies that predict these needs in advance can take advantage of new opportunities overlooked by others.

Competitive Innovation. It is no accident that the great innovations of our time—the car, the airplane, the television, the personal computer, and overnight delivery service, to name a few—have created new industries and caused the demise of others. Certainly, the buggy industry has never been the same since Henry Ford's invention became commercially successful, and the radio industry had to change in order to find a niche in light of the onslaught of television. When customers are exposed to innovation, they see new possibilities. They begin to visualize something better than what they have today, and that can be a powerful source of customer value change.

Innovation in support services, promotion, and distribution also lead to customer value change. Think about the impact of evolution occurring in distribution channels. Major discount retail operations such as Wal-Mart altered the way popular, brand-name products are sold and created their own private brand offerings with an attractive price-to-quality value. These private brands, in particular, have been especially successful at taking sales from national brands as consumers become more value conscious.

Predicting Customer Value Change

In the world of business-to-business marketing, just-in-time delivery has been a major source of change in relationships between suppliers and their customers. This innovation, which involves all aspects of businesses from manufacturing and logistics to marketing and finance, caused business customers to evolve new concepts of value for services from suppliers. As one outcome, large retail customers have been able to lower costs and become more competitive for consumer demand for everything from appliances to packaged products.

Organizations seem to have trouble seeing innovation coming in time to respond effectively. This observation is especially surprising when innovation comes from within an organization's own industry. General Motors, for instance, apparently did not pick up on how important safety features would become to U.S. car buyers. Consumers gradually learned to look for things like antilock brakes, airbags, engines that drop below the passenger compartment in head-on collisions, and all-wheel drive. European automobile companies stepped into the gap by emphasizing innovative safety features to meet consumers' emerging desire to feel safe in cars.[12]

More often, major innovations come from outside an industry that is serving a particular market. These changes are more difficult to anticipate, but they still open the door for new entrants. The Post Office, for instance, did not invent guaranteed overnight delivery of letters and packages. This oversight helped Federal Express create advantage by providing new benefits valued by many customers. Its pick-up service, package tracking information system, and record for on-time deliveries have set new standards for this industry.

It may be that established companies and industries tend to become too committed to current technologies. We often hear the popular saying, "If it ain't broke, don't fix it." The fact is that it is easy to fall into the trap of thinking that existing products and processes are the best ways to meet customers' needs. Only when someone comes along with a better way do existing companies begin to realize that something needs fixing or needs to be replaced altogether. By then it may be too late. Technology forecasting should be an essential business practice in all organizations.

Emerging New Markets. Almost by definition, emerging new markets herald new perceptions of value. Customers in these markets are different in important ways from those in existing markets, and they make new demands on suppliers. What they want may eventually become an important source of opportunity. Look what happened in the education industry when business began searching for quality improvements. That spawned a major new demand for executive education programs on quality initiatives, processes, and techniques. Some universities and consulting firms were first to see the opportunity and jumped into the new market with innovative programs. In another arena, consider the growth of environmentally conscious customers. One study found that 39 percent of Americans think of themselves as being concerned about environmental issues.[13] They value being able to use products that are less damaging to the natural environment. Similar environmental concern is emerging in other developed countries as well. It is still quite open as to what kinds of offerings will meet these needs.

New markets typically arise because one or more of the other forces drives them into existence. In fact, all of these forces are interrelated. For instance, consumers' environmental consciousness is spurred by debate about serious macroenvironmental issues between advocates, politicians, business spokespersons, and the media. You should look for insights from forecasts of these other forces to try to see what new markets may emerge.

Customer Use Situation. As we described in Chapter 3, our concept of a customer value hierarchy relies heavily on the notion of a use situation. Customers perceive value relative to the context in which a product or service is being used. That context is a use situation. For instance, in one of our research projects a mother talked about wanting to feel secure and in control while driving with her children in bad weather. To her, being a good mother means keeping her children safe during or just after a storm, which is the use situation, and so she values these feelings.

Use situations are just as important to business customers. Often a key to value lies on some characteristic of that situation.

One of the authors worked with a specialty instruments supplier who brought a new microprocessor-based instrument to market. The instrument was designed to give highly accurate temperature measurements in industrial applications. The microprocessor feature was supposed to be a strength of the new product, yet management was surprised to learn that potential customers did not see value to having microprocessors in these instruments. Subsequent research on the customers' use situation uncovered what was happening. A customer used temperative measurement instruments in a factory. In the typical use situation, someone pushed a cart carrying the instrument down long aisles with rough concrete floors. The instruments received considerable jostling along the way. Unfortunately, customers' quality engineers did not believe that microprocessors are rugged enough to stand up to this abuse. Armed with this new insight, the supplier launched a promotion campaign to demonstrate that the microprocessor in its instrument would hold up under rough use. Customers had to be convinced of the merit of the instrument's design.

Use situations are dynamic, and a change in them can trigger new perceptions of value as customers learn what it takes to satisfy new needs. Just by understanding the new situation, you may be able to anticipate what new value may emerge. Think about the temperature measurement instruments supplier again. Suppose a customer decides to construct a new plant. In the plant, designers planned built-in instruments at the site where measurements are made. Quality engineers will no longer have to roll an instrument over rough floors. We probably can safely predict that these engineers will no longer worry about the ruggedness of microprocessors. However, other value dimensions are likely to emerge, such as longevity of the instrument.

Build Your Own Framework

You may be able to think of other forces that influence your customers' perceptions of value. If so, add them to the framework in Figure 11.1. You must feel comfortable that you have identified the major forces creating change in customer value for your markets and segments. The next phases of the prediction process concentrate on these forces.

Predicting Customer Value

The framework in Figure 11.1 is the engine that drives our indirect approach to forecasting customer value. If you understand how these forces are likely to change, you will get insights into how your customers' perceptions of value will change as a consequence. Figure 11.2 describes a process that takes advantage of this idea. We want to derive value change predictions from forecasts of change in these forces.

Build an Industry-Specific Causal Forces Framework

The framework shown in Figure 11.1 is intended to apply across the board to many companies and industries. It only lists categories of forces that may affect customer value. However, your organization may have experiences and information that suggest more specific forces on which to concentrate. For this reason, the prediction process starts by modifying our framework to make it specific to your industry and markets.

Consider a luxury boat manufacturer with sales in the United States, Europe, and Asia. Its management knows from experience that a country's tax laws can affect customers' perceptions of the value derived from owning its product. If luxury boats are singled out for a special tax, the effective cost of owning a sport cruiser goes up. This change will shift the balance between positive and negative value consequences. In this case, tax laws are an industry-specific instance of macroenvironmental forces and should be placed on this manufacturer's list of forces. Figure 11.3 illustrates various forces to which a luxury boat manufacturer may want to pay attention.

If you miss a critical force, your forecast can be off the mark. So be sure that you spend enough time and effort to systematically search for all key forces. Personnel in your own organization are one important source for this information. Marketing, sales, product design, customer support, and other functions with customer contacts can bring different perspectives to the

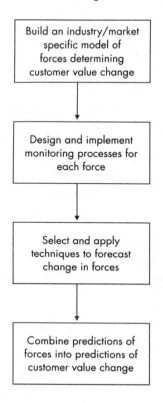

Figure 11.2. The customer value prediction process.

search. Of course, talking with customers can help, too. In addition, postmortem analyses of past customer value change predictions may be valuable. Often these analyses will uncover forces that should receive more attention in the next prediction effort. For instance, Sears no doubt learned from its previous underestimation of the impact of discount retail innovations on its business. If so, the company probably is devoting more effort to staying on top of emerging retail strategy trends.

Monitor Each Customer Value Change Force
Most change in forces that influence customer value perceptions occurs gradually over time rather than all at once. By monitoring

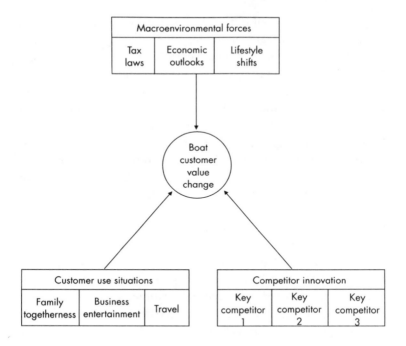

Figure 11.3. A luxury boat manufacturer's model of customer value change.

or tracking each force, you can develop an early warning system. Repeated measurement of a force reveals trends or patterns which can be extrapolated into the future.

Some forces are slow to change. In these cases, measures need only be made infrequently. Earlier, we said that the U.S. population is aging. This trend is highly predictable by looking at demographic research repeated every ten years by the Census Bureau. Aging is influenced by very regular and predictable birth and death rates. Other forces need more frequent tracking to see what is happening. Social attitudes and lifestyles evolve more quickly than do age trends, for example, and monitoring may be necessary every two or three years. Competitive innovation may need to be tracked continuously.

Some forces on your list may not be predictable. One that

occurs randomly would fall into this category. Suppose that a beverage manufacturer's management knows that unusual weather patterns, such as an exceptionally hot summer, affect how customers perceive the value in using nutrient-replacement drinks like Gatorade and Powerade. However, the technology for predicting weather patterns is not adequate for more than a few days ahead. This length of time is not far enough into the future to help the company make important decisions. Such forces are not actionable, and they should be screened out.

Data for tracking customer value change forces come from many sources, and the sources tend to be unique for each different force. Sometimes the data that you need can be purchased from a commercial service. For instance, if you want to monitor consumers' outlook on the U.S. economy, you can subscribe to any of several consumer-sentiment research services. To track other forces, you may have to collect your own data. Repeated research to identify customer value dimensions, for instance, may reveal trends in value dimension changes. Or suppose you want to track competitors' innovation. You may have to go to news stories from the media and reports that competitors make public such as stockholders reports. Observation of a competitor's products and service delivery may help as well.

While it is beyond the scope of this book to explore all the issues involved in setting up monitoring or tracking activities, we offer a few observations.[3] For one thing, it is likely that multiple forces will influence customer value change. You have to decide which forces to monitor, and these decisions are affected by the criteria that you use. Be sure that your criteria are made explicit and have consensus among data users. Some criteria to consider are: (1) the likelihood of a force exercising strong influence on customer value change, (2) the ability to forecast trends for each force, and (3) the cost of gathering and analyzing data required to monitor each force. For another thing, someone should assume responsibility for the quality and timeliness of these data. This person may be an information specialist, or an information function, such as a business intelligence department, may be designated. Finally, those who use tracking data probably will need training in how to interpret them.

Forecast Each Change Force

The next step is to predict what is likely to happen to each force. You can consult a professional, such as a futurist, for these predictions.[4] However, we think there is merit in making these forecasts internally. For one thing, the previous step in the process builds an appropriate database for this purpose. Who can resist seeing what predictions are supported by these data? Unlike the futurist's guesses, your database is tailored to those forces that management believes will influence your customers' perceptions of value in the future. Another reason for doing your own forecasting is that you can learn about the nature of and reasons for changes likely to occur. These insights encourage you to think about what the future has in store for you.

In spite of some skepticism about predicting the future, organizations seem to want to do it, or at least feel that they have to try. So, it is not surprising that many techniques have been developed and applied to forecasting a multitude of events, such as economic growth, company and product sales, and consumer sentiment. It is beyond the scope of this book to explore these techniques in depth. Those readers who want to know more about forecasting techniques may want to consult any of several forecasting reference books.[5] We also offer Appendix III which has a classification and brief overview of several alternatives. For now, we limit our discussion to the forecasting task.

Figure 11.4 lays out forecasting activities. First, select a particular customer value change force to forecast. (The previous step provides the list from which to choose.) Next, assemble data derived from the monitoring or tracking activity devoted to that force and evaluate it. You want to feel confident that these data are suitable for the forecast. This evaluation usually considers such factors as the quality of the data, its relationship to the value change force, and its cost to collect and analyze.

Your assessment of data suitability becomes a major factor in determining which of several forecasting techniques to use. You want to select the technique that best takes advantage of the

Predicting Customer Value Change

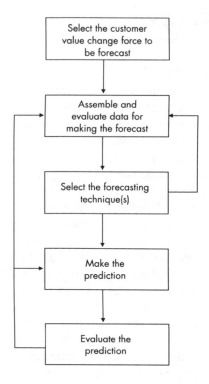

Figure 11.4. Forecasting forces that influence customer value change.

highest quality data available. As Figure 11.4 indicates, the forecasting process may recycle between data and technique selection as you try to determine the best combination to use.

Next, make a preliminary forecast by implementing the selected forecasting technique with the appropriate data. This task is a technical one guided by the requirements for the chosen technique. For instance, some techniques require a computer model and numerical data, while another may involve consensus building among a panel of experts (see Appendix III). Its helps to have expertise for this step because the accuracy of the forecast is highly dependent on the quality of the technique's implementation.

Finally, evaluate the forecast for reasonableness. No forecasting technique is perfect—they all may overlook something. One thing you can do to overcome this weakness in techniques is to assess whether additional factors need to be considered. It may be that a forecast should be adjusted to reflect factors that the forecasting technique and its data did not consider. We know of one case where a forecast was made of competitor innovation. It predicted a low level of innovation for the foreseeable future based on trends in the current industry. However, several managers believed that a new competitor was poised to come into the industry. This competitor would bring new product ideas with it. Based on this judgment, management decided to subjectively revise the likelihood of new innovation upward.

Customer Value Change Prediction

Finally, you have to convert forecasts of these forces into a prediction of change in customer value. As a starting point, we have found it helpful to combine the forces forecasts into one or more scenarios. These scenarios establish what the context will be like for customers in the future, and hopefully they will stimulate ideas about how value perceptions may likely change.

A scenario is a set of assumptions about a possible future.[14] In this case, the forecasts of each of the forces represent these assumptions. You have to assemble these forecasts and then assess how they fit together into descriptions of the future for customers. For example, the manufacturer of specialty temperature measurement instruments discussed earlier built scenarios based on forecasts of the likelihood of (1) stricter government regulation on the accuracy of measurements used for quality control in key customer industries, (2) economic growth, (3) competitor technology innovations in high accuracy instruments, (4) change in use processes of customers, and (5) new instrument competitors entering markets.

One way to deal with the uncertainty of forecasts is to allow more than one forecast per force. One estimate may be what you think is most likely to happen, while another might offer a less likely but possible alternative. For instance, you may think that a 2.5-percent growth in the economy is most likely, but a

1.5-percent growth is also possible. This approach encourages developing alternative scenarios to more completely capture what may happen in the future. Multiple scenarios allow you to consider the range of change in customers' value perceptions that might take place.

Table 11.1 shows two possible scenarios that the temperature measurement instrument manufacturer thought were possible. Scenario 1 paints a picture of significant changes that will affect customer value. Scenario 2 is quite different; it shows very little change during the period of interest. Note that management subjectively estimated the likelihood of each scenario occurring. Based on their evaluation of these scenarios, managers felt more comfortable with the "significant change" scenario and set about seeing how customer value might change as a result.

Applying Scenarios to Customer Value Change Forecasts. In the final step, consider how customers are likely to respond to scenarios with changes in what they will value. We think that those who will use the predictions should be involved in this step. You may want to bring together a strategic planning team, for instance, and ask them to reach a consensus on what the scenarios mean for customer value change. Brainstorming techniques help to encourage them to speculate about the kinds of changes that could occur in value dimensions and/or their relative importance. Or you may want to use a Delphi technique to avoid bias that may come from face-to-face interaction among team members.

Returning once more to the instrument manufacturer example, management predicted, based on scenario 1 shown in Table 11.1, that its customers' perceptions of value would change in two ways. First, new government regulation would cause customers to want more accurate measurements than they had in the past. In addition, customers' desire to cut technician labor costs would create a new value dimension described as "speed in reading instruments at the site in the customers' factories."

Ultimately, predictions of customer value change are subjective guesses. However, the purpose of the entire process shown in Figure 11.2 is to ensure that these guesses are based

Table 11.1. Multiple Scenarios

Source of CV Change	Scenario 1	Scenario 2
(1) Government regulation	Raise temperature requirement	Do nothing
(2) Economic growth	3.0%	2.5%
(3) Technology innovation	None	None
(4) Customer use situation	New desire to cut costs of measurement technician time during measuring process	No new customer needs
(5) Competition entry	One competitor enters market for high-accuracy instruments	No new competitor entry
Scenario likelihood	p = 0.070	p = 0.030

on reasonable pictures of what customers will face in the future. Managers must think about what the future holds and how it will be different from the present. We believe that spending time to consider your customers' future is a critical part of being truly customer-value oriented. One of the most important kinds of value that you can offer your customers is to anticipate their future and be ready to respond to changing needs when that future arrives.

From Predictions to Applications

Predicting customer value change should lead to better decisions. Again, one way this happens is when mangers have more lead time to develop new or improved value delivery strategies. You want to avoid the mistakes that come from making quick decisions under the pressure of a crisis. Further, predicted new value dimensions or change in relative importance of value dimensions should signal directions for strategy to take. If you think a particular value dimension will emerge later, you can look for ways to deliver that value. In fact, all of the applications of customer value information that we discussed in Chapter 6 can take advantage of our estimates of what customers' future will be like.

We know that just making predictions available does not guarantee that they will be used. Managers must feel confident that the information is worth considering. Perhaps the best way to ensure this confidence is to involve managers directly in the customer value prediction process. The process shown in Figure 11.2 offers several opportunities to bring managers in. For one thing, managers should be interviewed during step 1 to help identify forces likely to influence customer value change in their markets. Managers should also be brought back in at step 3 to help make predictions of change in these forces. Finally, as we said earlier, these managers should have primary responsibility for the final step of predicting actual customer value changes. Such involvement along the way ensures that managers understand how predictions were made and the rationale for them, which is a key to building the necessary confidence in them.

Summary

How customers think about value is dynamic, and so organizations must respond to these changes. Some are turning to quick-response strategies, and that trend will continue. We think more should try to expand decision lead time by predicting customer value change as well. The best of all worlds is to pursue a combination of both approaches.

We cautioned against relying solely on direct questioning of customers to predict future customer value. It may not hurt to try, but customers often do not know exactly what they will value down the road. We think that a more indirect forecasting process will help. You have to understand the forces that will influence customer value change. Our process for predicting customer value change depends on forecasting these forces.

We believe that the benefits of predicting customer value change lie as much—if not more—in going through this process as they are in the actual predictions themselves. All forecasts, whether of sales, market share, or customer value change, are guesses. No one can know for sure what the future holds. The real challenge is to develop an awareness of the possibilities. Out of the process for predicting customer value change should come strategies that are robust enough to deal with these possibilities. Jack Welch, chairman of General Electric, put it well when he talked about his need for "bands of possibilities," that is, rough alternative scenarios of the future: "I'm no guru. I'm not here to predict the world. I'm here to be sure I've got a company that is strong enough to respond to whatever happens."[15]

This book is about how organizations can make a difference to their customers. As we have argued, gaining competitive advantage will depend more and more on delivering superior customer value. However, it is one thing to say that you are customer-value oriented but quite another to put in place the internal processes to ensure that your customers receive superior value. Everything is in the implementation. You have to know your customers deeply, particularly what value they seek, before you can deliver it to them. And you have to keep up with how customers feel, over time, about the value that they receive. Your ability to change and improve value delivery in the future will make a critical difference to your customers, and to your ability to compete down the road.

Knowing your customers is an information activity. You can only be as customer-value oriented as your information will let you be. Every organization must take a hard look at its processes for gathering, analyzing, and using information to learn about market opportunity overall, and specifically about customer value. We believe that the customer value determination process presented in this book, which is based on the customer value hierarchy concept, is well suited as a framework for evaluating and improving your external information process. We think that it is crucial to make sure that this process is as good as it can be. After all, organizations with superior capability to know their customers will have a powerful source of competitive advantage in tomorrow's markets.

References

[1] Loomis, Carol J., "Dinosaurs?" *Fortune*, May 3, 1993, pp. 36–41.

[2] Waldrop, Judith, "Educating the Customer," *American Demographics*, September 1991, pp. 44–47.

[3] Gardial, Sarah Fisher, D. Scott Clemons, Robert B. Woodruff, David W. Schumann, and Mary Jane Burns, "Comparing Consumers' Recall of Prepurchase and Postpurchase Evaluation Experiences," *Journal of Consumer Research*, 20 (March 1994), pp. 548–560.

[4] Rose, Frank, "Now Quality Means Service Too," *Fortune*, April 22, 1991, pp. 97–110.

[5] Dumaine, Brian, "How Managers Can Succeed Through Speed," *Fortune*, February 13, 1989, pp. 54–59.

[6] Stewart, Thomas A., "Brace for Japan's Hot New Strategy," *Fortune*, September 21, 1992, pp. 61–74.

[7] Dumaine, Brian, "What the Leaders of Tomorrow See," *Fortune*, July 3, 1989, pp. 48–62.

[8] Sellers, Patricia, "Winning over the New Consumer," *Fortune*, July 29, 1991, pp. 113–126.

[9] Dumaine, ibid., pp. 58, 62.

[10] Hamel, Gary and C.K. Prahalad, "Competing for the Future," *Harvard Business Review,* 72 (July-August 1994), p. 128.

[11] Dychtwald, Ken and Joe Flower, *Age Wave*. New York: Bantam Books, 1990.

[12] Mitchell, Jacquiline, "Automobiles," *Wall Street Journal*, October 12, 1993, B1.

[13] Rice, Faye, "How to Deal with Tougher Customers," *Fortune*, December 3, 1990, pp. 38–48.

[14] O'Connor, Rochelle, *Planning under Uncertainty: Multiple Scenarios and Contingency Planning*. New York: The Conference Board, 1981.

[15] Henkoff, Ronald, "How to Plan for 1995," *Fortune*, December 31, 1990, p. 70.

Notes

1. For more on the importance of spending time on thinking about the future, see Gary Hamel and C. K. Prahalad, *Competing for the Future*. Boston, MA: Harvard Business School Press, 1994.

2. For more on applications of the focus group technique, see Bellenger, Danny N., Kenneth L. Bernhardt, and Jac L. Goldstucker, "Qualitative Research Techniques: Focus

Group Interviews," in *Focus Group Interviews: A Reader*, Thomas J. Hayes and Carol B. Tathum, eds. Chicago: American Marketing Association, 1989, pp. 10–25.

3. For more discussion of tracking activities, see Celente, Gerald and Tom Milton, *Trend Tracking*. New York: Warner Books, 1991.

4. For example, see Naisbitt, John and Patricia Aburdene, *Megatrends 2000: Ten New Directions for the 1990's*. New York: Avon Books, 1990.

5. A very thorough forecasting reference is Makridakis, Spyros and Steven C. Wheelwright, *The Handbook of Forecasting: A Manager's Guide (2nd Edition)*. New York: John Wiley & Sons, 1987.

THE CODING PROCESS

This appendix contains supplemental information about using a coding process to analyze qualitative data. Specifically, it addresses the tasks of developing and using a coding scheme, preparing a transcript for coding, preparing the coders, the coding, and reconciliation process and quality control.

Developing and Using a Coding Scheme

Essential Elements of a Coding Scheme

A sample coding scheme is shown in Table I.1. This is a portion of a coding scheme that was generated for the study of a health and fitness center.

Notice that the coding scheme has two levels of specification. At the first level, *major coding categories* are specified. These are identified by roman numerals. At this level, we have specified the major types of information which we wish to code; the object of thought, the point in time, attributes, consequences, and desired end states. The number of major coding categories that are specified determines the number of codes that are assigned to each thought within the transcript.

At the second level are *response categories*, identified by numbers which represent the potential levels or types of responses that are possible within each major coding category. For example, within the "object of thought" category there are four potential responses: the customer may be speaking about the health and fitness center where he or she is currently a member (response 1), about a previously attended fitness center (response 2), about fitness centers in general (response 3), or about fitness in general (response 4).

The numbers and types of response categories that are available within each major code category will obviously vary,

Table I.1. A Sample Coding Scheme

I. *Object of thought.* This category is used to identify the object of the customer's comment when talking about fitness or fitness centers. In other words, the subject of the sentence.
  1 = The fitness center to which the customer currently belongs. For example, "I like the staff here at (the present facility)."
  2 = The fitness center to which the customer previously belonged. For example, "My old fitness center was never kept very clean."
  3 = Fitness centers in general. For example, "They all (fitness centers in general) put this hard sell on you to get you to sign up for membership."
  4 = Fitness in general. For example, "More and more people in this country are getting interested in working out and having a regular fitness program."
  5 = Other
  6 = Not applicable.

II. *Point in time.* This category is used to note whether the customer is referring to experiences in the past, present, or future.
  1 = The customer is speaking about a past experience. For example, "When I first joined this fitness center, there were not as many members and it wasn't so crowded on weekends."
  2 = The customer is speaking in the present tense. For example, "They have changed the lighting on the racquetball courts and now you don't have to wait for them to warm up if you are here first thing in the morning."
  3 = The customer is speaking in future tense. For example, "I know that there are plans to add some additional aerobic programs, like step."
  4 = No mention of time or not applicable.

III. *Attributes (or product features).* This category refers to a product feature (either physical or service) that is part of the fitness center offering, including price, advertising, or other extended product features.
  1 = A tangible, physical product offering, including comments about the facilities and/or the equipment. For example, "They've added some new equipment."
  2 = Interpersonal characteristics provided by the staff, including administration, instructors, maintenance, and other. For example, "There is this one aerobics instructor that is really great because she somehow gets us all up and motivated at 7:00 a.m."

Table I.1. A Sample Coding Scheme, cont'd.

3 = The services that are offered by the fitness center, including parking, child care, swimming (or other) classes, individualized training programs, fitness assessments, and so forth. For example, "I was really disappointed in my fit test. I really expected more feedback about what kind of shape I was in."

4 = Overall comments, which may include several of the previous categories. For example, "I just think this is an outstanding center."

5 = Not applicable.

IV. *The type of consequence.* A consequence is any anticipated or actual outcome of the consumption experiences that results from the product or service or their use.

1 = Time. For example, "My workout uses up the entire afternoon."

2 = Money. For example, "The membership fee really straps my budget."

3 = Physical. For example, "I really feel stronger after a workout."

4 = Psychological. For example, "I feel better about myself."

5 = Other.

6 = Not applicable.

V. *The valence of the consequence.*

1 = A positive consequence; for example, "The fitness class gives me a good workout."

2 = A negative consequence; for example, "We really have to be careful about our other expenses so that we can afford to come here."

3 = A consequence that cannot be classified as positive or negative. For example, "It made me sweat a lot."

4 = Not applicable.

VI. *Desired end states.* Customers express a belief that they hold about some anticipated or desired end state they want to achieve.

1 = A personal value (or one that the individual holds about him- or herself) is mentioned. For example, "I just think that a healthy body also allows you to have a good outlook on life."

2 = An organizational value (or one that is held by a collective group) is expressed. For example, "My family believes in spending time together."

3 = A role value (or a desired end state that is associated with occupying a given position in a group) is expressed. For instance, "Being members here gives me the opportunity to spend time with my family and be a better dad."

4 = Other.

5 = Not applicable.

depending on the type (and specificity) of information that you desire. In the above example, four response categories were specified. For many of the major coding categories, researchers will want to consider multiple responses, such as those indicated in the sample coding scheme. However, at a minimum, two levels of response must be available for each major code; the characteristic identified by the major category may be either present (typically, response=1) or absent (response=0).

These response categories must be entered into the database in an identifiable manner. Therefore, each response category is assigned a unique *response code*. For instance, if a major coding category had only two responses—present and not present— these could be entered into the database as 1 and 0, respectively, or alternative response codes could be used (1,2 or A,B). The exact nature of the response codes will depend on the preferences of the researchers conducting the data analysis.

Obviously, the number and type of major coding categories, response categories, and response codes can and will vary for each individual research project. The content of the coding scheme is up to the discretion of the researcher. Regardless of the particular content, it is critical that clear, unambiguous definitions and examples be developed for each major coding category and response category (see the sample coding scheme). These will facilitate the coders in identifying exemplars of the categories and responses that are present in the transcript.

Refining the Coding Scheme through Testing and Iteration

It is important that the development of the coding scheme be an iterative process. Rarely will researchers develop the most thorough, effective coding scheme on the first draft. Typically, several iterations of the coding scheme must be tested and refined before it is "finished."

Once an initial coding scheme has been developed, several researchers (two at a minimum) should use it, independently, to code the thoughts of a holdout transcript. When the researchers come together after this trial run to discuss the effectiveness of the coding scheme, it is likely that they will encounter several possibilities for coding scheme refinement, including:

- *Unclear definitions.* The researchers may feel the need to further specify or clarify exactly what is being measured by each major code or response category. This should lead the researchers to reword definitions in a more precise manner and/or to provide clearer examples for the coders.
- *Unusable codes.* Often the researchers will find that they have overspecified their codes. In many cases, you may expect to find a level of detail in the transcripts that simply doesn't exist. In these cases you may want to collapse some of the overspecified response categories into broader categories or possibly eliminate codes altogether.
- *"Missing" codes.* At times tests of the coding scheme will reveal that there is additional information in the transcripts that has not been fully captured by the coding scheme. For instance, researchers may uncover important information that they did not anticipate when constructing their initial coding scheme. In this case the researcher should add the appropriate major coding categories or response categories to the coding scheme.

After refining the coding scheme, you will want to test it again by coding a transcript. This cycle of specify/test/refine may be repeated several times before you are happy with the coding scheme. Some of the initial coding schemes developed by our research team went through as many as six iterations prior to their use by coders. There is also the possibility that the coding scheme may need to be refined *after* the coders begin to use them. One should always leave open the possibility of using coder feedback to refine the coding scheme in process if necessary or desirable. Obviously, however, the sooner this occurs in the coding process the better, as any previously coded transcripts will have to be recoded following any change in the coding scheme.

Preparing a Transcript for Coding

The first order of business is to consecutively number each of the customer's responses in the transcript from start to finish (from 1 to n). The transcription should clearly delineate interviewer questions from customer responses so that this is quickly and easily accomplished. (We like to put the interviewer' comments in the transcript in bold type so that they will stand apart from the customer's words.) Each of these customer responses will serve as the base "unit" of analysis for the codes. Obviously these responses can vary in length, from one word (e.g., "yes") to many sentences. At least initially, we find it easier to consider a customer's entire response as a coding unit. In general, we have found that most customer responses during the grand tour are reasonably short and can be coded without difficulty.

In some cases, however, the entire response may be too large and may contain multiple "thoughts." When this occurs, it is necessary to subdivide responses into smaller units. If the coders find it necessary to subdivide a particular response during the coding process, and can do so with little disagreement, this option should be pursued. In this case, the coders should separate the larger response into free-standing "thoughts," each of which represents a unique point that the customer is trying to make or behavior that is occurring. When this subdividing occurs, it is easier to simply renumber the divided response, for example, response 26 into 26a, 26b, and so forth, rather than to renumber all of the subsequent responses in the transcript. You should be cautioned that subdividing responses can be a very time-consuming process, and there may be a significant amount of disagreement among the researchers about where, exactly, to best divide a response.

The opposite situation is also a possibility—that several responses may need to be collapsed into one. This may occur when it takes the customer several responses to the interviewer's questions before a complete thought emerges. In these cases it may be undesirable or even impossible to code the individual responses. When this occurs, the numbering of the thought should reflect this collapse (e.g., responses 3 through 6 were collapsed and renumbered "3–6").

Appendix I

Preparing the Coders

There are several issues to be considered with preparing the coders, including who and how many coders to use as well as how to train the coders.

The Number of Coders

Transcript coding is an inexact science. The application of codes is not always straightforward, and there is significant room for interpretation and inference. For these reasons, we feel it is imperative for at least two individuals to code each transcript. These two coders can provide a "check" on each other's work, they can cross-validate their interpretation of the transcripts, and they can discuss and reconcile any differences. (For the remainder of this discussion, we will assume that two coders are being used.)

We also think it advisable that at least one of the coders (and potentially both of them) should be a "naive" coder—that is, one who is ignorant of the research project objectives. Sometimes those who are too close to the research project are guilty of self-fulfilling prophecy, or seeing what they want to see in the transcripts. Ideally, the coding scheme should be so clear and straightforward that *any* intelligent person could pick up the transcripts, apply the codes, and come away with essentially the same interpretation. A naive coder tends to keep everyone honest and greatly enhances the validity of the findings. If the researchers are going to do the coding themselves, we suggest, at a minimum, that a naive coder be used to code a randomly selected subsample of the transcripts (such as 25 percent) in order to provide a validity check.

Training the Coders

The coders will require some training in order to accomplish their task. This training should include (1) a thorough overview of the coding process and the philosophies underlying it, (2) learning the coding scheme, and (3) coding at least one trial transcript as a learning experience.

The Coding Process and Philosophy. There are several issues that you will want to discuss with the coders prior to turning them loose on the transcripts. The first issue is how much of the transcripts should be read by the coder prior to applying the coding scheme. Although we have suggested that each customer response be considered a separate unit of analysis, it is usually easier to understand what the customer means if several consecutive responses are read together. Therefore, we suggest that the coders read larger sections of the transcripts (approximately one-half a page to a full page) prior to coding the individual responses within. This will not only provide the context for interpreting individual responses (see the discussion of the importance of context that follows), but the coders may decide whether it is necessary to subdivide or to collapse multiple responses into one, as described previously.

The coders should be trained in the importance of context for interpreting the customer's meaning. Very often an individual response is impossible to interpret without considering its surrounding context. For instance, it may be that a previous response or an interviewer's question or probe is needed to help interpret a subsequent response. There may even be instances where nonadjacent responses (e.g., something said on a previous or subsequent page) can help to interpret a particular response. If this is the case, the coders should feel free to code the focal response in light of the surrounding context. The point of coding is to provide, as much as possible, an accurate interpretation of what the customer *means*. To the extent that context facilitates this, it is important to use it accordingly.

A related issue that the coders should understand is how much room there is for interpretation in applying the codes. In other words, how literal should the coder be in applying the codes? ("Well, I know the customer said *this*, but what she really meant was *that*.") In general, the philosophy is to try to stay as close as possible to the customer's actual words. The coder should try not to infer beyond what the customer verbalized. The more successfuly this is achieved, the less room there is for disagreement among the coders and for criticism from others outside the process about the transcript interpretation.

Having said that, it is also important to know that customers don't always speak in complete thoughts and sentences. Some are also inherently more articulate than others. In short, sometimes the customer's meaning will not be explicitly and thoroughly verbalized. In these instances, it is often necessary (and advisable) for the coders to "fill in the gaps" with what they feel is the customer's intent.

Of course, doing this opens wide the door of criticism from outsiders. However, there are two points to keep in mind. First, the coders will be working independently. You can have more faith in the inferences of the coders if both, working independently, interpreted the same meaning from the transcript. This is where the agreement rate (discussed later in this appendix) is very important in assessing the quality of the codes as well as the coders "meeting of the minds." Second, the coders should be trained to use the "reasonable person" rule. In other words, would a reasonable person reading the transcript come away with the same interpretation? The further the coders get into speculation and far-reaching inferences about the customer's intent, the less likely a "reasonable person" would be to agree with the interpretation. In summary, the coders should stay as close to the transcript and the customer's actual words as possible and rely on interpretation only when the inference or conclusion is fairly obvious.

The Coding Scheme. A second part of the training process involves thoroughly reviewing the coding scheme. The coders should be given the opportunity to ask any clarifying questions about the codes and how they are to be applied *prior* to using them. Questions the coders have about individual codes or how to use them may even prompt the researchers to reconsider their coding scheme, definitions, and the like.

Coding a Trial Transcript. One important element of the training process is to withhold a sample transcript (or a reasonable portion of a transcript) that can be used to train the coders. Following the process described below, the coders should independently code this transcript according to their best interpretation and based on their training instruction. The trainer should then bring them back together after the coding, and the three of them should discuss and reconcile the codes that were applied.

This trial coding is a critical step in the training. First, it allows the coders to get a feel for how the actual coding will occur. Regardless of how well the training went, there is no substitute for actually coding a transcript to understand how the process really works. Often, for instance, codes that seemed very clear during training can prove to be problematic in application. The second purpose of this trial is to get the coders to discuss their rationale for applying the different codes. This often leads to better clarification of the code definitions and when or how to use them. Third, if one of the coders is misinterpreting a code, it is much better to catch the problem early than after hours of transcriptions have been coded. Fourth, this trial coding will give the researcher a preview of the quality of work he or she can expect from the coders. Again, any sloppiness or poor judgment should be identified early. Finally, following the trial coding and the (often lengthy) discussion surrounding reconciliation, all parties should have a higher comfort level about what is expected and be ready to tackle the larger set of transcripts.

Coding and Reconciling the Transcripts

As discussed in Chapter 4, the actual coding of the transcripts entails applying the coding scheme to each transcript unit or thought. Each thought is assigned a string of codes—one response code for each of the major coding categories. The goal of this process is to capture the meaning from the thoughts in the coding responses.

During the coding process, the two coders should work independently of each other, coding the transcripts without interaction. They can record their initial codes in one of two ways. The coders may choose to simply write the appropriate codes for each unit in the margins of the transcript adjacent to the customer thought. Alternately, they can use summary coding sheets, such as the one shown in Figure I.1.

After several transcripts have been coded, the coders should get together and compare their respective codes, identifying areas of agreement and disagreement. At this time, the coders will want to keep specific records of their reconciliation process that identify the number and type of agreements and disagreements the coders have across the transcripts. The better and more precisely defined the codes, the smaller the number of disagreements there should be. If the codes are ambiguously defined, the level of disagreement will be high and the coders will have a great deal of difficulty agreeing on the interpretation of the transcripts. In general, an 80-percent agreement rate or above suggests a high level of confidence in the coding scheme and process. A less than 80-percent agreement rate should cause the researchers to rethink either the coding scheme, the level of training which was conducted with the coders, or the competency or involvement of the coders themselves.

Figure I.1 shows the results of a reconciliation process. In the first column of the table, the subject number is entered. Each subject should be assigned a unique number between 1 and j. In the second column, the number corresponding to the response unit or thought within the transcript is entered. This should be a whole number between 1 and n, with the two exceptions previously noted: (1) if the coders have decided to subdivide a response, subnumbers will be assigned (e.g., n_a, n_b, and so forth) or (2) if multiple responses have been collapsed (e.g., "3–6").

In the third column, the coder is identified. If there is a discrepancy in the codes that must be reconciled, three lines will be entered for each response: one for each of the coders' original response codes, and one for the "reconciled" code. An example of this can be seen in Figure I.1. In the rows for subject 1, thought 1, the coders disagreed about the response to the second major coding category. The first line indicates the codes that the first coder (Bob) independently assigned to the thought, the second line indicates the codes which the second coder (Sarah) assigned, and the third line indicates the reconciled or agreed response of the two coders ("R") after they discussed and resolved their disagreement. If, on the other hand, the two coders independently agreed upon the codes to be assigned, only one line is

Subject	Response number	Coder	Codes					
			I	II	III	IV	V	VI
1	1	Bob	1	2	1	1	5	3
"	"	Sarah	1	3	1	1	5	3
"	"	R	1	2	1	1	5	3
1	2	Both	2	4	1	3	2	6

Figure I.1. Summary sheet to record coder reconciliations.

entered: one for "both" coders, along with the corresponding codes.

This type of summary sheet is necessary to assess the level of the agreement between the two coders. First, an overall agreement rate should be calculated. To do this, one should divide the number of codes on which the coders agreed by the total number of codes which were assigned. For example, on the first two customer thoughts, the two coders agreed on eleven out of the twelve codes that were assigned (where each thought contained responses for the six major coding categories). The agreement rate is then calculated by dividing the number of codes on which they agreed (11) by the total number of codes (12), for an agreement rate of 91.67 percent. Alternately, a disagreement rate can be calculated by dividing the number of disagreements by the total number of codes. By calculating an agreement rate across the entire set of transcripts, a rough estimate of the level of agreement or disagreement can be assessed. (A note of caution: a shortcut to counting all of the codes on the summary sheets [the denominator of the equation] is to simply multiply the number of major response categories by the number of response units that were coded. If you do this, be careful to account for thoughts that have been collapsed or subdivided, as this will decrease or increase, respectively, the total number of codes.)

A second level of analysis is also possible. It may be that, as opposed to coder disagreements being randomly scattered across the coding categories (which is desirable), the coders systematically disagreed on certain codes. To determine this, a separate agreement rate can be calculated by dividing the number of agreements *for each major coding category* by the total number of thoughts that were coded. If the agreement rate is significantly lower for one of the coding categories in the coding scheme, this might be an indication of an ambiguously or poorly specified category. Additionally, it might suggest the need to redefine that code and/or retrain the coders.

Quality Control Concerns

Finally, procedure is needed to assure quality control during coding. In many cases, it may be too time consuming for one of the researchers to participate in all of the coding and the reconciliation. If so it is desirable to have intermittent checks on how the coders are doing in order to identify any problems as quickly as possible. For this reason, we suggest two things. First, one of the researchers (ideally, the trainer) should periodically sit in on the coder reconciliation sessions in order to determine how the codes are being applied. Second, the researcher may want to periodically pull and review a coded transcript for accuracy.

IDENTIFYING STRATEGICALLY IMPORTANT CUSTOMER VALUE DIMENSIONS

The first step in the customer value determination process (see Figure 1.3) is to create a list of the many attributes and consequence value dimensions that customers want. These dimensions provide an input into the design of satisfaction survey questionnaires used to determine how well customers think our product or service offering performs on each one.

As we noted in Chapter 9, this list often contains more value dimensions than we can design into a single satisfaction questionnaire. Consequently, we have to determine which ones are strategically most important. Only these dimensions typically should go into the questionnaire. In our approach, we systematically screen the initial list of dimensions applying selected criteria (see Figure II.1). In Chapter 9, we introduced three such criteria: (1) similarity, (2) actionability, and (3) importance to customers. This appendix elaborates on how to apply each criterion.

Similarity Criterion

When analyzing transcripts from qualitative research, coders strive for completeness by recording all thoughts that are judged as customer value dimensions. The objective is to maximize the number of value dimensions found in the data. As a result, some dimensions may appear on the list that sound quite similar. Though customers use different words, they may be expressing a similar value idea. Suppose we are analyzing transcripts of customers talking about their experiences related to drinking beverages during a workout. From some of the data, we learn that customers want to "quench thirst." In other data, customers talk about "getting rid of the thirsty feeling." Both phrases make

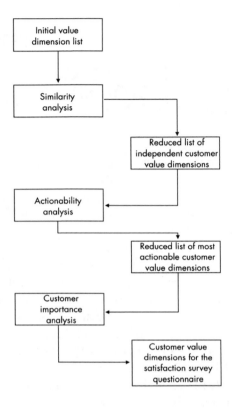

Figure II.1. Determining the importance of customer value dimensions.

the list of value dimensions. Yet, we may feel that "quench thirst" is just another way of saying "get rid of a thirsty feeling." When designing a satisfaction questionnaire, we probably do not need items that cover both phrases. But, how should we make this decision?

In one method for applying this criterion, judges determine similarity. They could be members of a research staff or customer "experts," such as product managers, research specialists, advertising managers, and the like. Their task is to scan the list of value dimensions and place them into categories based on the topic or object of reference. When two or more judges place the same phrases in a category, we gain confidence in the meaningfulness of the category. The next step is to scan the value dimensions within each category to judge whether any are so similar as to be redundant.

Let's return to the beverage illustration. The following lists show two categories of benefit consequences.

Category 1: Builds or Rebuilds the Body
1. Repairs my muscles.
2. Helps me grow better muscles.
3. Gets into my muscles and everything else that needs it.
4. Goes directly into my muscles.
5. Aids in muscle synthesis.
6. Gets your cells moving.

Category 2: Provides Energy
1. Gives me energy.
2. Gives me a boost of energy.
3. Brings my energy level back.
4. Provides a rush.
5. Gives me extra zip.
6. Pumps me up.
7. Makes me feel more energetic.
8. Maintains my high energy level.

The category labels emerged from the common referents of the phrases. As you can see, several of the benefits in each category appear quite similar (e.g., "pumps me up" and "makes me feel more energetic"). The similarity criterion says to eliminate redundant phrases within each category.

As a general rule, we want similarity to be interpreted from the customer's point of view. That is, two value dimension phrases judged as similar should mean the same thing to customers. This idea suggests a second approach; we can let customers determine similarity through their evaluations of product and service performance. If customers consistently evaluate a product or service quite similarly on two value dimension phrases, then they probably have the same or similar meaning.

To implement this criterion, we need to conduct research. A sample of customers from a target segment complete a questionnaire in which they rate performance of a product or service on each value dimension. Then, a data reduction technique such as factor analysis[1] is used to assess which individual performance ratings intercorrelate highly. These phrases form a "factor" and are assumed to have similar meanings to respondents. With this analysis, you can pare down the list of value dimensions by choosing only one or a few items that represent each factor. In effect, factor analysis of customer performance ratings takes the place of the judges used in the previous method.

Actionability Criterion

Data have value to managers only to the extent that they can act on them. If you know that there is nothing you can do to change value delivery on a particular value dimension, there probably is no point in collecting satisfaction data on it. The actionability criterion helps you screen out these value dimensions. For example, suppose you learn that customers in a high priority segment value "having the product easy to get where I play sports." Satisfaction data on this value dimension would tell you how well customers think that you are doing to make your product easy to get. However, suppose you see little chance of expanding your company's current distribution coverage to get the beverage to more sports sites. In this case, you probably would not benefit from satisfaction data on this value dimension.

We think that those who use the satisfaction data should be involved in applying the actionability criterion. Ask these managers to scan the list of customer value dimensions and try to imagine actions they would take in response to various satisfaction results. Choose those value dimensions for which actions are feasible. For instance, if ratings on a particular value dimension are low, indicating a performance problem, you should be able to suggest actions to take to improve the rating. If you cannot think of any actions no matter what you find out from the satisfaction data, then that value dimension is not actionable. It becomes a candidate for being purged from the list. As we stated earlier, measuring customer perceptions on a particular value dimension also implies that something will be done based on the responses. You risk greatly frustrating your customers if you continue to ask for feedback on areas where your organization cannot make improvements.

Actionability analysis can benefit from an internal assessment of the organization's capabilities. You want to know which internal processes are considered strengths. Customer value dimensions closely tied to these processes are more likely to have priority for taking action. If customers are dissatisfied with these processes, for instance, management will feel more pressure to respond with improvements.

Importance to Customers

Finally, we want to know which of the remaining customer value dimensions on the list are most important to customers. "Most important" dimensions are the ones that influence how customers evaluate and behave toward a supplier's offering. In other words, they are the ones that drive customer behavior. For instance, hospitals should know that "confidence that I will get well" is a crucial value or benefit consequence. Customers are unlikely to want to go to a facility where they have low confidence in getting well.

There are two quite different ways to find out which value dimensions are important: (1) direct measurement, and (2) indirect measurement.[1] Specific techniques representative of each way are shown below.

Direct Measurement

These techniques ask customers to tell us how important they think each dimension is. Current practice uses rating scales and there are several variations available.[2] A few examples demonstrate the range of alternatives. Some scales ask customers to think of each value dimension independently. For instance, probably the most frequently used scale in this category anchors one end with "extremely important" and the other end by "not at all important." Customers rate where each value dimension

Appendix II

- Direct scaling approaches
  - (1) Importance scale
  - (2) Constant sum scale
  - (3) Pricec comparison scale
  - (4) Competitive difference/importance dual scales

- Indirect measurement approaches
  - (1) Conjoint analysis
  - (2) Regression analysis

Figure II.2 Methods for determining value dimension importance.

falls between these two end-points or extremes. Five-, seven-, and ten-point scales are common. We have seen other anchor phrases tried from time to time. For instance, we have used an importance scale that varies from "no contribution to overall value" at one end to "extremely high contribution to overall value" at the other. Such phrases help to clarify, in customers' minds, what "importance" means.

Other types of scales ask customers to make comparisons of one kind or another. For instance, one technique asks customers to allocate 100 points to each of the several value dimensions so that more points indicate greater importance. Customers have to think about the relative importance of the different value dimensions. Or you might get customers to compare the value dimension to price by asking, "How much more would you pay for a supplier's offering that is superior to that of other suppliers on this dimension?" The corresponding scale might range from 0 percent at one end to, say, 50 percent at the other end. More important value dimensions are the ones where customers would pay more for superior offerings.

Dual scales also have been tried. For instance, some argue that customers should consider competitive differences between products or services in addition to rating importance of value dimensions.[3] The rationale is that more strategically important dimensions to your organization are those that customers (1) think are important and (2) perceive that competitors differ significantly in their ability to deliver that value. Two scales are needed, one for each aspect.

The rationale for the two scales is based on how customers make choices among suppliers. If competitors do not differ on a value dimension, even an important one, it probably will not affect the choices that customers make in the marketplace. You have to use some judgment with these scales. Suppose you know that all competitors are performing similarly but poorly on a value dimension. If you believe your company can significantly improve its performance on this dimension, you may want to consider it part of your strategically important list.

The first scale, importance, is measured in any of the ways described previously. The second scale, "competitor difference," can be anchored at one end by "extremely different" and by "no difference at all" on the other end. Again, five-, seven-, or ten-point scales work. Note that how important a value dimension is to customers is determined by their responses to both scales.

Look at Figure II.3. Value dimensions that fall in the upper left-hand cell (showing low importance and low competitive difference) are not strategically important. If you improve on these, customers may not notice, or they may think that your overall value delivery is not any better than it was before. In contrast, those value dimensions in the lower right-hand cell (showing high importance and high competitive difference) are highly important strategically. Customers think that they are important, and the differences between competitors sensitizes them to look for which competitors offer more value. You may find opportunities for creating advantage among these value dimensions.

Those value dimensions in the upper right-hand cell of Figure II.3 (that score low on importance and high on competitive difference) create competitive distinctiveness. High ratings on one or more of these dimensions may help you to stand out and be noticed by customers. For example, some airlines allow passengers to choose a special meal (e.g., a low-calorie meal) in advance of the flight. While this value dimension may not be

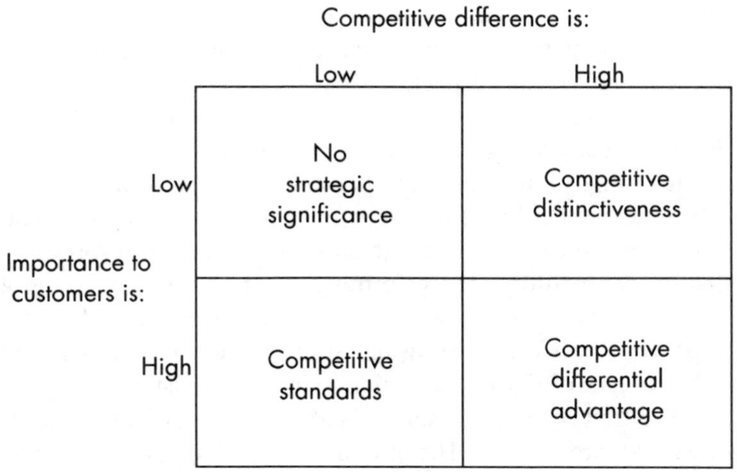

Competitive difference is:

	Low	High
Low	No strategic significance	Competitive distinctiveness
High	Competitive standards	Competitive differential advantage

Importance to customers is:

Figure II.3. Strategic importance of value dimensions.

highly important to your choice of an airline, it does provide the opportunity to be memorable or distinctive. Passengers remember the airline's "nice touch" of providing a personalized meal.

Finally, value dimensions in the lower left hand cell (high on importance, low on competitive difference) are competitive standards. You may not stand out relative to competition by the way you deliver value on these dimensions, but your performance had better be perceived as good as competitors. These value dimensions are important to customers. Also, if you can distinguish your offering from those of competitors, you may create advantage by moving this dimension to the lower right-hand cell.

Indirect Measurement

These techniques infer value dimension importance from customers' evaluations of product or service alternatives. One approach is based on the following idea: When a customer evaluates a seller's product or service offering, more important value dimensions will contribute more to his or her overall evaluation than will less important dimensions. This idea is applied by examining the relationship between various value dimension evaluations and some measure of overall value. If the overall evaluation measure is a continuous variable such as overall satisfaction, then regression analysis is appropriate for finding out which value dimensions are most important. Note that the importance weights (i.e., the regression coefficients) are derived from the data. On the other hand, if the overall evaluation measure is categorical, such as different satisfaction groups (e.g., highly satisfied respondents versus dissatisfied respondents), then discriminant analysis becomes appropriate.

Another approach derives importance weights from respondents' relative preferences among competing product or service alternatives. We assume that customers choose a supplier that performs better on the more important value dimensions. Conjoint analysis is a popular technique that applies this idea.[2] Respondents are shown product/service profiles (or combinations of value dimensions), usually two profile sets at a time, and asked to state which one they prefer. A computer algorithm searches for a set of importance weights that, when added together, would best reproduce the rank order of the preferences provided by respondents.

Applying Importance Criteria

No one criterion is likely to do the whole job of identifying the most strategically important value dimensions from an initial list. We think that you should apply multiple criteria in sequence (see Figure II.1). The first step is to screen for redundancy using the similarity criterion. The result is a reduced list of independent customer value dimensions. A selected group of managers search this list for the most actionable ones. Those deemed not actionable are removed, and the list gets pared again. Finally, this reduced list becomes the focus for measuring customer perceptions of importance. Those value dimensions that customers say are of low importance are purged, providing a final set of dimensions that are fed into the design of a satisfaction survey questionnaire.

Appendix II

References

[1] Wyner, Gordon A. and Hilary Owen, "What is Important?" *Marketing Research*, 5 (Summer 1993), pp. 48–50.

[2] Dutka, Alan, *AMA Handbook for Customer Satisfaction*. Lincolnwood, IL.: NTC Business Books in Association with AMA, 1994.

[3] Alpert, Mark I., "Identification of Determinant Attributes: A Comparison of Methods," *Journal of Marketing*, 8 (May 1971), pp. 184–191.

Notes

1. It is beyond the scope of this Appendix to provide an explanation of factor analysis. For a more thorough description of this technique, see A. Parasuraman, *Marketing Research*. Reading, MA: Addison-Wesley Publishing Company, 1991, pp. 757–764.

2. There are several good sources for more extensive explanations of conjoint analysis and its application, including Paul E. Green and Yoram Wind, "New Way to Measure Consumer Judgments," *Harvard Business Review*, July/August 1975, pp. 107–117; A. Parasuraman, *Marketing Research*. Reading, MA: Addison-Wesley Publishing Company, 1991, pp. 771–775; Paul E. Green and V. Srinivasan, "Conjoint Analysis in Consumer Research: Issues and Outlook," *Journal of Consumer Research*, 5 (September 1978), pp. 103–123; Dick R. Wittink and Phillippe Cattin, "Commercial Use of Conjoint Analysis: An Update," *Journal of Marketing*, 53 (July 1989), pp. 91–96; and Paul E. Green and V. Srinivasan, "Conjoint Analysis in Marketing: New Developments with Implications for Research and Practice," *Journal of Marketing*, 54 (October 1990), pp. 3–19.

CUSTOMER VALUE CHANGE FORECASTING TECHNIQUES

In Chapter 11, we laid out a process for predicting customer value change. This process depends heavily on forecasting forces that influence customer value as well as customer value change itself. To implement this process, we have to choose specific forecasting techniques. In this appendix, we present a classification of available techniques. For more detail, you may want to consult any of several good forecasting references.[1]

Figure III.1 classifies alternative techniques that we think are most suitable for forecasting forces that influence customer value changes. They fall into one of two categories: (1) *formal modeling techniques* or (2) *informed judgment techniques.*

Formal modeling brings the power of statistics to the forecasting activity. It begins by building a mathematical model that describes the relationship between a "dependent" variable—the one you want to estimate—and other, "independent" variables that you think are related to that variable. For instance, to estimate the future state of "business entertainment expenses," a force driving the value that customers perceive from owning certain products like luxury boats, you might model future expenses as a function of past spending on business entertainment (the independent variable). Two kinds of formal models are briefly reviewed in the following sections: (1) trend models, and (2) causal or descriptive models.

Informed judgment approaches rely on the ability of "experts" (e.g., managers, personnel from support firms such as advertising agencies, consultants, and the like) to subjectively make a prediction based on what they know. The challenge is to draw out these judgments from experts, and for that we turn to technique. Examples briefly described later in this appendix are:

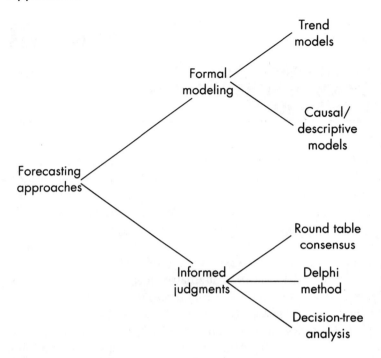

Figure III.1. A classification of forecasting approaches.

(1) round table consensus, (2) the Delphi method, and (3) decision-tree analysis.

Trend Models

Trend models take advantage of the fact that customer value change forces evolve over time. If we know what has been happening in the past, we may be able to project that history into the future. In essence, trend techniques allow you to see what a force will be like in the future if the historical trend for change continues in the same direction and at the same rate.

These models search through historical data to find patterns of change (the trends). When a pattern is found, it is extrapolated into the future. For example, suppose the force that you want to predict is a lifestyle attitude toward health and fitness. You have been monitoring that attitude by purchasing the results of a research supplier's annual lifestyle survey. Over a period of several years, the health and fitness attitude scores have been going up. You can use a trend technique to find out how much scores have been increasing and extrapolate that increase into the future.

Sometimes it is possible to forecast a force in one market locale by examining trends from another locale where the phenomenon has been occurring for a longer time. You have to be willing to assume that the phenomenon will evolve in the locale of interest just as it did in the older locale. Consider the application of retailer strategies in Britain. Recently, French, Asian, and American retail competitors introduced discounting into British markets.[1] Suppose you want to predict how this phenomenon will progress for the next several years. You might look at how discounting strategies have evolved in U.S. markets where it has been used for a long time. In effect, you assume that the pattern of growth of discounting that was experienced in the United States will occur in a similar way in Britain.

Trend techniques can be applied to most any of the forces of customer value change shown in Figure 11.1. The only requirement is that data, whether quantitative or qualitative, be gathered over time. Many organizations collect such data routinely. They track any of a number of relevant forces, such as economic growth, legal regulations, competitive innovation, and customer uses for product or service offerings.

Causal or Descriptive Models

Sometimes an organization may have data that describe variables thought to be "causes" of a force that influences customer value change—or at least highly correlated with it. These data may be used to build a model describing how the force will change in response to changes in these causes. Instead of forecasting the force directly, you predict what is likely to happen to each cause included in the model.

For instance, in the early 1990s several forecasters predicted that unexpectedly high growth will occur in the U.S. economy during the next several years. We can see a causal or descriptive model reflected in the reasons given for the forecasts: (1) increased capital spending, (2) more hiring by organizations, (3) lower interest rates, (4) paying off debt by consumers, (5) increasing willingness of banks to lend more to small businesses, and (6) more favorable export trade. The descriptive model shown below translates these six causes into a forecasting model. After forecasting what will happen to each force, the model yielded a forecast of economic growth of about 4 percent by 1994 and 1995, an unexpectedly high rate.[2]

Economic growth = f(capital spending, hiring, interest rates, consumer debt, lending rates, exports)

Round Table Consensus

What happens when you cannot use a formal model, such as when you do not have tracking data? Forecasts of customer value change forces are still possible through the use of informed judgment techniques. One such technique, round table consensus, takes advantage of the fact that certain people may have special knowledge of a particular force. For instance, United States Surgical, a manufacturer of surgical instruments, regularly sends its sales people into the operating rooms of American hospitals.[3] They have a wonderful opportunity to observe what goes on in this use situation, including what the doctors and nurses are saying about surgical procedures. Salespeople track what changes are occurring in these procedures and note the needs of their customers. This information is brought back into the organization to influence new product decisions, among other things.

To apply round table consensus, a panel of experts is assembled and asked to reach a consensus on what will happen to a particular force influencing customer value change in the future. The group might be comprised of a company's key managers and sales personnel, outside consultants, people from service firms such as advertising agencies and research firms, and even the customers themselves. Through round table or face-to-face discussions, these experts pool their knowledge, experiences, and opinions into a consensus forecast.

In one application, a publisher formed a team of editors and authors to develop a new text. The team met periodically to assess likely competitor innovations in text design and promotion methods. Various team members brought to the table information gathered from observations of competitive text offerings; conversations with customers, competitors' sales persons, and other authors; and the results of the publisher's marketing research. The team talked through the possibilities suggested by the information to make predictions about what competitors would likely do during the several years it would take to design and introduce the new text.

As this illustration suggests, you must be able to identify "experts" who have special knowledge and then draw out their insights about the future for customers. Face-to-face discussion is simply a way to do the latter. By talking about their observations of the future and the reasons for them, the round table consensus technique combines the knowledge of several experts, no one of whom is likely to have all relevant information, into a consensus prediction.

The Delphi Technique

This technique is intended to overcome some of the objections to round table consensus. A common fear is that when people talk face to face, extraneous factors may influence the forecasts. These factors stem from characteristics of the participants, such as their communication skills, reputation, and job positions. None of these has anything to do with knowledge and insights into what a particular force will be like in the future, yet they can easily affect the outcome of the discussion. The Delphi technique is popular because it eliminates the need for face-to-face interaction in reaching a consensus.

A panel of experts is assembled, but each participant is not told who else is on the team. No face-to-face interaction occurs. Instead, self-response questionnaires elicit from each expert both a forecast of the phenomenon of interest and a list of facts and opinions that justify that forecast. Consensus is reached through an iterative series of questionnaires filled out by the team members. Each subsequent questionnaire includes (1) a list of the forecasts from participants from the previous round of questionnaires, but without any identification of who provided what forecast; (2) a listing of all the reasons given for the forecasts across the team, but again not identified by participant; and (3) a request for a revised forecast and reasons for it. In effect, each iteration pools the knowledge and insights of the various team members, and over the several questionnaire iterations, the participants' forecasts tend to come closer together. The iterations continue until a consensus is reached.[2]

Decision-Tree Analysis

One last example of an informed judgment approach is decision-tree analysis. This technique encourages the forecaster to consider the possibility that more than one change outcome is possible. Further, more than one customer value change force can be considered simultaneously.

For instance, suppose a company's customers are just beginning to use its product in a new use situation. Management believes that the speed of competitor innovation will be affected by the forecasts of potential sales in the new market. If the new market evolves to high potential, competitors will be more likely to develop new product innovations within two years than if the potential turns out to be moderate. Competitors will not innovate at all if potential sales stagnate. Figure III.2 shows what a tree diagram describing these events looks like.

A decision tree graphically shows the alternative possibilities and the dependencies of one customer value change force on another. Subjective probabilities are estimated to show how likely each branch of the decision tree will occur. These estimates allow calculation of expected values. For instance, if dollar amounts can be attached to high, moderate, and low market potential, then an expected market potential can be calculated using the probabilities shown. An expected value can

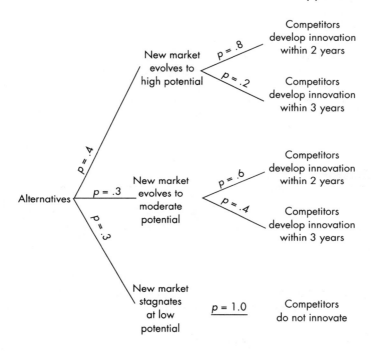

Figure III.2. A decision tree for emerging new markets.

also be calculated for the number of years it will take for competitors to bring out product innovations.

Choosing a Forecasting Technique

Each of these forecasting techniques has both strengths and weaknesses. If a particular forecast is critical to a decision, you may want to try several techniques to see if the estimates merge. If they do, then you can feel more confident that a forecast is not an artifact of a method. If there is no convergence, then you can examine how the forecasts were developed to discover reasons for differing estimates. These reasons may help you assess the risks you are taking by adopting any one of the estimates. Or, more likely, you may want to develop contingency plans to deal with the possibilities represented by different forecasts.

References

[1] Associated Press, "British retailers are shaken by new concept: discounting," reported in *Marketing News*, October 11, 1993, p. 3.

[2] Harper, Lucinda, "U.S. May Be on Verge of Stronger Growth, Some Signs Suggest," *Wall Street Journal*, October 12, 1993, A1, A6.

[3] Reese, Jennifer, "Getting Hot Ideas from Customers," *Fortune*, May 18, 1992, pp. 86–88.

Notes

1. For example, see Makridakis, Spyros and Steven C. Wheelwright, eds., *The Handbook of Forecasting: A Manager's Guide*. New York: John Wiley & Sons, 1987; and Charles W. Gross and Robin T. Peterson, *Business Forecasting*. Boston: Houghton Mifflin Company, 1983.

2. For more on the Delphi technique, see Linstone, Harold A. and Murray Turoff (eds.), *The Delphi Method: Techniques and Applications*. Reading, MA: Addison-Wesley Publishing Company, 1975.

INDEX

Index

customer service
    and customer value
        determination, 137–8
customer value
    versus customer satisfaction,
        94–102, *98, 233*
    definition of, 54–64
    dimensions of, 109–12,
        315–23
    hierarchy of, 64–80
    See also value hierarchies
customer value changes, *291*
    response to, 279–82
    sources of, 282–9, *284*
    See also value prediction
        research
customer value determination
    (CVD), 12–16, *14,* 105–25, 277
    and business decisions, 127–53
    defined, 6
    and market opportunity
        analysis, 34, 35–40
    process of, 108–25, *110,*
        315–23
    techniques of, 155–299
    See also value delivery
customer value orientation, 132
customer value strategies, 278–9
CVD. *See* customer value
    determination

data, 118
        collection of, 25–30, 42
        customer value change, 292
        customer value determination
            and, 122–3
        See also external data;
            internal data; performance
            data; qualitative data;
            quantitative data;
            satisfaction data; value data
data-driven management, 108, *124*
decision influencers, 166, 208
decision makers, 166
decision-tree analysis, 330–1, *331*

Delphi technique, 296, 329–30
Delta Airlines, 140
Deming, W. Edward, 85
descriptive models, 327–8
devaluation process, 63
diagnosis analysis, 263–5
direct measurement, 165, 319
disconfirmation, 87–90, *89,* 240–2,
    250n4, 252
distribution
    and customer value
        determination, 141–2
Domino's Pizza, 142
Drucker, Peter, 4, 28
D-T scale, 244

Eastman Chemical Company, 86
Eastman Kodak, 244
Echo System, 280
Edwards, Daniel, 244
electronic data interchange (EDI),
    31, 67, 138, 280
emotions
    and satisfaction, 93–4,
        216, 244
executive education, 44
external data, 24, 42, 46

facilitators, 166
factor analysis, 318, 324n1
Federal Express, 130, 151, 286
flexibility, 130
focus groups, 13, 42, 172–4, *176,*
    190n1, 194, 282, 300n2
    See also interviews
Ford, Henry, 285
Ford Motor Company, 5, 69, 244
forecasting activities
    and value change, 293–5,
        301n5, 325–31
frameworks
    for value prediction, 289–90
frequency
    and customer value
        determination, 119–22

Index